Wildlife Photography Field Skills and Techniques

Paul Hobson

Short-eared owl. 1Dmk4 500mm, 1/800, f4, ISO 800, from a car. Lincolnshire.

Photographs, words and design by Paul Hobson

www.paulhobson.co.uk

ISB: 978-0-9570265-9-9

Printed on FSC certified paper.

Wheatear. 1Dmk4, 500mm +1.4 converter, 1/1200, f5.6, ISO 1000 handheld. Fair Isle.

Introduction

There are countless books about wildlife photography. These can be great if you want to learn about lenses, cameras, exposure and composition. However, most of them lack any detail about how to get close to the actual subjects whether they be birds, mammals, reptiles or insects. This book is different - it will give you in-depth guidance that, with practice, should allow you to master some of the arts of fieldcraft.

Wildlife photography is a rapidly changing pastime. The introduction and immediacy of digital photography and its rapidly developing technology has captured the interest of thousands. When we also consider the use of the internet and the huge

It would be great if we could all learn by trial and error but our diminishing wild creatures possibly couldn't handle the onslaught of such pressure. Never has wildlife been so precious and valued yet the huge increase in attention from photographers and those simply wanting to experience the ultimate thrill of getting close to a wild animal has never been higher and in all probability will increase more in the near future.

Many TV programmes, voluntary wildlife organisations and the government's own Natural England have a strong remit to engage far more people directly with the natural world. However, the flip side is that some of Britain's best loved wildlife sites have already been damaged by a small but significant number of photographers and in a number of situations some animals have

Red deer stag at dawn, IDX, 500mm, 1/500, f4, ISO 1000, tripod. Derbyshire.

quantity of accessible information, wildlife photography has never been so easy. In tandem with this technology has been the evolution of workshops and trips.

It is now very easy to amass an amazing portfolio of images of some of our most iconic species from the large number of pay-as-you-go hide set-ups around the UK. It might seem that the need for basic field skills is over. This is far from the truth. It could be argued that the need for field skills has never been greater as fewer and fewer of us now have them. To spend time stalking an otter and have it fill your frame without it having any idea you are there is an amazing buzz.

actually changed their behaviour because of human pressure.

We should not try to disengage people from wild creatures. The benefits contact with nature brings us are enormous. The aim of this book is to encourage such access but in a responsible way - one that gives that thrill but does not threaten the very animals we love so much.

Some wildlife conflicts have occurred at honey pot sites - those where generally access is simple and the ability to find out about them very easy. It's not difficult to see how these situations arise. We all want to stand next to the animal and get that ultimate thrill and image. The thing we all tend to ignore is that so do hundreds of others and when they all arrive on the same weekend the inevitable happens. Only a few honey pot sites suffer this way where, at times, the heaving throngs of humanity far outweigh the numbers of bewildered wild animals.

One of the main aims of this book is to show you that there is an alternative. You can forge your own way in new places and get close to wild animals without disturbing them and retain that feeling of still working in wild places.

I started my wildlife photography career over thirty years ago when I learnt the art of bird nest photography at the hands of an expert. If I actually took a picture one day in ten I would be doing well. We spent most of our time moving hides and watching and learning about the birds' behaviour. It was a slow but incredibly rewarding grounding in wildlife photography. I progressed from there to include mammals, reptiles, amphibians, insects and fish in my portfolio. With each new subject I researched as much as possible. However, my best sources of guidance were the 'old school' photographers who had acquired a superb set of field skills over decades. I supplemented these nuggets with as much additional information as I could find from my local gamekeepers.

I am the first to admit that I am no expert but the vast majority of the information here is from my own personal experience. In some cases, where I have little or no expertise, I have sought the guidance of other photographers who have worked with specific species. I make no guarantees that the guidance contained here is the definitive article - it worked for me but it may need tweaking in some situations. Wild creatures don't all read the same script. They may stick to the same menu but will often have their own ideas and individuality. The art of field skills is to know the basics but also to be able to adapt to each new situation, learn to read the signs and act accordingly.

The Ethical Question

As society evolves our relationship with wild creatures changes. As a general rule we become more compassionate and considered about the state of the natural world and how we impact upon it as time goes by. We are also bombarded with conflicting issues and concepts such as the need for cheap food and the impact of modern farming on our wildlife which has created incredible declines in many farmland bird populations. We are all aware of this yet virtually no one calls for food prices to rise so farmers can farm in a more wildlife friendly way. We care, but only so far. Perhaps in generations to come they will look back and condemn many of the methods we use today just as we look into our own history and condemn otter hunting and bear baiting.

There are three basic codes we should be aware of - our own personal code, the RPS's code of conduct (Royal Photographic Society p215) and the letter of the law as it pertains to wildlife in the UK. We need to be familiar with all three yet individually we will still operate differently when it comes to wildlife in the UK. The largest killer of badgers are cars on our ever increasing and busy road network, yet most of us will still drive to get around. We are aware of the increasing levels of CO_2 in the atmosphere and its huge global impact yet we still will look forward to that overseas trip.

As wildlife photographers we should always put the welfare of the animal or plant first. That should be our overwhelming mantra and we should only use techniques that cause the minimum amount of disturbance possible. In many cases it's actually impossible to photograph without any disturbance at all. The same applies to wildlife watching but at the same time we shouldn't advocate that no one ever goes into the countryside because some disturbance will occur. We have to think and act sensibly within the compass of the world we live in but at the same time be aware of how we operate and how society views this.

Some of the approaches once commonly used in the past are frowned upon by some today - such as playing tapes to attract birds nearer to the photographer. The ethics of wildlife photography are ever changing - what was acceptable yesterday may not be tomorrow. They may not be illegal but for a variety of reasons become unacceptable. You must adopt your own personal ethics and be prepared to work within them and stay honest to them. The onus is always to stay within the letter and spirit of the law and put the welfare of your subject first.

You should also find, as I have done, that your own ethics will change over time as you age, mellow and become aware of how the public and a variety of organisations change their opinions about how we work as photographers.

If you intend to enter your wildlife images into competitions you will need to read the rules carefully. Many now expect full disclosure of your techniques and do not allow any form of baiting or the use of lures or tapes. It is possible that many of the changes to the wider perceived ethics of wildlife photography are driven by the major wildlife competitions as they respond to their audiences. One reason is that the public want to think that what they see in an image is honest. They expect the photo to show a truly wild animal without it having any knowledge of, or influence from, the photographer. In some cases it seems obvious that this can never be so. Wide angle shots of owls with claws extended only a metre from the camera do not show wild behaviour yet the public expect it to be so.

Slow worm in autumn, Canon 5Dmk3, 180 macro, 1/60, f16, ISO 1600, tripod. Derbyshire

One of the most contentious issues today revolves around the use of live bait to attract your subject. It is illegal to use any vertebrate to attract a predator if that vertebrate suffers unnecessary suffering (mental and/or physical). Some photographers are happy with using fish but not everyone is. The use of mice is reprehensible and should not be countenanced. In the future we may think differently as the ethical base of our work shifts.

This raises one other issue - your honesty when labelling an image. If you think the end user should know something about how you took the image you should declare it. I suspect that as we move forward we will be expected to declare more about how we took an image and that aspects of how it was created will influence its sales and use.

The bottom line is to be honest to yourself and your work. There will be techniques that I have discussed or described that you may find unsuitable in your approach to wildlife photography. That's fine, I leave it up to you to decide which techniques and skills you are comfortable with.

Licences

Virtually all wildlife is protected by the law in some way. The Countryside and Wildlife Act (1981 Ammended 1985/91) set out precise schedules (lists) where different species were given different levels of legal protection. Since then various European directives have influenced the act.

the birds. Barn owls are on Schedule 1 which means you must have a licence to work at, or near, the nest. So in the winter, no problem, they are not breeding. In spring, no problem in the next field but close to the old building a licence is required.

In terms of wildlife photography licences are needed for specific things - to work at or near the nest of all Schedule 1 bird species, to work at a bat roost or hibernation site or to handle or move a great crested newt or crayfish.

Red-throated diver. 1Dmk4, 500mm, 1/1600, f5.6, ISO 1000, +1/3 exposure compensation, tripod. Iceland.

It is imperative that when you decide which species you want to work with you make sure you are aware of which schedule they are on and whether you require a licence or not. For the vast majority of species and situations you will not need a licence. However, the same species in different situations may require one. For example, you find a good set of fields with hunting barn owls. In winter you work hard to produce a series of flight shots (no licence needed). Later in the year a pair breeds in an old building. You watch them hunt and bring food back to the building. There is an excellent spot right next to the building to put in a hide, which you do carefully. You have now broken the law, even if you don't think you have disturbed

The law is clear about baiting animals. At the moment it is fine to feed mealworms or waxworms to birds, many already do so. In the UK for photography purposes (without a licence) it is illegal to use any live vertebrate as bait for a predator though dead animals are fine. It is also illegal to put live fish into a river unless they were caught in that river. You can only do this if you get a licence from the Environment Agency.

Applying for photography licences is done via Natural England (England), Scottish Natural Heritage (Scotland), Natural Resource Wales (Wales) and Northern Ireland Environment Agency (Northern Ireland).

You can apply on-line or download the form and post it. Licences are given for one species, for one location (though this may be a county) for a specific time period. For example, when I had a barn owl licence it was for Derbyshire and valid from April to September for that year only. At the end of this period I had to submit a report detailing my activities and the breeding success or not of the owls.

I photographed this barn owl in Linconshire where it reguarly hunted at daybreak for a few hours and was feeding large young in a nest. I didn't need a licence because the nest was over 200m away and I was working from a public hide. 1Dmk4, 500mm, 1/2000, f5.6, ISO 500, beanbag on window ledge.

The first time you apply for a licence you will need at least two referees. In the case of Schedule 1 bird licences one of the referees must be someone who has worked with you on a number of non-Schedule 1 species at the nest and he or she must be a licence holder. You will also need to produce a series of images of your nest work. For species apart from birds you still need referees, usually someone who has a licence for that species and has allowed you to work with them. Unfortunately once you have held a licence it does not mean you are guaranteed licences without referees in the future.

For Schedule 1 birds you will need to start the whole process from scratch if you have not had a licence for over three years. The same may apply for other species as well. Having held a licence in the past is no guarantee that you will get another in the future.

One other major issue is also worth considering when applying for a licence. Since European directives have influenced our law it is no longer appropriate to apply simply for photography alone because you want to work with that species to produce images for yourself and to show your friends. You must have a conservation aspect included in your application. For many of us this should be straightforward. If you give talks to RSPB or local bird or natural history groups you should be discussing the conservation issues around your work with that species. It should also be part of your photography to support local conservation initiatives such as your local Wildlife Trust. Free images will help them promote their work. Doing this adds a useful purpose to your photography and will help with any licence applications.

If you want a licence and are struggling to make a sound application then phone Natural England and seek advice. The hardest part is often finding a suitable referee. Start by asking at your local wildlife group or the local branch of Natural England. They may be able to recommend someone.

Clothing

How we dress ourselves as wildlife photographers has evolved over the years. Traditionally, scruffy clothes or ones from a country background were the norm. Today, partly due to the influence of the American hunting fraternity, a bewildering array of clothing and accessories exist. You can now purchase a full head to toe outfit in a variety of camo designs and colours. One question that is often asked is 'Are these really necessary or are there other reasons to wear them?' In terms of camo gear (coats, trousers, shirts, socks, wellies, hats, even binoculars) there are only a few situations that really merit their use, such as stalking wild roe deer. On the whole simple soft, dull browns and greens are just as good.

There is one issue that does need raising and that is the effect of a big bloke, head to toe rigged out in camo rising up out of the long grass or heather in front of an unsuspecting member of the public. They must think they have walked into a military invasion! This may seem a bit of a joke but this issue was raised by a Peak District ranger a few years ago. He had received a number of negative comments about photographers pursuing red grouse on the moors. Some of the members of the public actually said that they felt threatened and were very wary because of the military overtones.

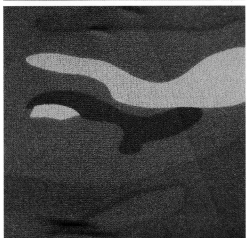

Modern, oak camo material (top) and the older, Army style camo design.

So what is the ideal clothing? One of the most obvious considerations is comfort and weather proofing. You may be crawling around or sitting for hours so comfort is a serious issue. Your clothing must stand up to the elements - once you get wet and don't dry out it can be miserable. Many favour walking trousers that are designed to dry out quickly. If you are kneeling or crawling around ones with built in knee protection are ideal. Pockets that zip up are a bonus. Velcro can be noisy when you're close to animals so try to avoid it. Choose a good, light storm-proof jacket and for warmth light layers underneath that you can take off. Try to keep all clothing green, brown or grey.

Another point to consider is how noisy is your clothing. Soft cotton or ventile materials are very quiet. You don't want stiff, crinkly, noisy materials when you're trying to be as quiet as possible.

With all your clothing pockets are something that you should look at closely. When you're crawling through seaweed, snow or mud you don't want pockets that are going to fill up with debris. You do though need pockets that are easily accessible and have flaps on to stop things falling out. It's fine to keep spare cards in your camera bag but when you're stalking you often won't have your bag handy so you need somewhere to stow spare cards, a battery, possibly a converter etc. A photo vest may be the answer. These are not as popular in the UK as they were twenty years ago but in certain situations they are ideal (possibly not for crawling) when you're sitting in a hide or walking.

For many of us one of the most noticeable parts of a human is our pale face and hands, especially if it's sunny. It's hard to keep these still. Gloves are good to hide the hands - greens, browns or black are ideal colours. Think about soft gloves that still allow you to operate all the camera controls. You could try fingerless gloves but you may find that your fingertips freeze in winter. On your head wear a green/brown soft hat. A balaclava is worth thinking about for situations where

Camo gear. In this case coat, trousers, gloves and net balaclava do help to disguise you in woodland.

you think you need to hide your face, for example when you're lying down waiting for hares. Some people recommend face paint to dull the skin. I must admit that I have never tried this, it has always seemed to be a step too far. Another option is to try camo netting but you may find it restricts your vision.

One item that is indispensable is light, but strong, waterproof trousers. These are brilliant when your are stalking any animals where you have to lie down or kneel. It's never pleasant to slowly get wet when you're lying down for a few hours! Make sure you buy a good pair with strong knee pads and robust zips that won't get clogged up.

Footwear is also something that needs thought. Try not to buy cheap, lightweight walking boots that are supposed to be waterproof. They are OK in summer but on wet ground your feet will be soaking. Today there are lots of options. It is worth considering spending your money on good quality hiking boots that are really

waterproof, not shower proof. If you know it's going to be very wet then a pair of neoprene wellies can be brilliant. They are light, warm and very comfortable.

There may be a few situations when you may have to try some alternative ideas. I was told that a white oversuit was needed to stalk ptarmigan in the snow. I guess it may be a benefit but I have found that ordinary browns and greens are fine for both these and mountain hares.

Clothing is not just something you wear, it should be something you consider for your camera and lenses too. Canon pro lenses are white and very reflective so often you need to have some form of covering. Most other manufacturer's lenses tend to be black so disguising them is not so important. You could try camo tape but this can be a nightmare to get off if and when you come to sell the lens.

Camera body and 500mm lens with protective camo lens cover.

Many manufacturers now make lens coats. Some are definitely better than others. The cheaper ones are thinner with weaker stitching. Good quality ones are designed for your specific lens and are made of thick neoprene. These have the benefit of not only 'hiding' the lens but reduce damage and scratches when you're working in the field and not using a tripod or beanbag. You can also buy protective covers for your camera body. These won't hide it (it is black anyway) but they do reduce the chance of scratches and damage if you drop it.

Alongside these covers you should seriously consider a waterproof bag to stop rain or damp when you are working in wet weather. Many manufacturers now market specific ones for camera and lens combinations and these are usually in nice soft cloth with a waterproof lining. They are often in a camo design as well. There is no reason though why you can't make one yourself. Remember to design it so you can operate the camera easily and see through the view finder (or live mode screen) and leave a space for the lens to mount onto a tripod. Many people simply use a plastic bag!

In many situations you may lie down for extensive periods (such as when photographing hares) so if the walk is not miles take a waterproof blanket - one that has a plastic liner on one side, often sold for picnics. This helps to insulate you from the cold and wet of the ground.

Camera equipment

The aim of this book is to explore field skills and projects relevant to wildlife photography. However, it would seem a little remiss not to give a brief outline of the main photographic gear used today.

At the moment most wildlife photographers use digital SLR cameras with a variety of lenses. The two most popular brands are Canon and Nikon, both offering a wide variety of camera bodies and lenses at prices from budget to professional. If you are on a tight budget consider starting with a second-hand body and lenses.

The more you spend on a camera body generally the better it is. This does not necessarily mean it takes better shots. Often the model below the flagship one has the same technology but is in a cheaper, less robust body and may cost a lot less than the top end one.

The big thing is that once you start with one brand you tend to stick with it for a very long time because as you accumulate lenses, flashes, cable releases etc the cost of having to replace everything becomes prohibitive.

A few things you might want to consider when buying a DSLR body

- How good is the auto-focus?
- How does it perform in low light? (the ISO range. Newer bodies are much better).
- Can you attach a cable release? (virtually all bodies can).
- Does it have a depth of field preview button? (not all do).
- Does it have over exposed highlights in its menu? (a quick way to see if you're over-exposing images as you review them on the back of the camera).
- Does it allow live view? (most, if not all, new bodies do).
- How big is the back screen you review images on? (the bigger the better).
- How does it feel in your hand and how easy is it to use the main buttons?
- What are the focus sensors like and what pattern are they in? (some are in a grid and easy to move around, others are in an oval pattern with sensors at various hours like 12, 3, 6, 9 and one in the middle, not so versatile but not a real problem).
- Can you customise the white balance?
- Does it have WiFi? (not essential but something you might consider in the future?)
- How showerproof is it? (always worth knowing).
- Can you lock the mirror up for times when the shutter is very slow?
- Has it got a cropped sensor? (which acts like a converter magnifying the image by 1.3, 1.6 or 1.7 times) or is it full frame? (Traditionally the most expensive bodies tend to be full frame because the sensor is larger and the image quality higher. Cheaper bodies have cropped sensors. This is not a bad thing because they act like converters and create images that look larger. However, they are a hindrance if you like wide angle work because they reduce the wide angle effect of any lens).

Lenses

The choice of lens will depend on both your budget and the type of wildlife you want to work with. In general a lens is defined by the size of the glass at the front and thus how much light it lets in. Big glass lenses like a 300mm f2.8 will cost £4000+, a 300mm f4 about a £1200 and a 300mm f5.6 zoom lens £300+.

Basically the bigger the lens the better. A 500mm f4 is great but expensive. A 150-500mm f6.3 zoom is good and much cheaper. In the past it was always considered that zoom lenses (like a 70-300mm) were lower quality than a fixed focal length lens like a 300mm. Today this is not true. Some zoom lenses are of outstanding quality. Zoom lenses clearly have the advantage of flexibility when composing images but generally they are higher f numbers like f5.6 and slower to autofocus.

If you can't afford a 500 prime or 500 zoom look for a 300 that will take a converter. Some manufacturers make a 400 f5.6 which may be available second-hand at a good price, though it may not auto-focus with a 1.4 converter.

If you do decide to add a converter to your kit bag try to buy one that is the same make as your lenses. Many photographers prefer the smaller converters like a 1.4 or 1.7 and feel that 2x converters lose too much quality and slow the auto focus. However, the new ones coming out are a distinct improvement on the older versions in terms of sharpness.

Most manufacturers will have a zoom that is ideal for wildlife photography. Canon have a 100-400 f4.5-5.6 zoom. Version two has just been launched and is reasonably priced. The older model is available second hand at reasonable prices (under a £1000). The top of the range zoom is the 200-400 f4, an amazing lens but its cost is high. Nikon make a fantastic 200-400 f4 zoom, not cheap but very good and used by many wildlife photographers. A cheaper Nikon alternative is the 80-400mm f4.5-5.6 zoom.

Brand lenses of the same make as your camera can be expensive, especially the bigger, high-quality ones. Independent manufacturers like Sigma and Tamron make some superb lenses that are usually just as sharp and often at a lower price compared to brand lenses.

A mid-range zoom will be very handy, a 70-200 is ideal. The f2.8 works well with converters but the f4 version is much cheaper. They are ideal, particularly when you want to include more landscape into your wildlife images.

You should also have a standard wide angle zoom, again low f number ones (f2.8) are expensive but a f4 version would be ideal. I use a 16-35 zoom a lot for wide angle close ups and in my underwater bag (see p136).

If you are thinking about macro photography a macro lens is essential. They come in 3 size ranges - 60mm, 90/100mm and 150/180mm. The latter two are good. However, many believe that the 180mm is the best option because it has its own tripod mount (great for turning the lens from portrait to landscape and not having to mess about with the tripod head). It should also allow you to attach a converter. The most

A 180 macro lens with 1.4 converter and extension tubes.

important factor however is that you are much further away from the subject than a 100mm or 60mm to get the same image size. This is a major issue when working with flighty insects. The downside is it's bigger, heavier and costs a lot more. A good compromise is a 90/100mm macro. The f2.8 version is available in brand and independent makes. It is also fairly easy to get second-hand ones.

A cable release, tripod and a set of extension tubes are highly recommended. Once you decide this is definitely a hobby you want to pursue you could look to get a big lens later. The choice is dependent on your purse.

Tripods

A good quality tripod is an essential part of your kit. They come in a bewildering array of designs and makes. Choose one with legs that open fully (without a centre column) so it can be spread flat on the ground. This allows you to work with a low position of view (pov). If you have to get one with a centre column make sure it can be taken out or moved so you can get down low. Manufacturers tend to make them in two materials - carbon fibre and aluminium. Carbon fibre tripods are lighter to carry. When you buy one get the shop to put it up and twist the top. You want it to be firm and stable. Remember it may have to hold a big lens firmly. You might not have one now but get the tripod in anticipation of possibly getting one later.

Tripod heads

Tripod heads also come in a range of styles and sizes. Basically there are 3 main styles - ball, pan head and gimbal. Each has its own advantages.

Ball heads (top right) are great for smaller, lighter lens and camera combinations but tend to let the lens droop or simply can't hold a big lens firmly. They are ideal for macro work and come in a range of sizes. The larger ones are better at holding heavier lenses but they do cost a bit more. However, the extra investment should be worth it because they should last many years.

Pan head and tilt are good for fine tuning but a nightmare if you want to follow a

moving animal around.

Gimbal heads (below) look odd and are a fairly new design. They are brilliant for bigger lenses because the lens is balanced which makes them ideal for tracking moving animals.

For macro work a ball head is great but for birds and mammals a gimbal is the head of choice. The price of all of them reflects quality and brand name. A good name gimbal (Benro or Wimberley) can be £300-500 but cheaper alternatives exist at sub £100.

Extension tubes

These are a cheap, essential part of any wildlife photographer's kit bag. They are simply a set of tubes without any glass. You pop them between the lens and camera like a converter. Their effect is to allow the lens to move closer to the subject. In a sense they allow non-macro lenses to become macro lenses. They can transform a 300 or 500 lenses into an effective macro lens that creates superb backgrounds. They are relatively cheap and can be as low as £30.

Spirit level

You can get this to fit on your hot shoe to help you get your horizons straight. You may use it infrequently but when you do you will be glad it's in your bag. Most modern DSLRs now have a spirit level built in that you can see on the live view screen.

Cable releases

Many photographers still use the old style cable releases. They are very reliable and allow you to fire the camera when it's on the tripod without vibrating the camera with your hand. You can get electronic, wireless versions which can be cheap and very good. With some of the newer cameras you can use its in-built Wifi and fire the shutter with your phone.

My basic photographic technique

The following is purely how I photograph most of the time. I am comfortable with this method but if you talk to other photographers or read other books you will come across a wide range of styles and

The older fashioned style cable/remote release (top) and an independent make electronic remote shutter release. This has the advantage of allowing you a bit more distance and flexibility. However, it needs batteries which can have an annoying habit of running out just when you need it!

approaches. Each is probably as good as mine, I am just comfortable with my method.

I shoot almost entirely in aperture priority (Av). I select the f number I want to get the type of background I am looking for. So a low f number like f4 or f5.6 gives shallow depths of field (dof) and blurry backgrounds. If I am using a wide angle or macro lens and want a larger depth of field I will choose a higher f number like 16, 22 or 32.

Shutter speed

I always look at the shutter speed to make sure it's high enough for either hand holding the camera or if it's on a tripod. If I am handholding the camera I try to get a speed higher than the lens size, e.g. 1/500 with a 300 lens, 1/750+ with a 500, 1/200+ with a 70-200. If I can't get the speed high enough I use a tripod and cable release.

Many modern lenses now have IS or VR (image stabilisation) systems built in. They are designed to allow the lens to produce sharp images at lower speeds. I only switch mine on when I actually need it, i.e. when the speed drops and I don't want to increase the ISO any further. There is no point in having it switched on when the speeds are high. All it will do is use up the battery faster and delay the first image by a fraction of a second.

ISO

To get the speed higher I choose a higher ISO. This makes the sensor more sensitive to light. It's always a trade off because if the ISO gets too high the images become grainy (called noise). The more modern the camera the better it performs at high ISOs. A few years ago I tried to keep the ISO below 1000, now I can shoot at ISOs above 1000 and still get good quality images. The thing is to test how high an ISO you are happy with. Do a set of images with everything the same but at a different ISO (say 200, 400, 800, 1250, 1600, and 2000). Print them off and see how far you are happy to go.

White balance

Most people shoot with this set to AWB (auto white balance). I have mine set to cloudy (customise at 6200). This tends to saturate the images more and gives them a warm feel. White balance is the way the sensor interprets colour at different light levels or different sources, such as bulbs.

Reviewing images

I review my images on the back of the camera quickly and have the over-exposed highlights switched on. If it looks too dark or they are blinking merrily (over-exposed) I use the +/- button to exposure compensate. Remember the camera will try to under-expose whites and over-expose blacks so be prepared to compensate. I sometimes use the histogram but generally not. I usually don't have the time in the field.

Background and composition

When I photograph and am looking through the viewfinder I am constantly checking the background and composition. With composition the best place to start is to use the rule of thirds, it basically will get the composition right most of the time. It simply means I keep the subject to one side of the frame so it looks into the space on the other side of the frame.

Bearded reedling. 1DX 500mm +1.4, f5.6 1/1000 ISO 2000 +1/3 exposure compensation. Norfolk,

Once you get comfortable with this start to experiment and break the rules. The background is vital. More images are ruined by a poor background e.g. hot spots of sky or white twigs or tree trunks which lead the eye away from the subject. Get into the habit of looking around the picture. Does it all hang well together? If not change it or move position to improve it.

RAW or JPEG?

I shoot in RAW for three reasons. The main one is that the maximum data is preserved in the RAW file. When the camera produces a JPEG it compresses the image file and some data is lost. In the vast majority of cases this is virtually impossible to see. Another reason is that a lot of competitions now ask for the RAW image if the image reaches the latter stages. This is to ensure no computer manipulation beyond the competition rules has occurred. The last is that some agencies may want to see the odd RAW if a client wants authentication of an image's integrity.

Shooting in RAW does have some disadvantages. RAW files are large and can slow the frame advance down if you shoot lots of action as the buffer fills up. Choosing the fastest cards does help to speed things up. The other big downside is that you have to convert the RAW to either a TIFF or JPEG before you can work on it. I don't mind this because I can do most of my image manipulation in Lightroom (an Adobe programme) when I convert anyway (p211). The last drawback is that you have to store far more files (the RAW and the worked TIFF or JPEG) in your hard drive, so it fills up quicker.

Shooting in JPEG should be considered if you don't want to enter any competitions, are unlikely to be producing huge prints and want to cut down on time spent in front of your computer. It will also mean you get more images on your card and the buffer is less likely to fill and slow down the frame rate. However make sure you choose the highest JPEG quality setting possible to get the highest detail in your images.

Storage cards

All digital cameras write their images onto a card (SD or CF) which you place into the camera. They come in a bewildering array of makes and sizes. As technology advances their capacity to hold more data is leaping ahead. Choose intermediate sizes like 16 or 32 GB cards. If you shoot all your work on a trip onto one card (like a 128 GB) and it goes wrong you may lose all your images. If you have changed the card a few times at least some work is safe. Cards do go wrong but it is rare. I have had three cards fail in ten years.

Always buy cards with the fastest write speed possible. This really makes a big difference when shooting extensive action photography. Slower cards allow the buffer to fill quickly so the camera's frame rate slows and you could miss potentially good images. These cards cost more but the price is worth it and they should last for years.

Camera traps - Trail cams

These are simply a small compact camera in a waterproof housing that is triggered when an animal walks past. They are brilliant for taking some of the leg work out of field work. You set the trap up and point it to an area you want to watch, switch it on and leave it. In theory every time an animal walks past it takes an image. You then simply pop along later, take the card out of the camera and view the images. It is a huge benefit and lets you know the time of activity in your desired location.

There are numerous situations where you can use them – at a badger sett to get an idea of when they come above ground and if there are cubs around, at your fox set-up, at a spot you think an otter is sprainting or on a path you think roe deer walk down. They are not excessively expensive, introduction models cost just below £100 and do a good job. They are rainproof, record either stills or video, work in daylight and at night and use SD or CF cards (if you choose big ones like 16 or 32GB they will last for ages). Many use AA batteries which means you can use rechargables to keep the cost down. When you buy one check that it has a screen to view the images on.

The only consideration is placing them where they won't get stolen. They come in camo design so are not too obvious but if you use them in popular places it may only be a matter of time before they disappear.

Some competitions now allow, or even have, camera trap categories. Many photographers still like the idea that they are physically at the scene and that means they have to use some skill and knowledge to get the image. There is far less control over camera traps. However, the winds of change are forever blowing!

GoPro cameras

These have been around for a few years now and are a firm favourite with extreme sports fanatics who want dramatic video. The latest GoPro, the Hero4, is also able to shoot stills and has WiFi connection so you can use your phone or their gizmo to remotely trigger it. It can take bursts of 30 frames per sec or you can choose time-lapse. It is waterproof and can be used underwater. The images are very wide angle and can look incredibly dramatic. Very few wildlife photographers who shoot stills use them but there are many situations where they could be used to create innovative images in situations you would not want to commit your DSLR. At just under £500 for the latest model and some accessories it's not a bank account buster.

Compact and bridge cameras

Some of these can be used for wildlife photography but they all have various limitations. Most will not shoot in RAW, only JPEG, and the zoom is often limited if you're working with animals such as birds that are at a distance. They are often slow to autofocus and the frame rate can be very slow. Another problem is that many are difficult to use away from the auto settings which reduces your control, or at least speed of control and creativity. However, if you have one they are great for keeping in a pocket on walks.

If you are serious about becoming a wildlife photographer I would suggest you start with a digital SLR. However, if you have a compact or bridge already there are many situations where you can use it and produce some really excellent work. They can be very good for macro work. One or two makes now have optical zooms that go to the equivalent of a 600mm lens on a full frame SLR and can produce some very good images.

Flash

The need to use flash has changed over the years. With the rapid development of digital cameras and the ability to set high ISOs it can be argued that it is not so essential today.

Flash is used generally in two situations - as full flash to completely illuminate the animal in very low light situations (such as an owl at night) or as a fill-in to add a dab of warmth and brightness to a daylight situation. There is very little literature about the effect of flash on the animal itself.

A few years ago I had a commission to work photographically at a marine aquarium. I was asked not to use flash at all. I asked why and was told that many marine species suffer badly even to the extent of the flash killing them if repeated many times. I now have some misgivings about using full flash with some insects and birds at night because I suspect that it may temporarily blind or even in extreme cases harm the animal.

Many photographers feel that fill-in flash has no effect. The pupils are already dilated and adjusted to daylight and the power of the flash is low so the animal never even notices it, let alone is harmed. Fill-in flash is particularly useful for adding catch lights in eyes, reducing shadows and boosting the animal's colour in dull light.

Hides

There will be many occasions when a hide (or blind as they are known in the USA) is necessary. A hide is simply a structure like a shed or tent that allows the photographer to remain hidden, yet close, to the subject. Hides come in a large range of sizes and styles. You can buy off-the-shelf designs or you can build your own. There are a number of questions you need to ask yourself before you commit to buy one.

- How long do you want it to remain in position? (only on a daily basis, left for a week or two or left up for months, possibly years)
- How far from your vehicle will you be working?
- How well disguised do you want to make it?
- Can you afford for it to be stolen or vandalised?

The following are a range of popular hide designs that you should consider - for each style the potential advantages, disadvantages, workings and approximate costs have been outlined.

The bag hide

This is simply a sheet of camo material that you throw over yourself and camera. It is very versatile, cheap (£50), light and portable. It will fit into your camera bag easily. Commercially made ones have a bit of scrim to look through, the ability to stick your head out and holes for a lens and tripod legs. It does give one level up of concealment from wearing camo gear and usually you should wear this or the type of clothing recommended earlier. The best situation to use it is if you can get some vegetation around you e.g. in scrub, the edge of a wood or by a hedge.

The basic idea is to set up your camera and tripod, focus on the area you think your subject will appear, sit comfortably (either on a low stool or the ground. A gardener's mat

Bag hide covering me with a 500mm on a tripod. I am only looking through the camera so my sight is a bit limited.

will help to keep your bottom dry) and throw the hide over you. Get it hanging comfortably, make sure you have a decent view and put your hands ready on the camera. Now simply wait - and that's the problem. If you know it's only going to be minutes that's usually fine but if it might be an hour or two then it can become problematic. Every time you move or turn your head the bag hide also moves and if that happens any fox or roe deer will usually be well away. So to summarise - it's quick to put on, light and very portable and works well if you don't think you have to wait for long but any movement by you is easily seen and it's difficult to sit perfectly still for hours at a time.

Modern canvas hides

These come in a variety of designs and prices. The most popular today is the round dome hide. These retail at about £250/300 for a good-quality, durable and waterproof one down to under £100 for one that is of a lesser standard. Some use poles that you have to thread through, others have the poles inbuilt and simply expand up to size when you take it out of the carry bag.

A modern dome hide in leafy oak camo.

They usually come in modern leafy camo design. You can get them in a variety of colours, even whites for snow work. You can also buy low height models for lying down photography. They are portable and it's no hardship carrying them long distances. If you decide to buy one check that it has pockets at ground level which allow you to put stones in to help weigh it down in windy weather, the gaps you look out of are nice and large and it has sown-in scrim to hang around your lens.

The inside space is usually generous and you can fit in your camera bag with no problem. Some have sown-in groundsheets. These are a matter of taste - if the ground is wet they help to keep your gear dry but stool feet pierce them eventually. Many prefer them without a groundsheet because they are more versatile. You have the opportunity to move them around with you and your tripod if you don't tent peg them down. With a bit of care it's possible to shuffle it around with you and your gear without alarming the subject - saving you having to get out and be very visible.

They are nice and robust and can be left up for a week or two as long as you anchor them down properly. (You may have to add your own guy ropes for this).

At £250 you don't want them stolen and this is an issue in today's world. Sighting them is a consideration. They are not so good on steep hillsides as the poles are fixed and don't allow one side to be erected at a slightly higher height. They also tend to be either fully up or down, there is no halfway house if you want to introduce it slowly to a nervous subject.

The traditional box hide

Many wildlife photographers cut their hide teeth with these and have a real love for them. They are simply a green, waterproof box tent with four poles and cross struts, three foot square and four feet in height. They are not quite as easy as a dome hide to put up and at first glance are not as versatile. You can move a fully erect dome hide around, but not so easily the box and pole design.

An old fensman hide, now not commercially available but not too difficult to make yourself with poles from camping stores. (see p221)

They do have a number of major advantages. The main one is that they can be erected at various heights. So if you are moving it up on a bird's nest you can start with it at a low height and build the height up gradually. A great advantage. You can also leave it at half height when you're not in it - less chance of it being seen by others and less stress to the animal.

It is fairly easy to construct a Dexion square with small tubes welded to the four corners. This is excellent for use in streams or on rocky ground. The hide poles simply fit into the tubes and hold it steady. The square is also ideal if you are using scaffolding. It allows the hide to be put up slowly and securely on top of the scaffolding if you do any photography of birds in trees. This type of hide is excellent on sloping ground where you can adjust each pole height. Dome and chair hides fail a bit in these situations.

Poles and Dexion frame for a square canvas hide.

One major issue unfortunately is that they are not commercially available today but they are easy to build. Use tent cloth and tent poles. You could buy camo cloth (though it can be expensive) but make sure whatever cloth you use it is thick enough not to show your outline when it's sunny. Add pockets at the bottom for stones, ties on the openings and create a large hole on the front for your lens. (See p221 for a design plan)

Use scrim held up with safety pins to hide your face and hands and drape it around the lens front. Don't forget to shape a couple of cross poles for the top with a slight curve so the roof has a slight dome to it. This will stop rain pooling up on the top.

Disguising the hide

This seems a bit daft at first but for some animals and birds it does help. It also makes it less likely to be discovered by others and stolen. A large bit of army scrim draped over the hide works well. You can buy this from many Army and Navy shops. It's a net with plastic bits built in to add as camouflage. On its own it helps disguise the hide but you

Disguising a canvas box hide with scrim and heather at a merlin's nest in Derbyshire.

can add suitable vegetation which you can weave into the scrim. Heather on a moor or seaweed on the coast can effectively disguise your hide. Don't forget to peg it down thoroughly, you don't want it blowing around in the wind and scaring your subjects. Make a hole for the lens and to look out through.

The chair hide

These are as the name says, a hide built around a comfy chair. They retail at approx £80+ and are very flexible and easy to put up. They weigh a bit more than a dome hide and you might not want to carry one for miles

with all your camera kit as well. The major advantage is that they are easy to get in and out of and you can move the hide around with yourself in it. An example of their use would be at a bird feeder where you can't leave a hide because it might get stolen. The chair hide is excellent because it allows you to move it around with yourself in it as

can't really have your bag in as well so you need to have everything you need in your coat pockets.

They are not good on sloping ground where you tend to tip over along with your tripod and camera! You probably wouldn't leave it out for any length of time either though it should be OK for a few days as long as it does not get windy. Two-man versions are also available.

Permanent hides

If you intend to run a baiting session over years then you might think about building a permanent hide. This obviously takes a lot more effort though it's quite easy to buy a small shed from garden suppliers. They cost approximately £100+ and take a lot of the effort out of the equation. You will probably want to cut extra holes alongside any windows and add a shelf or two as well. If you want to build the entire thing then it's simply a matter of building a framework with good 2x2 timbers, using ply sheets for the roof and sides and not forgetting to add a door. Plywood is not cheap and you will need to waterproof it or buy marine ply.

Other ideas

Sometimes you don't want to use one of your conventional hides and need to improvise. I have built hides using straw bales on the side of fields. I once saw a hide made out of an old metal water tank! It's also possible to improvise your bag hide by cutting 4 poles from small trees and pushing them into the ground and draping your bag hide over the top, not brilliant but it works in an emergency.

Working with the hide elevated

If you intend to do any serious work in the tree tops then you will need to either rent or buy some scaffolding. Aluminium is best because it's lighter and does not rust but is very expensive. However, if you search hard enough you can come across the section type of scaffolding where you build up a tower in sections that face each other. It's very quick to put up and with the cross struts quite stable. The Dexion square helps hold the hide on the top with planks as a support for your chair.

A canvas box hide on scaffolding at a long-eared owl's nest in Derbyshire.

The square has 4 short pieces of tube welded onto each corner which fit the poles of a square hide. Since it's most likely you will be putting this up next to a tree make sure you securely tie or brace it with a couple of struts to the tree. You climb up it on the inside and enter the hide through the floor, moving a couple of planks to the side.

If you only want to level your hide on sloping ground or go up a metre or two make a frame scaffolding with Dexion. This is like giant Meccano and comes in various lengths which bolt together. It's brilliant stuff and incredibly versatile. As with scaffolding it's not too hard to find second-hand.

A few bits of Dexion help level up a hide on sloping ground.

Your vehicle as a hide

Many birds that perch on hedges close to roads have learnt that cars are seldom a threat, especially when they whizz by. Wildlife photographers often discuss what the ideal car is for this approach. Some think that red or white cars scare birds but it is unclear if it's true. However, since they are fairly large the colour is not too important. Some people prefer 4x4s because of the elevated position but you could argue this is just as likely to be a disadvantage for birds or small animals on the ground as you're not as low as in an ordinary car. Then again, they get stuck less often in muddy fields when off road. It's really a matter of personal preference.

You can do a few things to increase your vehicle's ability to be a successful hide. A piece of Velcro fixed across the top of the windows (on the inside) can be used to fix a piece of scrim. This is a real benefit to hide you, your face and hands when you're parked up in position but don't drive with it still fixed. There are many devices to support your camera on the window sill. However, a heavy beanbag is simple to use and offers good support.

The main consideration when using the car is how you approach the subject, for example a bird on a hedge. You should try to spot it in advance and have the camera already on the beanbag with the shoulder strap secured in the vehicle to stop it falling out. Approach

Scrim and a bean bag to support a 500 lens on my van window.

gently and turn the engine off and coast up the last 20 metres or so. You need to check before you start where the sun is and how you intend to use its position when moving the vehicle to get the best light. It does work but you will need to practise a bit. The worst bit is if you misjudge the coast in because you have to start the engine again and this can startle the bird or mammal.

Another approach is to coast in with the car in neutral but the engine still idling. You can then move again by slipping the clutch gently. You must be very conscious of other road users - it's easy to forget who is behind you.

Floating hides

Low position of view (pov) images have become very popular today. They are created by having the camera and lens almost on the ground or water's surface and firing across at the subject. Many photographers love this viewpoint because of the blur in front of and behind the animal. If you want to work with water birds most people would work from the bank and lie on the ground. If you look hard enough you will find some dams or reservoirs have concrete water exits where the excess water leaves. Sometimes

these can be ideal places to stand and allow you to get that low pov. However, you may decide you want to venture out into the water itself. A floating hide is just that and over the years many designs have been developed. The simplest is to use a boat like a low-sided rowing boat or rubber dingy and to lie down and throw a bag hide over you. More complex designs involve using large blocks of polystyrene and planks. The key point is to create one where you have a hole in the middle. You stick your head through this and wade around, or swim if the water is deeper. Your camera and lens is fixed on the front and looks out of a low hole cut into the canvas that forms the roof. Try to keep everything nice and low and make sure you design a system that stops the camera from sliding out into the water.

One main consideration is if you want to move around in it or have it anchored in one spot, such as at a bird's nest or a place where ducks or herons congregate or fish. Moving around is always a problem. The simplest way is to push it whilst you swim in a wetsuit and flippers. If you want to save your energy a small, electric outboard motor is nice and quiet but a much larger investment.

A floating hide in Norway

The best floating hide I have used was in Norway. It was a large permanent wooden structure that allowed a number of photographers to lie down and shoot from portholes at water level. You could stand and it even had a loo! It was anchored in one position but if it needed to be moved it was towed by a boat.

A word of caution. The places you can operate a floating hide are very restricted in today's health and safety conscious world.

You must have the land owner's permission and you must be clear with them what you are actually doing. Always have someone with you who can help if you get into difficulties - and have an exit plan! Water can be very cold and dangerous. Prolonged immersion can leave you totally powerless and very weak when you least expect it. And lastly, as we were always reminded when we were kids, there are often weird currents in lakes and submerged weeds or trees that can snag you and cause all sorts of problems.

Hide comfort

It is easy to spend long hours in a hide and be really uncomfortable, all due to a lack of preparation. In winter it can get really cold. The obvious thing is to wrap up well but it is easy to forget just how cold you get when you're not moving at all for hours on end. The best theory is that you can always take something off, you can't put it on if it's not there. On your feet wear thick, wool socks with thermal liners. Sometimes if it's very cold thermal underwear or even ladies tights (which are thin but amazingly warm) help greatly. Thermal lined trousers are now available and for extra warmth pop your waterproof trousers on as well. Your top layers should be thermal t-shirts and a fleece under your coat. Never forget gloves and a hat. If the hide is on frozen ground a gardener's kneeling mat to put your feet on does make a bit of difference and you can leave it in the hide. If you are using a fairly large, substantial wooden hide then try a simple paraffin burner. They are not large and produce a superb amount of heat, just be careful of the build up of fumes. For longer stays try using a sleeping bag. You can sit in it and it's amazingly warm. Again you can leave it in the hide after each session.

One problem that sometimes occurs when you get into the hide early in the morning is the lens fogging up. It's hard to stop this. You can either leave it in the hide and keep wiping it until it stops or keep pulling it in if it's out of the hide. Obviously any animal may now see it moving. Luckily it's not often that lenses fog up.

Summer is less of a problem. Many people sit in the hide in their underwear, not the most pleasant of sights possibly but the best way to keep cool! One major problem in summer are midges. These are always worst in still, muggy air at both ends of the day. I remember one day in a hide on open moorland. It got warmer and I must have been there on their annual hatch. It was as if the heather was smoking. A gradual mist rose right out of it, including in my hide. I had forgotten my midge spray so it was a nightmare. I could only stand it for 30 minutes then when the bird had left I bailed out. I now make sure I have a small bottle of bug spray with me for hide work in summer.

The choice of chair is important. A light-weight stool may seem ideal but you may get back-ache after an hour or two so choose a chair with a back. The cheap picnic chairs with arms and back that fold up and are often sold for a tenner on motorway service stations are very good. The other thing to consider is its legs. Straight pointed feet have a bad problem of sinking into the ground. You may have to find some stones to perch on and hope it does not slip off. Chairs or stools with metal that runs from one foot to another as braces are much better and sink in far less. If you are in position for a while take a couple of cut planks to rest the chair legs on.

It's always a good idea to have your gear handy and ready in the hide. There is nothing more frustrating than having to contort yourself round and work with noisy zips to get your spare cards out when the action in the front of the hide is in full swing. If you have built the hide yourself make sure there are good pockets to pop cards, batteries, converters, food etc into. Another option is to hang a cloth bag from the frame with a bungee clip. Cloth is nice and quiet.

Never forget drinks and food if you're in for a long haul and at some point you will have to consider toilet issues. A large plastic bottle for men will suffice, a bowl for ladies. I never pee directly onto the ground. I know some photographers do and it can be really unpleasant to follow them into a well-used hide. Another problem is that the smell may attract vermin to the hide and whatever you are photographing.

Even food wraps should be thought through. Paper rustles, clingfilm is quiet. Crisp packets sound loud as do many sweet wrappers. It may seem a bit OTT but with very nervous animals every little thing planned will increase your chance of success.

Stalking

Stalking is the art of getting close to wild animals whilst on foot, your knees or even your belly. Different species will require slightly different approaches and these will be explained in the species specific texts later. This section reviews the main ideas behind stalking.

One key concept is to understand how your subject understands the world around it (its sensory awareness), particularly the way it detects danger. Some animals like deer and foxes have excellent eyesight whereas badgers are relatively poorly sighted. Other animals have incredible hearing. Most animals use their noses a lot and a strange scent is something that will make them wary, possibly flee. Unfortunately many animals

have all three main senses well tuned! Luckily most birds have no real sense of smell so this is something that you can ignore when stalking them.

Most animals are able to detect movement by the stalker, often simply a slight turn of your head. Skylines are definitely to be avoided as you stand out like a sore thumb. The trick is to be aware of how the animal lives in its environment and to perfect your technique to suit the weather (specifically the wind direction), the local cover and the animal's reaction to your approach.

Before you set out you will have to decide how you will dress. Again you should be able to make the correct decision based on the animal and place you will be stalking. For many species camo gear is not really needed though in some cases it's an advantage. Think about your hands and face, pale skin can show up amazingly well when you move your head or hands. Dark hats and gloves can reduce those flashes of pale skin and increase your chance of success. Don't forget to take your bins, these are valuable to look ahead and check what is around.

A roe deer at dawn, 1Dmk4, 500mm, 1/500, f4, ISO 800, stalked, tripod. Holland.

Wind direction is one of the first things to check. If it's strong this is easy to judge. If it's mild it can be harder, especially if you have a lot of gear on. Some people like the idea of wetting a finger and holding it up. Another technique is to pick something light, such as a piece of grass or a dry leaf, and let it fall. Some experienced stalkers carry a small bag of feathers for this precise job. If the weather is cold your steamy breath is usually quite a reliable indicator. The key point is you don't want the wind to blow from you to the animal.

Next check out all the cover. Anything that can help, such as hedges or any dips in

place each foot down slowly and let your weight down carefully. You will quickly get the hang of this and be able to feel any possible noisy sticks or stones. Try to look for mud, grass or moss to step on. They are nice and quiet but not always available.

Remember your camera bag on your back. It can get snagged on branches causing noise and movement. It also makes your body shape larger and it makes you heavier, especially if you have a full bag with big lenses. This makes walking harder and you more clumsy with your footing.

the landscape to hide your approach, need looking at. Remember that hedges and woods have gaps and if you pass across one you can be easily detected by something on the other side. It will probably be only a change in light but it will cause the animal to watch far more closely. If you approach such a gap go down onto your knees or even crawl across. As you walk, look at the ground to see where you will place your feet. Don't step on twigs or anything that will crack or make a noise. Dry leaves can be a nightmare, as can shingle or gravel. If you are not sure

Farmland in the English Midlands with a healthy population of roe deer. The deer graze the fields at dawn and can be easily spotted with binoculars from a vehicle parked on one of the tracks. Planning the stalk should take account of the wind direction and the position of the many small woods, hedges and old walls. These can all be used to allow you to get into photographable range.

As you progress keep an eye on the animal at all times. The biggest mistake is to rush. Think about taking minutes walking only a few metres. When unsure stop and wait. It may take you an hour or more to move into position. Obviously this is determined by how long you anticipate the animal being in the key area.

As you look at the animal watch how it behaves. If it's continually feeding it usually means it's relaxed but most animals will stop and glance around. If it starts to look nervous, head held up, ears clearly pricked and continually sniffing and staring in your direction stop and wait until it relaxes again. Keep checking on the wind direction, this can have an annoying habit of changing!

In some cases the animal will be able to see you at all times. Every species has something we call the fear circle, a distance from it that once you step closer it gets nervous and is likely to move away. Often once this starts it is impossible to complete the stalk, the animal usually remains wary. The fear circle distance is both species and individually determined. Some individuals of the same species will allow a much closer approach than others. In many cases this is the animal you are searching for and it may take a few goes before you find that confiding, photo-friendly individual. Mountain hares are well known for having the odd 'tame one'.

If the animal can see you then it's best not to approach it in a straight line. Walk slowly or even crawl on your knees at an angle. Don't look straight into its eyes but glance out of the corner of your eye. Approach slowly, keep the noise to a minimum and try to keep your scent from blowing across the animal. Remember it knows you are there. If you suddenly disappear behind some bracken it can become nervous and wary. As you get closer go slower and have your camera and beanbag or tripod ready. (You don't want to be undoing noisy zips when you're close).

Take insurance shots as you get nearer. You never know when it may flee and it helps you to judge its reaction to the noise of the camera. If you have a silent drive mode then definitely have this set before the stalk. In fact it's a good idea to have all the settings adjusted before the stalk - focus mode, ISO, white balance etc.

Once you get into position and the animal is not aware of you then hunker down (sit or kneel) and try to get your back against a tree, rock or large tuft of heather or bracken. Pick anything that will help disguise your shape. Often it may be that your final approach is hidden by a tree or rock or dip in the ground. The very final approach will take you into the animal's sight line. This is the time when you go very slowly, move your head up carefully and find the animal. If it's looking at you freeze and don't move until it resumes feeding and relaxes.

Once the animal looks comfortable or you think it has not seen you wait until it looks away or feeds and get your camera into position. This might mean adjusting the tripod, monopod, beanbag etc so be slow and silent. Eventually you will be in position with your camera ready to take a shot. Have all settings, including silent drive, set when you were hidden.

Wait until the animal is relaxed, not staring straight at you. Take one shot and don't move at all. Keep viewing the animal through the viewfinder or with your non-focus eye. Watch how it reacts. It may take no notice at all or jerk its head up and stare at your position. Remember it won't know you're there so keep still and watch and wait until it relaxes again. Give it a minute or two and take another image. Hopefully as you repeat this the animal will increasingly relax and will allow you a good photo session.

Photography is usually finished by the animal deciding to move away. However, you may want to leave with the animal still feeding or sleeping. Moving away should be as slow and carefully executed as your approach. The perfect stalk is one where the animal has never been aware you have ever been there. This means that next time you work this site you will have another good chance of success. You definitely don't want the animal feeling nervous and wary when it next feeds here, or even worse to abandon this spot.

29　In some cases you may not be stalking an animal or bird but getting into a position where you expect it to turn up, so you may be able to walk confidently to the spot. In most cases though it's a good idea to anticipate that the animal may be around so whilst you may not take an hour or two to move into position it's good to use the previous guidance to help you get there quietly and not alarm a hidden subject.

Brown hare running alongside a hedge at dawn. I had arrived a few hours before sunrise and lay on a mat in the hedgerow base. My camera was on a beanbag on the ground. All I had to do was to wait until a hare came running towards me.
1D mk4, 500mm, 1/800, f5.6, ISO 500, beanbag on ground. Derbyshire.

There are about 60 species of terrestrial (land dwelling) mammals in the UK. Some of these are natives, such as badgers. Others have been introduced over the last 2000 years and include brown hares, rabbits, grey squirrels and sika deer. The state of our mammal populations is in many cases precarious - hedgehog, red squirrel and water vole numbers have declined dramatically over the last forty years with numbers alarmingly still plummeting.

Some species are probably stable in numbers such as badgers and foxes with approx 250,000 of each. In a few cases some are actually increasing which is certainly true for all deer species. One mammal has certainly seen an amazing change in fortune. Otters were almost at the brink of extinction yet with dedicated conservation their number has risen amazingly and luckily they have become much more visible at long last.

A wary hedgehog in a church yard. 5Dmk2, 16-35mm at 3.2 secs, f16, ISO 1200, tripod, fill flash. Sheffield.

We also have internationally important populations of some species such as grey seals.

Most mammals are difficult to watch. They are usually very wary, often nocturnal and in some cases still persecuted. The larger mammals are all watchable in the wild though a few, like Scottish wild cats, are very secretive and scarce. Most of the larger species are stalkable with care though in some situations you may be able to get closer than others - such as foxes in towns and gardens and deer in deer parks.

The smaller mammals, whilst often very common, can be difficult to photograph in the field, though not impossible. It is with some of these that an alternative approach can work well, though this will not be to every one's taste - live trapping. Mice and bank voles are common and the stress is fairly low if you carry it out well. Many photographers are fine with the idea of trapping a small mammal like a wood mouse or bank vole, keeping it in captivity for a period of time and working with it photographically. If you are not, simply don't do it. For some species, such as the shrews, a licence is needed because they need special care when trapping and keeping healthy in captivity. I would urge you not to photograph shrews until you are very experienced and only after spending time with one of your local experts.

Some small mammals are virtually impossible to photograph in the wild so captive bred animals are used. Two good examples are harvest mice and dormice. If you want to work with these species you will almost certainly have to use captive animals. Again, if you are not comfortable doing this, then don't. However, there is a good argument that far less harm is caused when a captive bred animal is photographed than the potentially large amount of disturbance which can be caused when trying to work with a wild one and in the dormouse's case a protected one.

A badger climbs over the wall on the edge of a wood where the sett was located. I left a few peanuts each night to tempt it to stop for a few seconds. 10D, 1/200, f16, ISO 100, 2 flash guns at -1. Derbyshire.

Badgers

Badgers continue to have a chequered history in Britain. They are the only British mammal that have their own act of parliament, yet we continue to persecute them. The recent culls in SW England highlight just how vulnerable wildlife is when other vested interests can dominate. Badgers are widely distributed across Britain. Their preferred habitat is deciduous woodland but since we have chopped down the vast majority of this badgers have had to adapt to our changing landscape. Setts can be found on moorland, dune systems, gardens and in fields and hedge bottoms - basically virtually anywhere that provides good feeding and the ability to dig a dry home underground.

Badgers are mainly nocturnal. They do venture out in daylight in the evening during summer in some places where disturbance is minimal but on the whole they confine their activities to the dark of night. Badgers eat a variety of food. It is mainly a diet of earthworms to which they add the odd nestling bird, small mammal (including hedgehogs!), carrion and fruit during the year. Photography is often confined to areas around the sett but it is possible to work with them away from it as well.

Locating an active badger sett is not too difficult, it will just take a bit of field work. Many woodlands contain badgers setts, large woods often having a few. Each group of badgers will have a number of setts, perhaps three or four. They tend to use the main one (which is the largest) most of the time but they often have out-lying setts which they may visit for short 'holidays'. I would suggest that you use the winter/early spring months to locate any setts in your area. It should cause less disturbance and the lower level of vegetation makes spotting tracks easier.

The best time to start photographic work is in spring and summer. Adult badgers are very wary and require a lot of effort. Young cubs come above ground in May and are far more confiding. You can build trust up over the summer which increases photographic potential and reduces stress. By September they are adult size. If you follow through with your work over the next few years you will have a group of adults that are photographically workable.

Badger clues

Badgers are creatures of habit. They like to use the same paths to and from favourite feeding grounds so they leave quite visible tracks through woodlands (easier to see with less plant growth in spring). Other animals like deer and foxes may also use these. If the surrounding vegetation closes over the top then it's not likely that deer are using them. On your first exploration simply walk around the wood, especially away from the human footpaths, and look for any animal paths. If they look like they are fairly well worn then follow them. You have two chances really - the path will either go back to the sett or it

A badger trail in a bluebell wood.

won't. If it looks like it might be leaving the wood turn round and follow it the other way. Sooner or later it should lead you to the sett. If it doesn't simply scout around for another path.

Badgers go to the toilet in a very civilised way. They dig a small pit 5 to 10 cm deep and deposit their business there. Badger scat is quite soft and dark brown-black. The pit is the big clue.

Badger latrines. The upper image is a fresh deposit, the lower one is much older.

Eventually you will come across an active sett. First thing, NEVER walk over it. Treat it as if some badgers are just below the surface listening for you, which they may well be. As you approach try to keep downwind and tread slowly and as softly as possible. Look around for any clues of activity. This may be freshly dug soil and bedding (piles of leaves/bracken) left out for an airing (mainly in dry weather in summer). Use your bins to scan as many holes as you can see and check for cobwebs across the entrance holes. Some holes may be hidden by vegetation so be careful. If you feel the sett is in a safe area you can leave a camera trap set up covering the main part of the sett and the hole you think looks most active. If you think this is going to be the sett you will work scatter a few handfuls of peanuts around.

Other badger signs include hair caught on barbed wire when the path crosses fields etc. Many books mention this but in reality it is seldom met with. However, always check any low fences for snagged hair. It is a clue.

Badgers have a range of calls. The most common one is described as whickering and is often heard from cubs when playing. They are noisy feeders and snuffle a lot. Males can be a bit noisy during the mating season in spring with a low level, gruff throaty sound.

The right sett

This is an important consideration. Don't simply find your first sett and think it's the one to use. It might be but there are a number of questions you need to consider. First, make sure the landowner is fine with your ideas and make sure you explain about night time work with flashes going off. Next, check with the local badger group. They will probably be aware of the sett and will need to know you will be there working on it extensively over the summer and possibly beyond.

It's most likely you will be using a flash gun or two. Can these be seen going off from local houses and roads? If they can you should let the local police know what you're doing. It's very embarrassing having a couple of Bobbies appearing in the dead of night. They won't have a clue what you're up to and will probably approach with some firm, if in your case misguided, ideas about your activities! It is better trying to find a sett that can't be seen from a road or footpath. It will cut down embarrassing encounters. It's also worth mentioning that you will be sitting quietly in a wood at night. You need to be sure you are safe and OK with the idea. If you're in an area where badger diggers are active, you definitely don't want to come face to face with a gang. I have once and it was a scary experience.

Check all around the sett and try to work out where you will be doing your photography. Does it offer good potential? It could be there is too much local vegetation to make it worthwhile.

Getting started

Once you have found the best sett and have sought all the necessary permission you can start to put some groundwork in. Scatter a few peanuts around the sett each day, not loads and not in the morning - early in the evening when it's just light. This stops wood pigeons finding them and effectively hoovering them all up. You should aim to start serious work in late May. This may vary across Britain so check out with your local badger group for best dates when cubs first come above ground. When you're ready to watch approach the sett as you always should, keeping downwind and walking softly to your chosen viewing place. The best viewing spots are up in trees because the wind will carry your scent over the top of the sett but it's a real pain in the butt to sit on a tree branch for a few hours! Choose a tree to lean back on, making sure you don't cut any skylines and are not on one of the badger footpaths.

You can leave an old, worn (not washed) t shirt lying in the place you will watch from. It is never clear if this works but it may help them start to get used to your scent. They will smell it eventually anyway. You don't need to use a hide. Just wear dark, neutral coloured, soft clothing (including gloves and a balaclava). Make sure there are a few peanuts about and wait. Start your watch a couple of hours before it gets dark. It might be a long wait but you definitely don't want to turn up when the badgers are above ground. Try to choose evenings when it's likely you will be able to see after dark. Moonlight is a great help so check when the moon is up and at what time and if it's going to be cloudy. Then lean back and wait. If it gets to about 2 or 3 hours after dark and nothing has appeared then consider giving up and aim to return the next evening. Hopefully, sooner rather than later, you will see a badger poke its head out

of one of the holes. If you let a few peanuts roll down the hole you can actually hear the badger munching away before you see it, a good clue to be ready.

When the badger does show up don't move, just watch. It will be cautious at first sniffing the air and looking around. Remember its eyesight is poor but its hearing and sense of smell are acute. If one badger emerges others will probably follow. They tend to stick around for a bit of grooming and play then will depart on their nocturnal forays. Certainly don't take any images yet. In fact rather than be tempted leave your camera at home.

What you're really waiting for are the cubs. They may appear or you may be too early, or possibly there are none in that sett that year. If you get to be a week or two beyond the date you think they should appear you need to make a decision. Try another sett or return next year. You could try a few images with the adults if there are no cubs.

Occasionally you may find a sett that is right out in the open, such as in a farmer's grassy field. Obviously now you can watch from some distance and get a good feel of the activity there. It might be ideal for more environmental images, particularly if the badgers come above ground on light evenings in the middle of summer. However, it may be harder to work closely because there is not much cover to hide your human shape.

Feeding badgers

Many photographers, including myself, feed badgers. Don't use any food with sugar. Some well intentioned, misguided people feed badgers every night in their gardens with Sugar Puffs. The badgers love them but they are long lived animals so tooth decay is a very possible outcome, leaving them in permanent pain. Fatty foods are not good either for obvious reasons. Food sources that are cheap, nutritious and loved by badgers are peanuts and dog nuts.

The second consideration is dependency. Your badgers must lead normal wild lives at all times, especially when you pack up photography. Never use bucket loads of nuts, a couple of handfuls a night is ideal. It gives them a tasty snack to start the night and gets them to hang around your photography area. For the vast majority of the night the badgers should be roaming and searching for natural food.

There is no harm using natural food occasionally. I have cut blackberry bushes and placed them near the sett to get images of the badger feeding on the fruit. I must admit it didn't work brilliantly. I had to use a few peanuts to keep it interested and eventually it did eat a few blackberries but never really looked that keen. 10D, 1/200, f16, ISO 200, 2 flash. Derbyshire.

Lighting the sett at night

Once you are ready to have a session taking images you will need to consider how you intend to light the badgers and be able to see enough to focus. My tried and tested method is to use flash and a red light. You can fix a torch to your lens with an elastic band and cover the end with a piece of red plastic so it shines with a red light. This does work but you tend to wiggle the lens around and it might not be pointing where you want to watch. Badgers don't seem to notice red light at all. The only drawback with using a car battery system (see photo) is that you have to carry it. Depending on how long you leave it on and the power of the bulb it should last at least two to three nights. You can use the same idea and experiment with weaker bulbs and smaller batteries. The key thing is to get your lens to autofocus because it is difficult to critically manually focus in low light levels. If the badgers are not too active you might find live view can work

I made a simple rig using an old stop light from a car. I taped this to a pole and ran it from a small car battery. I cut a dimmer switch into the circuit so I could turn it off and on and slowly bring up the brightness. It's strong enough for my lenses to auto focus and me see well helping you to all the action and the focus . badgers are not bothered in the slightest.

Many photographers use flash to photograph badgers most of the time. A good system uses 2 guns on poles with a unit on the camera that fires the guns directly. Many systems allow you to vary the power of the guns from the camera so you can take a shot, see what it looks like, then vary the power to get modelling (shadow) into the image without having to get up and disturb the badgers.

When you start photography bury the peanuts under a centimetre of soil/leaf litter in the area you want to photograph the badgers. They will quickly find them and you won't have to clone peanuts out of all your images. Wait until the badger is feeding, set the camera to silent and take one shot. The badger will probably retreat, possibly back underground, hopefully not. If it goes back into the sett wait until it comes out again and watch but don't take any more images that evening. If it flinches but does not run off give it five minutes than take another shot. You should now stop for the evening and let it snaffle up the rest of the peanuts. Repeat the next night but take 3 shots and build it up this way. It won't be too long before it does not show any reaction to the camera noise and flash.

Once you have the badgers used to the camera and flash it's now up to you to be imaginative. You may simply be content with images around the sett. However, you might like to get a wider range of pictures. Once your badgers are comfortable with your presence you can start to arrive at the sett five minutes earlier every evening. Within a

Two young badgers at the sett. 10D, 1/200, f16, ISO 100, 2 flash guns at -1. Derbyshire.

couple of weeks they should be coming out in the last rays of the evening sun.

I mounted my camera and wide angle lens with one flash gun on a tent peg at the far end of the tunnel (which I had made at a local saw mill). The other end had 2 flash guns aimed at the entrance to create a rim lit effect on the badger's fur. I baited the tunnel for a week until the badger was really confident then took my first shot firing the camera with an infra red remote. The badger didn't even look up! The only problem I had was that he would often come and nuzzle the camera leaving the lens covered in badger slobber! 10D, 16-35 at 20mm 1/200, f16, ISO 200, 3 flash guns, 1 at -1, 2 at -2, remote trigger. Derbyshire.

Badgers do climb amazingly well so try using short stumps baited with peanuts to get them to rear or climb up.

To get a shot of a badger drinking you may need to bait the banks of any small stream that runs near the sett. It should only take a few nights before they find the nuts and a couple of visits before you get one having a drink. They obviously drink naturally but the places where they can get a drink are so varied it's unlikely you will be there when they stop for a sip.

One shot I always wanted was a badger taking bedding into the sett but I never saw it happen when I had my camera handy. I thought about it and in the end simply collected a load of ferns from the wood, dried them out at home then spread them into a rough mass in front of the sett. On the first night I did this the badger sniffed through the pile and then grabbed as much as it could get into its front paws and shuffled backwards underground. I must admit I was really chuffed it had worked so well and so quickly. EOS 5, 70-200, tripod, 1/200, f16, ISO 100, 2 flash guns. Sheffield.

If you feel that the badgers are really confident with your presence it is possible to follow them on their night time forays. This is taking the situation to another level and the care you need to take is huge. If at any time you feel the badgers are stressed or not behaving naturally retreat and pack up the idea. Remember the golden rule - the welfare of the subject is more important than your images.

You should aim to work the sett most evenings from May until at least September. There is no reason why you can't keep working all year though activity does slow in winter. As you approach the time you intend to finish the project start to leave slightly less peanuts out each night until it's really only a few. This way the badgers learn not to depend on them too much. During my projects working with badgers at the sett I have worked with one other photographer. This is a great help as it reduces the work load greatly. If neither of us intended to photograph one of us would always go and chuck a couple of handfuls of peanuts out. We tended to avoid very windy evenings for photography. Badgers are not keen because their hearing and sense of smell are reduced.

Many people now feed badgers in their gardens and they can quickly lose a lot of their natural inhibitions. If you think you have badgers visiting your garden it is fairly easy to bait them in the ways described earlier. Unless the badgers are used to being photographed take the same precautions as when working for the first time at the sett. This way you should be able to build up their trust with the promise of many fruitful evenings ahead.

Some of the more modern DSLRs now have the capability of setting very high ISOs. This offers the opportunity of photographing nocturnal badgers without flash. There are two ways you can go about this. One is to set up a lighting system that will illuminate the area the badgers feed in - something like the powerful motion sensor lights that are used on doorways. If you allow these to become brighter over a week or two you can easily provide sufficient light to work with. You will need to experiment with your white balance to get the colours as natural as possible.

The other option is to try to use moonlit nights and photograph in totally natural light. Luckily badgers are often fairly static when feeding. When they are coming regularly try to distract them with a little noise, say a click of the tongue. With any luck they should look up for a second or two and allow a shot. Unfortunately they soon learn that these noises are harmless and they cease to be effective if used a lot.

A far more adventurous idea is to try to work with urban badgers by street light. There are many setts in urban areas and these badgers will be out and about, often on a footpath or road that is lit. Here a bit of fieldwork beforehand watching where and when they go should allow you to predict some likely spots to try for images. If you try this it is a good idea to let the local police know - it saves some embarrassing conversations later!

The top badger sett is an old established one with a well defined path leading to it. The bottom sett shows a lot of recent activity with a large amount of newly dug earth making it very obvious.

A young fox stares hard at my hide which was set up in a field of barley next to the edge of a wood. EOS1 100-400mm, 1/500, f5.6, ISO 100, tripod. Sheffield.

Foxes

Foxes are common right across the British Isles. They are found in an incredibly wide range of habitats including towns and cities. Foxes are smaller than many people imagine. They are members of the dog family and are very intelligent. This means they are resourceful and adaptable. In Britain there is only one species of fox, its full name being the red fox. This species also occurs in the USA and widely across Europe.

We can divide, if a little crudely, foxes into two groups based on their relationships with humans - urban and rural. Urban foxes live in towns and cities where they live cheek by jowl with us. They are often fed in gardens or they may scavenge from bins and rubbish tips. They can become amazingly tame and may allow a really close approach. Rural foxes on the other hand are one of the most wary animals you could ever work with. They have a long history of being hunted, chased and shot at. Working with them photographically can be demanding indeed.

Foxes have their young underground in an earth. This may have been excavated and enlarged by them or it may be a natural hole or one dug by badgers. Young fox cubs come above ground in spring, sometime around May and are often amazingly confiding, though the parents are usually the very opposite. Oddly, as you work with fox cubs you find that they become increasingly wary as they age, the opposite of badger cubs which become more confiding the longer you work with them.

Fox clues

You can almost guarantee that foxes will be living near you, the hardest part is to locate them. In cities they are often spotted in the car head lights crossing roads. Probably the quickest way to locate your local foxes is to ask around. You will be amazed at how many people have seen them and you will get some great nuggets of information such as who might be feeding them or possible earth locations. In the countryside woodland edges in farmland are one of the best habitat types and offer some of the best potential for photography. It is a matter of getting out at dawn and dusk and watching.

Foxes walk around the countryside using distinct paths, though these may be the same ones used by badgers. It is possible to follow these but they often wander all over the place and perhaps won't lead back to the earth anyway.

Fox scat is often deposited in obvious places on the edge of their territories as a way of telling each other who is around. The scat is quite thin and long and has tapered/pointed ends. It is usually grey/brown/black with a twisted squiggly appearance and is full of hair if the foxes are eating a natural diet of rabbits, mice etc. It will also contain small bones. In more urban environments where foxes are dining on chilli kebabs and biscuits it resembles more of a dog-like deposit but still with pointed ends and a bit thinner than most dogs.

Fox scat. This one was found on a prominent stone on a frosty morning. Note the tell-tale pointed end.

Foxes are fairly silent through most of the year but they call a lot in December when the mating season is at its height. The call is very distinctive and a bit eerie. The best place to guarantee to hear it is on Midsomer Murders - they love the call of a fox! If you have never heard it start watching 'Massacres' or find a site on the web that has auditory files where you can play the call.

When the cubs are above ground and feel safe, especially in the early morning or at

A young fox next to a hedgerow. EOS1, 100-400, 1/800, f5.6, ISO 100, hide. Derbyshire

dusk, they like nothing better than a good romp and scuffle with each other. They can be quite noisy with high pitched squealings, yips and yelps.

The best clue by a long way is the smell. Foxes have a really distinctive smell. It's sharp, tangy, animal-like, a bit sweaty and quite strong. If you are checking out an area and you suddenly notice a whiff it's almost certainly a fox. It's not unpleasant and if it fades turn around and go back a bit.

See p223 to help recognise fox footprints which resemble dogs but are a bit more diamond shaped with the toes closer together. They are usually about 5cm long.

Watching foxes

Foxes have all their senses tuned to the highest degree. Sight, hearing and smell are all top notch so it's not easy to outwit your local fox. Urban foxes are so used to humans and their smell that they can often be easy to watch. Rural foxes are a different matter altogether. When you set out to watch have a good walk round and select likely places, such as a hedge with a track down the side, a track on a woodland edge or one running across a field. Wear greens/browns and make sure you are downwind of the area you want to watch. You can climb into a tree as long as it's comfy and allows a good view around. A hat and gloves are necessary. The best time is dawn so try to be in position an hour or two before sunup. Sunny, still mornings provide ideal conditions. Then it's simply a matter of waiting. If you put the hours in you will see foxes, that's almost guaranteed.

Photography

The big decision is how and where you want to photograph - at the earth with pups or one of the adults walking along a path. If you want to work at the earth you will need to find it. It will resemble a badger's and it may even be in an old badger's sett. There will be holes, though not as many or with such huge earthworks as a badger's. A good clue is if there are any food remains around - bits of fur, chewed rabbit bones etc. Foxes

41 are messy around the earth, badgers don't tend to leave remains around. If the pups are above ground surrounding vegetation may be trampled by their play.

Not all wild foxes are nervous of humans. This wild fox in Norway was amazingly tame. 1Dmk2, 300mm, 1/500, f4, ISO 500.

If you think you have found an earth then extreme caution is needed. If the vixen becomes in the slightest bit nervous she will move the pups to another earth. Don't go close if you can help it. Try to make sure you don't go trampling all over the earth and surrounding area. Don't go looking for it at dawn or dusk when there is a risk that mum or dad may return and catch you there. You probably wouldn't even know they were around and had seen you. Mid-day, with bins and quiet footfalls is best. Check out any likely spots - hedge bottoms, woodland etc until you have found it. If you are then going to watch the earth you really need to be as far away as possible and completely hidden. Here camo gear can be a help. Again dawn is best as this is the time you are most likely to see pups about or an adult returning. A camera trap watching the fox paths that lead to the earth can help to get an idea of any activity.

In an urban situation like a garden where they are fed and used to humans you probably won't need a hide or other method of concealment. In a more rural area you will almost certainly need to use a hide.

Photographing a fox on a path is never easy and you will have to put a lot of preparation in first. Winter is probably the ideal season - the foxes are set in their territory and food is harder to find. They tend to be secretive and extra wary in spring and early summer when they have pups. Once you have found a path that is well used you will have to decide where you will put your hide. The best spot will be alongside the path that allows you a good vantage point but far enough away for the fox hopefully not to notice it.

Remember to consider where the sun will be shining at dawn. Start the hide low, covered with scrim and disguised with local vegetation. Leave a dummy lens with lens hood so they get used to seeing it. Make sure you have loads of scrim in the hide to drape around the lens so there is no chance of any movement from you being spotted. The foxes will see the hide but the idea is that they don't consider it a threat. Leave it for a week or two, then bait the path with raisins, bits of biscuit, chicken bits etc in the area you want to get your image. It is best to bait at dawn or in the evening. If you bait during the day wood pigeons and magpies quickly find it and scoff the lot! Try not to get your scent on the food. Hopefully the fox will get used to these little snacks and wait a minute or two here at dawn each day.

When you want to start pick a day where the light will be ideal, lay out the bait at the usual time, get into the hide and get really comfy. (I would suggest an hour before dawn). Check you have a good view and wait. When the fox appears stay still and watch. Hopefully it will stop and eat its snack. Move your gloved hand slowly to the camera and lens. You will have to decide when to press the shutter. Have all the settings adjusted before the fox turns up, including silent drive. Try to pick a moment when it glances to the side of the hide, not when its head is down. Focus on the eye with the autofocus and press the shutter. The fox will certainly hear it and may stare hard at you, or even leave. Freeze in the hide and wait until it does one of two things - starts feeding again or disappears. If it's the former give it a minute and try another shot.

It is probably best to stop then and wait until it leaves. Once it has gone wait for at least 30 minutes so that hopefully it has left

I had watched this fox on a number of early mornings as it patrolled a path alongside a wood. I set up a hide which I tucked into the vegetation and left it for a week before I started my photography. I only ever managed a couple of shots because when the light was good it tended to create hot spots which normally I don't like but in this case I think they add a bit to the story. EOS 1, 500mm, 1/250, f4, ISO 100 slide film. Sheffield.

the area. If it sees you get out of the hide (remember you don't know where it is) then you have blown it for good. If all goes well try another morning. Adult foxes rarely stop being wary and you will seldom get them to become tame so exercise the highest caution every time you work on that path.

Working at the earth requires even more caution because if mum gets any inclination you are there she may well shift the pups to another earth. Again you will have to use a hide and it will have to be well placed and disguised. In a hedge or bush is ideal so it's not like a new shape appearing in the area. However, saying this, the last time I worked at a fox earth we placed the hide in a field of growing wheat facing a hedge where the pups came to play. The wheat helped to disguise the hide a bit but it did stick above the vegetation.

Many gardens in urban areas are visited by foxes. Occasionally these become tolerant of humans and appear in daylight. Suitable food left out for them will encourage them to visit more often. This fox patrols through my garden every few days and sometimes it just watches as I crouch down and take images. 1DX, 500mm, 1/250, f4, ISO 800, Sheffield.

43 Exercise all the same precaution as if working with an adult on a path. Pups like sweet things so try a bit of honey (in moderation) on a few peanuts and dog biscuits to tempt them to stay in the area of the hide. The best situations are when the hide can't be seen from the earth.

Pups are really confiding when very young but as they age they quickly adopt the necessary wariness of their parents and photography becomes harder the longer you proceed with the project. It is possible to add some natural food - the odd roadkill rabbit can provide a nutritious snack for the pups and can make for some great photography.

This young fox was sunbathing in my garden. 1DX, 70-200mm, 1/800, f4, ISO 800, handheld. I tried to keep it around for the next week by putting out food. All I ended up doing was feeding the local magpies!

I used my trail cam to photograph this fox which visited my garden every few days. This allowed me to work out where and when he showed up so I could plan my photography better.

Otters

Once virtually extinct in huge parts of England otters have now returned to all the English counties and remain healthy across much of Scotland and Wales. A decade or two ago virtually all wild otter images were taken on the Scottish coastline as trying to capture usable images of an otter on a river was virtually impossible. Today, refreshingly, this is not so. A number of 'river' otters have grown up who don't see humans as a threat and are active during daylight. It's not wise to give precise locations. By the time you read this book they may no longer be there and other sites will have been found. And it's not the brightest idea to overload a site with hundreds of photographers chasing an otter as happened in Norfolk recently. I have seen otters on rivers and have photographed captive ones but the majority of my work with wild otters has been on the Scottish coastline.

Signs

Otters leave footprints and sometimes large dog otters drag their tail which leaves a line in the sand or mud. The best sign is their scat, called spraint. Otters like to advertise their presence to others by leaving spraint in certain places, a smelly marker of who is around.

If you are searching for signs of otters you need to be familiar with spraint, and also make sure you can identify mink scat as well. (Probably the only other scat that is likely to be in similar places). Otters stick pretty much to the coastline or river bank and spraint in familiar places. On the coast look at rocks on small headlands, prominent boulders or rocks that remain dry and, at low tide, prominent piles of seaweed. The latter are only likely to show spraint if an otter has been there in the last few hours. On rivers look on prominent stones, under bridges and big tree roots. If you walk the bank make sure you take your time and keep glancing under it. It's easier to find spraint by actually walking in the river itself with waders on.

Female otter. 1DX, 500mm, 1/800, f5.6, ISO 1250, handheld. Scotland.

Otter spraint on the coast showing crab shell bits and fish scales. The colour is pink - reflecting the crab diet.

The state of the spraint will give a clue as to how old it is (though this can depend on if it has rained recently). The key thing is to tell if it's from an otter. If you don't fancy picking it up poke it with a stick and look for fish scales - it should be full of them. Smell your stick. It should be sweet smelling and actually pleasant, sort of like damp hay. The colour is very variable, usually dark and bound by a sticky tar-like substance which dries out grey in colour. Spraint is about 5cm long. The key identifier is the smell.

Mink scat (often confused with otters) is 6-8 cm long, usually black or dark, occasionally lighter, twisted a bit like rope and tapered at both ends. It will usually contain some bones, some fish scales and fur. It however stinks (from the mink's anal glands).

If you find spraint and lots of it, then it's a good clue that otters are around and your chance of seeing one is increased.

Otters live in underground holes called holts. These are usually near or on the bank of a river (often under and among old tree roots). On the coast they can be up to 50, even 100 metres, from the shore line. It is perhaps not the best idea to look for the holt. Disturbance is too much of a risk especially as it may contain their young. If you stumble across a potential holt then retreat quietly and leave it alone.

Watching otters

Once you have found an area to work the next thing is to find your otter. Traditionally river otters were nocturnal, mainly to avoid people. It was not that long ago that hunting for otters with hounds was legal practice. Today a number of otters on some rivers are definitely losing their wariness and have started to be active during daylight. It is almost certain that as time goes by this will increase dramatically.

Otters on the Scottish coast are dominantly active in daylight. There is a lot written about which state of the tide is best. Often it's suggested that a rising tide is ideal because fish follow the tide in. I must admit that I now pay no attention to the state of the tide. The best time to work with coastal otters is in winter because the shorter days increase your chances of an encounter. Otters will fish at high tide, low tide and on both rising and falling tides. Your main philosophy should be to watch from dawn to dusk whatever the state of the tide.

This otter had come on shore and was checking some spaint, possibly left by another otter. Once it had taken a good sniff it turned round and left its own calling card. 1Dmk4, 500mm, 1/1600, f5.6, ISO 1000, handheld. Scotland.

Coastal otters' territories are two to three km long, with dogs having bigger territories that overlap a number of females. On a river the territory can be anything from four to twenty km. You have two approaches - wait at a likely spot or walk the river or coastline and watch.

Many photographers prefer the latter as they feel that it increases their chance of

Female otter on her favourite seaweed resting place. 1DX, 500mm, 1/1200, f4, ISO 2000, hand-held. Scotland.

coming across an otter. In coastal situations you may have some choice as to which piece of coast you want to work.

Rocky coasts are much better at concealing you and are much easier to get close to the otter. Unfortunately they don't offer as many good photographic opportunities as flatter, seaweed-covered beaches. The problem with rocky shores is that the otter often chooses a hidden spot between two boulders or strips of rock so your viewpoint is partly obstructed or your angle is not so good. Flatter beaches are far harder to get close to the otter but if it does come ashore in front of you the backgrounds tend to be better.

On the coast look carefully with your bins at any rocks or seaweed that an otter could be snoozing or feeding on. It is also a good idea to watch the activity of other animals as well for clues. It does not happen all the time but occasionally a group of hooded crows flit around a feeding otter hoping for a few scraps. If you spot anything like this take a much longer look. Always make sure you don't cut into the skyline and are suitably dressed. You don't need camo wear - matt browns and greens are fine. Gloves are a bonus. They help to disguise your hands and protect them from barnacle encrusted rocks which can be really sharp. Waterproof trousers help as you will be lying on wet seaweed or sand, sometimes actually in the sea itself!

After checking for any possible otters on shore make sure you constantly scan the sea. Otters tend to dive for about 30 seconds or so. When one surfaces its head bobs up and if it has caught something you can watch it eat it if the fish is fairly small. It's actually possible to hear it feeding. Even if its 30 to 100 metres from the shoreline you can sometimes hear the otter merrily chomping away.

When the otter dives the tail sticks up and is followed by a splash. It is sometimes the white splash that first draws your attention. Confusion occurs with diving birds like ducks and cormorants. They are about the same size and look similar when diving. However when they pop up their distinctive bird shape gives them away. If it's possible try to choose the calmest days, rough seas are a nightmare to try to spot fishing otters.

Once you have located an otter it's then a case of how to get close enough to photograph it. This depends on whether it is fishing at sea or on the shoreline.

Getting close for photography

If it's fishing, or diving and travelling the approach is to only move when the otter is under water. The trick is to try to decide where on the shore it could come out if it caught a large fish or crab. If it catches a small one it will eat it at sea, large ones are usually brought ashore. Try to watch the otter from a lying down position. Then attempt to determine if it's moving along the coast or fishing in one spot. If it's moving or you want to improve your position wait until it dives then (camera in hand) get up and run for 10-12 seconds, counting elephants (seconds) as you jog along. On 12 elephants dive down again and wait. Hopefully you will spot the otter surface so watch without moving. Try to ensure the wind is blowing away from the otter to you and not from you to it. If the otter is always moving along during each dive keep repeating the process as you follow it along the shoreline.

If it catches something large you can usually spot this as soon as it surfaces and you now know it will work its way to the shore. Most of the time it will swim on the surface with an occasional dive. When it dives try to work yourself into a position where you can photograph it and where you predict it will come to shore. Don't stand up when it's swimming and break the skyline!

If you feel that to crouch and move will cause the otter to spot you belly crawl, using as much cover as possible, into position before it comes to shore. You don't have much time to do this but don't rush it. In many cases it will come to shore in an unphotogenic position or simply in a place you can't see it. Sometimes this will be the end because it will be impossible to work into a position to get a shot. If this is the case, such as if it's on the seaward side of a large rock, don't be tempted to try to get into a bad position. The risk of scaring the otter it is too high.

When otters are swimming they are generally doing one of two things - either fishing or travelling. If they are fishing they can stay in the same spot for a few dives and tend not to move far between dives, though they may move further out to sea. You should pay particular attention to these otters because they may come to shore with a large catch.

At other times the otter may simply be travelling. It becomes obvious because it never catches anything and it travels a fair distance during each dive. It may also swim

This female otter has caught a large fish and swum with it to shore. The art of stalking is to be in the right place as she approaches and comes ashore. 1DX, 500mm, 1/500, f4, ISO 1000. Scotland.

on the surface. It is now making its way somewhere. If it's a female it may be going back to its holt or to a favourite haul-out site in seaweed. If it's a male it may be cruising looking for females or again going back to its holt. If you choose to follow one of these it may travel for over a mile. If it's going back to its holt it will eventually veer towards the shore and once there run from the sea and into cover. It may use a small stream to move inland.

Once back in its holt it will probably stay there for quite a few hours. If it uses a stream to travel to its holt it is possible to lie on the bank well back from the holt and wait until it either returns or leaves. As long as you keep back and don't let your scent blow across the otter you should cause no harm.

If the otter is in a potentially photographable position on land but you're not there yet, you will have to stalk it. This should be done on your belly if you're on a flat, exposed shore line. If there are rocks to give cover use these. Even on your belly seaweed lumps can disguise your approach. Keep downwind and approach as quietly as possible.

Choose seaweed or bare rock to crawl on, shingle can be very noisy. Put one hand down slowly and feel it sink into the seaweed, let any shingle or stones move slowly and quietly as your weight is taken up, slide your camera ahead and repeat with the other hand, using your knees to move forward. Take your time, don't rush, and watch the otter all the time.

Try to move when the otter is eating. If it stops and looks at you, freeze and don't move until it starts to chomp away again. Move slowly into position. When you're there carefully move your camera into a place where you will take your first picture. This may be on a rock if one's available. You will find that more often than not you use your knees or actually handhold the camera because there is nothing high enough to use. You might think a tripod would help but they are a nightmare when you're stalking and really difficult to put in position when the otter is only a few metres in front of you. A short mono-pod can be good. You could take a beanbag when you are stalking and hope a suitable rock or mound of seaweed is available.

If you are stalking on a river the idea is the same but you will be on the bank so there is likely to be more cover. It may be the case that the otter goes to the bank you are on and feeds underneath. I met a photographer where this happened and he quietly retreated, sprinted up river a 100 metres, waded across and stalked from the opposite bank so he could get a shot.

The taking of your first shot is the same as with any new situation. Use silent drive, take one image when the otter's distracted (such as when it's eating) and watch. If it looks up wait until it relaxes again and repeat. You will usually be able to take many this way, perhaps even be able to switch on the fast frame rate as it gets used to the noise.

Occasionally the otter may start to move towards the shoreline without a fish and it may be slowly getting closer as it swims along. When this happens there is a good possibility that it may be coming to the shore ahead of you for a groom and brush up, even a snooze. Try to look ahead and see if there is a prominent heap of seaweed it may use. If on a previous day you had found sprint on some seaweed this may be a clue, or you may have seen the otter on the shore. If this is the case try to run into position to get to that place as the otter dives. You are now ready and waiting if it chooses to come to shore. It does not always work but it is well worth considering. When the otter does come onto the shore be very quiet. It will first watch using seaweed to disguise itself and you may not spot it so it's a good policy to be very quiet and still if you are not sure where it is. It will often surprise you when it does appear.

The end of your session is usually the otter finishing its fish or crab dinner and leaving. However you may stalk it when it is asleep on a pile of seaweed. It could be here for eight hours or more so try not to disturb it too much. Then, when you want to leave, use the same method as your approach. Don't stand up and scare it thinking you have all the shots you want. In some areas of Scotland otters no longer snooze out in the open because they have been disturbed so much by photographers!

Two otter cubs, 1Dmk 4, 500 mm+1.4 converter, 1/500, f5.6, ISO 800. Scotland.

A weasel emerges from a leaf covered wall in autumn. 1DX, 300mm with extension tube. 1/800, f2.8, ISO 1200, tripod. Sheffield.

The smaller mustelids - stoats, weasels, mink and pine marten

The smaller mustelids have a particular attraction all of their own. They all share a common body shape - long and sinuous with short limbs. They look like they have been designed to get down as small a hole as possible, which in fact they love to do. They are fast, very active and usually very difficult to observe easily. All are carnivores and excellent hunters. Stoats and weasels are common across the whole of the UK. Pine martens, also a native species, are having something of a renaissance, having been actively persecuted for centuries and driven back to the wilds of Scotland, Wales and Ireland. They became virtually extinct in England.

Mink is an introduced species having escaped or been released from fur farms. They are very fond of water and now occur along many of our rivers and canals. They are certainly having an effect on our native species and the sad demise of our water voles is partly due to the rise in mink numbers. The silver lining (if one does exist) is that mink and otters don't get along and as otters are increasing the hope is that mink numbers may decline.

Stoats and weasels

Stoats are often confused with weasels because our glimpses of them tend to be fleetingly short. They are larger, about 30cm long, and have a characteristic black tip to their tail. In winter a few turn white (ermine) in Scotland and England but it is quite rare in southern England. In Derbyshire most gamekeepers have only ever seen the odd white stoat in their lifetime.

Like weasels, stoats are common and exist much closer to us than we think. Both are active hunters of other mammals, particularly mice, voles and rabbits. An adult stoat can kill an adult rabbit and many have heard tales

about how they mesmerise the rabbit and literally run circles round it.

The best place to watch for stoats is at a large rabbit warren where you might be lucky to see one hunting in the open. Their metabolic rate is high so they have to hunt for quite a time every day. Very cold days in winter when the demand for food is higher will make them bolder and increase your chances of getting a view.

The most bizarre place I have seen a stoat was right out in the middle of a frozen lake as it ran from one reed bed to another, obviously looking for food. This stoat shows its black tipped tail well. 1Dmk4, 500mm + 1.4 converter, 1/2000, f5.6, ISO 1600, tripod, from a hide. Yorkshire.

Stoats can have up to 12 kits but usually 5 or 6 is normal. They are born in spring around May to June and will venture above ground in a few weeks. As they get older and bolder they can play right out in the open around their den. If you are lucky to ever come across this you should certainly have hours of amazing viewing ahead.

Weasel scat, thin and with a twisted rope - like appearance and usually full of hair. Stoat scat is similar.

This weasel was fed small bits of chicken on an old wall where I built the set with a rusty pipe. 5Dmk3, silent motordrive, 300mm, 1/1000, f4, ISO 1600, tripod. Sheffield.

Most encounters with stoats and weasels are fleeting, usually the animal is darting across a path or road. However, if you have your camera at the ready and spot one streak across a path walk quietly up and sit down. If you can make a squeaking noise with the back of your hand there is a fair chance it will pop back out for a glance. They are incredibly curious animals. If this does happen have the camera ready on a tripod so you can squeak and be prepared for the shot.

It is possible to bait both stoats and weasels. They love linear systems like hedges and old walls where they can hunt for mice and voles. Place small pieces of chicken or rabbit into the wall. Make sure you hide it well inside the wall. (You will be amazed at how resourceful magpies are at finding any food). Unfortunately stoats and weasels don't always hunt the same area every day so you may need to bait for quite a while. It does work but is a bit of a lottery.

If you see a stoat or weasel around a certain place definitely bait up there first. You don't need a hide. Just sit very quietly, dressed in greens/browns with a hat and gloves. Have the camera already set up and keep your hands close to the controls. Once you spot it be ready for it to poke its head out of any suitable hole. Try to remember which ones have meat in them.

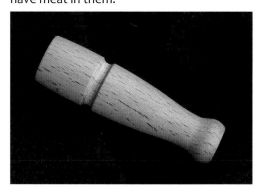

A gamekeeper's rabbit sqeaker.

Stoats can be called up with a rabbit squeaker. It does have to be relatively close but if you spot one or are in an area where you know there is a good population you could try this. One word of warning though, not everyone is keen on the idea of fooling animals with squeakers and you have to think carefully about how you want to generate your images. I certainly wouldn't do this in a public area and would only use the squeaker judiciously.

If you can get the animal coming regularly you can try to put the bait a little further away from the wall, say hiding it in fallen leaves or under moss. The stoat or weasel may start to explore and find it. If you do get to this stage or get one coming for food try to work it as often as you can. They tend to be very ephemeral animals and may turn up every day for a week or two them simply disappear again.

Mink

I have had limited photographic experience with mink though I have seen many over the years. I often spot them as they swim across a river and it's easy then to see how they can be mistaken for an otter.

Mink are a non-native species that we've allowed to escape from fur farms. They are fairly firmly anchored to water systems, using rivers and streams to hunt along or move across country. Droppings are a clue. They are much smellier and unpleasant compared to otters and have a tell - tale twist. The best way to watch mink is to station yourself on a suitable river or canal at dawn and watch with binoculars. A check for droppings in similar places to otters should let you know if they are about. The rest is a bit of pot luck. If there are fishermen about it's always worth asking them if they have seen any mink and can give you some clues.

Mink often leave footprints because of the nature of the river bank and these can help you decide where to concentrate your efforts.

I have not heard of anyone baiting mink but I would guess that small bits of fish in strategic spots under the bank, on stones etc may work. I would certainly choose very hard, cold weather because they will be far keener to find food. The big problem is other things eating the food, like magpies or herons.

Pine martens

One of our most drop dead gorgeous British mammals, pine martens are larger than stoats and far more arboreal, loving to climb and explore in trees. They were persecuted vigorously in the past and were driven back to the more remote parts of our Islands where they tended to shun the presence of man. Luckily that situation is no longer true and some holiday lets in Scotland now feed pine martens in their gardens.

This adult pine marten was coming to bait (peanuts and a few raisins) every evening in the summer. It would usually arrive with enough daylight for photography. 10D, 300mm, 1/250, f4, ISO 800. Hide and tripod. Scotland.

They are slowly re-invading their old haunts as the persecution of the past has relaxed and are present now in much of highland Scotland and in small pockets of Northern England and Wales.

In England and Wales, unless you are very lucky, sightings are hard to come by. In Scotland there are many places now where they are fed at dusk and before you start a project try to visit one of these to become familiar with the animal. Probably the best way to get to grips is to find an area where they are already fed by locals, holiday lets or a wildlife organisation. Booking a holiday cottage where someone else has done all the hard work of habituating the martens to human presence and getting them coming regularly to food is by far the easiest way forward. You can build your own sets to create unique images. Most sets involve mossy logs or stumps.

They have a sweet tooth and will take bread with jam or peanut butter, custard creams and eggs. It's best to use food they are accustomed to but try to keep the sugar content low and hide it so it does not show up in your images.

If you want the reward of completely creating your own project you will have to find an area where pine martins exist. Instead of trampling around miles of forest in Scotland ask around (local forestry workers) until you find an area that sounds ideal. Learn to identify their scat which is about 6 to 12 cm long with a twisted appearance. The colour is variable depending on what they are eating but look for signs of fur and seeds, especially in autumn. It can be confused with fox scats but is sweeter smelling.

Activity is mainly after dark so try to bait a selections of sites with suitable food and keep doing this for a while. Once you know the food is going hide up with a good view a couple of hours before dusk and watch, or set up a trail cam. This will save you hours of watching and will tell you if it is a pine marten taking your bait and at what time it visits. With luck you will have attracted a pine marten and if you do this in mid summer you may be lucky to get mum with her kits.

The big advantage of working in mid summer are the long hours of daylight. With high ISOs it is possible to work into the late evening and produce images of the animals in natural daylight without resorting to flash. It is best to start with a hide but once you have the martens coming regularly they often become fairly tolerant of the photographer and you may be able to sit with your back to a bush or tree and work free of a hide.

Pine marten scat showing some fur and bones.

Hedgehogs

Hedgehogs are ingrained into our wildlife folk-lore. We have all heard of Mrs Tiggy Winkle and old names include urchin and hedge pig. For many of us the most familiar sighting though is a very flat one on a road in spring and summer. Hedgehogs are fairing really badly in the UK at the moment. Some surveys are suggesting that they may have declined from around 30 million in the 1950's to possibly less than one million today. The reason for their decline is not clear but larger, chemical sprayed fields, loss of hedgerows and effective garden fences plus the almost unstoppable rise in cars and roads are all probably responsible. The idea of a hedgie snuffling about our gardens on summer nights is getting to be a scarce thing indeed.

Hedgehogs spend about a third of the year in hibernation so photography is really restricted to the spring, summer and early autumn. The first hogs tend to emerge around late March to April. Mating takes place in spring and if you ever get to watch (or more likely listen) it can be a really noisy affair - not surprising really considering the prickles!

Hedgehogs, unless you are very lucky and have a garden visitor, are actually difficult to find. Their preferred habitat is deciduous woodland and areas of small fields of old pasture with good hedgerows. They are usually totally nocturnal, not venturing out until about an hour after dusk. So if you want to find one this is the best time to look. One tip though, don't concentrate on woods or farmland where there is a good population of badgers. They think nothing of eating hogs and usually hogs are rare where badgers are common.

Hedgehogs are quite noisy as they explore and feed, particularly if there are lots of dry leaves about. They continually snuffle and sniff as they explore for food. However, if they hear you they will freeze and become silent. The best way is to use really well walked paths that allow you to move silently

This hog visited my garden for a few weeks one summer. I baited the step with a bit of dog food and snails. 1Dmk4, 16-35mm, tripod, cable release, small fill-in flash. 1/60, f3.5, ISO 500. Sheffield.

and you should walk very slowly around the wood or area until you hear a hog rambling about.

For those that are lucky enough to have a hedgie regularly visiting your garden you can do a few things to keep it around for longer. Many people feed hogs but you must be careful with the food you use. Never use bread and milk. It's unnatural and gives them diarrhoea, which can eventually prove fatal. A few small chunks of dog food are good.

The hogs natural diet is insects, worms, slugs and small snails. It is a bit of a myth that they eat all snails. Many hogs can't break the shells of the big ones. One trick is to gather up a selection of the larger snails then tap each one to break its shell and place them around the garden in photogenic spots at dusk. The hogs love them, noisily chomping them up with real gusto. They sound just like they are eating crispy, spring rolls!

If you are not sure you have hogs in your garden you can look out for their droppings on the lawn. They are usually dark to black, squiggly and about 5cm long. You can also put food out and simply sit and wait after dusk for a few evenings. A low powered torch will help but you are really waiting to hear if a hog is visiting your garden. Unfortunately the absence of any food the following morning is not a sure sign as your local cats and foxes may snaffle it up. If you don't want to wait all night to see who is scoffing the food use a trail cam.

Photography

Photographing wild hogs is not as simple as it sounds considering they are slow-ish animals. Any noise from you will usually cause them to stop and curl up. Now is the time to try for a shot. Lie down in front of it with your camera on a beanbag. In time it will slowly unfurl. Annoyingly though it will often curl up again and flinch at any shutter noise. Certainly use the silent mode if your camera has one. This is something you should seriously consider when you buy a new camera body.

Hedgehogs are nocturnal so working with wild ones will probably mean the use of flash and since you will probably be moving around the flash must be mounted on the camera. As a rule they tend not to be too bothered by the flash, it's more the noise of the camera. If the animal does seem reluctant to perform then the best policy is to leave it alone and let it get on with finding its food.

If you build up a good working relationship with a rescue centre it may be possible to keep some of their rescued hogs for a while feeding them until they reach the critical release weight. Then, with their guidance, you can release the hogs into suitable places. It's now that you do the photography whilst you carry on feeding these 'wild' animals.

Most of my hedgehog work has been done with rescued animals. I have an excellent working relationship with a local hedgehog rescue centre. There are many of these dotted around the country providing a vital lifeline. Some are big concerns but others are simply caring individuals who want to do something positive. They may be open to discussing their work with you and sharing their experiences. Gifts of dog food and photographs can go a long way to establishing a good working relationship. This rescued hog had been released into a local woodland. 1Dmk4, 180 macro, 1/160, f4.5, ISO 800, tripod. Sheffield.

Some disappear immediately, probably finding better spots. However, some do hang around and can be worked with over the coming weeks. The main advantage here is that you are not stressing out a totally wild animal and as a bonus they are already slightly habituated to your presence and camera noise. You should get a warm feeling that you have played a small part in helping the rehabilitation of hogs in your local area.

If however, you come across a hog wandering around in daylight you should consider picking it up (with gloves), placing it in a strong box with newspaper for bedding and getting it to a rescue centre as soon as possible. Hogs that wander around in daylight tend to be ill or severely underweight. If it proves to be fine simply return it straight away to where you found it. It is a difficult call because if you leave it and check later with a rescue centre the chances are you won't find it again.

A rescued hedgehog in one of my local woodlands. 1Dmk4, 70-200mm, 1/250, f4, , hand held, ISO 800. Sheffield.

I used this rescued hedgehog to create this image for my local hog hospital who wanted to remind people of the dangers of cars to hogs.1Dmk4, 70-200mm, 1/500, f4, hand held, ISO 800. Sheffield.

Mice, voles and rats

There are a number of different species of mice, voles and rats in Britain. Some, like the Skomer vole, are restricted in their range but most are widely distributed. In terms of mice the one that is most photographed is the wood mouse (or its close relative the yellow-necked mouse). House mice are oddly much rarer than in days past but do make good projects. Both species can be photographed in either the wild or in captivity. They are easy to trap in humane mammal traps and adapt well to a week or two in a large tank.

Working with wild, small mammals in captivity is something that is now becoming frowned upon as we rightly continually review how we relate to the natural world. Certainly images produced this way should have it stated in the caption. I have trapped wood mice in the past and kept them in specially made large tanks. I never felt it was cruel or that the mice suffered in any way. However, in response to the changing ethics of wildlife photography I believe it is not appropriate to describe or encourage anyone to work in this way now.

Dormouse in captivity as part of a breeding and release programme. 1Dmk3, 180mm, 1/250, f4, ISO 500, fill-in flash in daylight. Somerset.

Dormice

The dormouse is arguably the most drop-dead-gorgeous of our small mammals but is protected and very difficult to photograph in the wild. The vast majority of images are from captive individuals and a licence will be needed. If you want to work with this species you will have to find someone who is part of a captive breeding project and hope they can help you.

Dormice are nocturnal and most images are taken with flash. Some photographers now have misgivings about the over use of flash. I have worked with dormice on a number of occasions over the years and the mice hated it. They do have a neat trick to avoid predators, they freeze when they feel threatened. This can appear that they are comfortable but they are not - it's a defensive strategy. The ears, like harvest mice, are held flat against the head when they are very nervous. If you do get the chance to work with one be aware of this, it makes for an unnatural and unpleasant image.

Harvest mouse in summer breeding nest in natural grasses. The nest was found after it had been used by wild mice. Captive mouse. 1Dmk4, 180 macro, 1/250, f8, ISO 800, tripod.

Harvest mice

Harvest mice are small and not far from dormice in the cute stakes. There are very few, if any, true wild harvest mice images. A trained researcher and mammal expert who surveys harvest mice and has been doing so for over 25 years told me that he has only seen two wild mice in that time and on both occasions they shot off. Most images are taken in captivity from captive bred stock.

Longer macro lenses such as a 100 or 180mm are ideal. The mouse will wander

I have bred harvest mice for a number of years now and they make fascinating animals to photograph. They are probably the easiest mouse to work with - they do not jump and I photograph mine in natural light in the open. I simply put a bunch of weeds or canary grass in an old school chemistry clamp, boss and stand. I then place the mouse in the vegetation and let it clamber around. This harvest mouse is photographed among blackberries. Here I was a bit nervous of the sharp thorns so I clipped them all off with a pair of nail sissors first. Keeping the set and props faithful to natural situations should be an important aspect of your work. 1DX, 180 macro, 1/800, f2.8, ISO 800, tripod. Captive.

around a bit on your set so mount the lens on a tripod. This will allow you to keep your hands free to make sure the mouse comes to no harm. Make sure the background is pleasing and wait until the mouse relaxes.

A relaxed mouse is an important point because if it is stressed or nervous (which is not surprising) it will have its ears flattened. Lots of harvest mice images are of scared mice because the photographer is not aware of this. Even some that do well in competitions look scared stiff (the mouse that is!). If you are gentle and patient with them they soon relax and their ears adopt the normal upright pose. Try not to work with them in hot, bright sunshine. The mice will over-heat and become uncomfortable and the high light levels can create hot spots. Warm, bright, overcast skies are best.

One other issue well worth mentioning is the appropriateness of the props or vegetation you use. It is certainly odd (if understandable) that many images of harvest mice are still published with them on stalks of modern wheat or barley. Harvest mice have not lived in fields like this for decades. The habitat is far too harsh. There are no weeds for food and for making nests and storms of toxic chemicals are devastating. Most harvest mice that dwell in Britain choose weedy areas or often wetlands with reed canary grass. Every time a shot is published with the mouse on a cereal the myth is further enhanced.

Voles

The two most common voles are the bank and short-tailed vole. They do overlap a bit in their preferred ranges but basically short-tailed voles are larger and much more restricted to grassy moors, dunes and rough grassland. Bank voles prefer a more wooded habitat and are easy to work with in the wild. Short-tailed voles are harder, partly because they tend not to respond to being fed like bank voles because their diet is less varied and their habitat (grassy fields or moorland) is far larger and difficult to work in.

Water voles are Britain's fastest declining mammal, an unenviable record to hold. As Ratty of Wind in the Willows fame they are well loved and another one for the 'gorgeous' league table. They are noticeably larger than the other voles and are very photographable in wild situations.

Photographing wood mice, house mice and bank voles

Whilst all three species are small they can be photographed in the wild by feeding them. You will probably notice that when you run a bird feeder in the winter it is not too long before a wood mouse or bank vole appears on a regular basis in daylight snaffling any fallen sunflower seeds and peanuts. It is quite easy to take this a step further by putting food in a spot where you have created a nice photogenic set-up.

This bank vole is snacking on spilt seeds from a bird feeder placed on the wall above. I was only visiting this site for one day but if I had more time it would have been a simple matter to create a more photogenic set to photograph the vole which was used to the camera and bright sunlight. 1Dmk4, 500mm 1.4, extension tube, 1/1000, f5.6, ISO 250, tripod. Wales.

Choose small hollow logs (about a mouse width in size) scatter nice vegetation and leafs around and bait the site. Ideal situations would be hedge bottoms, edges of a wood or clearing or somewhere in some rough weedy ground. Make sure there is an area where you can lie down not too far away with a clear view of the set. It won't take too long before a mouse or vole is visiting the site every day. To increase your chances bait in the morning so the animal gets into the habit of appearing in daylight. However, try

to hide the bait in a way that the mice find it but the flying 'Dyson' on wings (the wood pigeon) does not!

This bank vole was baited at a bird feeder I was running over autumn and winter. I simply created a set around the base of the bird table and took the image from ground level. 1Dmk3, 300mm, 1/500, f5.6, ISO 1000, beanbag. Sheffield.

On the day you want to produce some images clean the site up, make sure everything looks good through the camera (no distracting grass stalks across the place you want the vole to come to) and hide the food (peanuts, apple, sunflower seeds etc). Try to use a big lens, say a 300mm, with extension tubes. This allows you to be a little distance away but still get a good image size. You can use a hide but if you lie or sit still they quickly get used to you and the camera noise.

Start with the camera on silent drive mode if you have it to get them accustomed to the noise. They move really quickly but they will often stop in the entrance of the hollow log and watch, which makes a lovely image.

You can use these ideas to bait and photograph house mice in abandoned buildings. Bait inside old discarded boots or anything that you think has a lovely derelict feel to it. Flash tends not to bother them if it's fill-in flash. If you plan for a long term project wild bank voles and wood/house mice can become incredibly tame.

Another approach if you just want to watch them is to build a wooden tunnel from the base of your bird table to a box that you place next to your lounge window. Leave one side

I took the baiting approach much further with a wood mouse that lived wild in my garden shed. I wanted something a little different so I baited the mouse on the window sill of the shed. I placed typical garden utensils here as well. When it was coming regularly (which only took a day or two) I lit the inside of the shed with candles, and took the picture from the outside. By under-exposing I managed the silhouette I wanted and the candles gave a lovely orange glow in the background. 1Dmk4, 180 macro, 1/160, f3.5, ISO 1600, -1/2/3 under exposure, tripod. Sheffield.

of the box open and push this against the window. A hatch that you can open on the top will allow you to add bait. If you run it for a while it won't take long before they are feeding every evening in your box. You can leave the house lights on dim initially but as they get used to them increase the intensity. It's great to sit and watch the mice feeding only a couple of feet away.

House mice are the ancestors of all the white mice that make popular pets. It is possible to buy grey, natural-looking pet mice which are house mice but captive bred. Many wildlife film makers and photographers use these to create intimate mother and baby images. It's much kinder and less intrusive to produce images this way than to cause the mouse stress and risk desertion or harm coming to its nest and youngsters. They are simple

to breed and by making a set of clean, but natural litter, it's a great way to get this type of image. The same approach can be carried out with brown rats.

Rats

Britain has two species of rat, the black (or ship) rat, which is native (or been here so long it is usually considered so) and is very rare and the introduced, abundant brown rat. Many will be breeding close to where you live, possibly even in your garden. Not to everyone's taste perhaps but they make fascinating subjects to work with.

Photography is basically the same approach as with mice but they are often far more cautious so you will probably have to take more time over it. There are many places where rats can be seen running around and these may be a good start. One issue you must be aware of is the opinion of others, not everyone will be happy with you feeding and encouraging your local rat population! A good approach is to find an area that has a lot of rats (field margins, ponds and river banks) and bait an area regularly.

Rats will eat virtually anything but never use any meat products. Once you are sure they are coming regularly set up a hide if

Water vole nibbling reed stems. 1Dmk4, 500mm, 1.4 converter, 1/800, f5.6, ISO 400. Derbyshire.

you can but in many situations this is not possible. Suitable clothing (not camo) and patience whilst sitting quietly is usually enough to allow them to behave naturally in front of you. As with mice, rats will quickly get used to new situations and can become quite tame.

Water voles

Water voles are still fairly widespread but are becoming increasingly scarce. Mink, water pollution and loss of habitat have all had a serious impact on their number. The best way to start is with a little research checking out which rivers, ponds and canals near you still have healthy numbers. Once you have worked this out then a little field work will be needed before you attempt any photography. Water voles leave three main clues that advertise their presence. The first are holes in the bank. These can be in the side of the bank or even on its top. They are much larger than mouse holes, about 5-6 cm width. Some holes look active with fresh or flattened soil around. Others can look older in grassy areas but are still in use. Some holes are below the water level but you tend not

to see these though you can work out where they are by watching the voles when they take food into the burrows.

The second clue is their latrines. Water voles like to leave their droppings in the same places each day so they tend to build up. They are easier to find on canals and ponds where the water level rarely changes. Look for areas of bare soil or stones near the water's edge with droppings on. They are approximately 1 cm long and brownish-green in colour.

Water vole at a latrine. The greenish pellets can be seen on the stone, bottom left. 1Dmk2, 500mm, 1/250, f4, ISO 500, tripod. Chesterfield.

The third clue is their mini-lawns. Water voles graze an amazingly wide range of plant species, well over a hundred. One favourite are the lush grasses that grow on the bank side. Over time these start to look like small, well mowed lawns, as if someone has come by with some nail scissors and cropped the grass in small areas along the river or canal.

Water voles can be active any time during the day. They seem to be slightly more active at dawn and with the stunning light it is the best time to start your search. They will feed and move around for up to an hour at a time. They then tend to retreat underground for a

Water vole at dawn in a canal bank. 1Dmk3, 500mm, 1/500, f4, ISO 400, tripod. Derbyshire.

snooze for an hour or two before venturing out again. They are very territorial so once you have found one specific vole it will usually be around that area each day. Males have much bigger territories. If you spot one feeding in one specific spot it will usually use it again but they will have a number of favourite dining tables.

When you look for voles use your bins and scan the bank for any that are having a snack. Make sure you also scan both banks for ripples. If these are clearly coming from one spot or moving along it's worth a closer look. Be careful though. A huge shape leaning over the bank and cutting the sky above will send them straight underwater and they will usually disappear. When you choose a site try to find one that allows you to photograph them on the opposite bank, so a pond, narrow canal or thin stream is ideal.

Once you spot a vole crouch down and move quietly and slowly into position. If you take your time it will usually stay out feeding.

You may be following one along the river so adopt the same method to keep up with it. If the area you are working is well walked then the voles are usually much tamer but exercise caution at all times.

If you find a particularly photogenic spot that is used but could do with a bit of improvement it may be possible to introduce a nice moss - covered stone. Onto this and close by place food such as apples that are cut into small bits, not quarters! I watched one photographer once who assured me he knew what he was doing throw quarter apples out. Once the vole appeared, it grabbed one then disappeared below ground to munch away. We didn't see it for another two hours! Think of a size that allows it to nibble for 15 seconds then seek out another piece. You will have to feed them fairly frequently because if there are any moorhens around they will happily tuck into your apples!

An attractive, natural food that works well is willow flowers. Water voles love young pussy willow and this looks natural when they eat it.

The time of the year is not critical though you might think summer is better, and in some areas this may be true. However, in many places late winter and early spring are ideal. In summer the masses of vegetation make seeing the voles almost impossible. In early spring, the winter storms have often knocked down the tall dead vegetation and seeing and photographing the voles is much easier.

A water vole nibbling a large leaf. 1Dmk4, 500mm +1.4 extender, 1/500, f5.6, ISO 800. Derbyshire.

Shrews

Most, if not all, shrew images are created by live - trapping the animals and keeping them in captivity. To do this you will need a licence. I would strongly suggest you don't even consider this as the risk to the animals is very high unless you really know what you are doing. If you want to work with shrews make sure you contact your local mammal or wildlife group and get to know your mammal recorder. They will probably have a licence to catch live shrews for surveying purposes and they may be willing to let you work with them to build up your experience.

Before you even consider photography you must apply for a licence and will need references (see the section on licences on p8). It is not an easy task but you should also try to find someone who has worked with shrews in captivity and seek all the advice you can get. It most likely will end up with you being refused a licence. If so just move on to something else.

Water shrew, 1Dmk2, 300mm, 1/800, f4, ISO 800, fill flash, beanbag. Devon.

Water shrews are the exception. It is possible to photograph these in the wild because not only are they larger but also because of their habitat, they have more defined boundaries. If you can find a stretch of a pond or stream where there are water shrews you can put food (such as earthworms or mealworms) in suitable areas like small mud banks and stones. With patience and simply lying down it is possible to get shots. You will be better off with a bigger lens and extension tubes and auto focus. Choose a high shutter speed

because they move very quickly. As long as you are still and silent they tend not to notice you at all.

Bats

Working with bats is fraught with the same difficulties as shrews. You need a licence just to visit a bat roost let alone photograph a bat there. Again the advice is simple. Contact your local bat group and go on a number of field meetings. As you build up your experience and knowledge you will start to generate some ideas about photographing them. Many bats are very nervous and prone to disturbance at the roost. Again only work here with expert help.

It is possible to photograph bats in flight though it is very difficult. You will almost certainly need a high speed flash unit and some form of remote trigger. Most bats have an incredibly erratic and rapid flight though they are more predictable when they leave the roost. Some bats, such as noctuals, hawk over water and it is possible with flash to get images of these. If you want to work at a roost as the bats leave remember you need a licence and you should seek help and advice from your local bat group.

It is possible (though with a very low success rate) to simply pre-focus the camera and set the flash to manual and simply fire away as bats fly around feeding. The trick is to guess roughly how close they

Many bat images are taken of captive rescued bats such as this long-eared bat. Working with rescued animals still needs lots of care and patience and you must listen to the advice of the expert whose bats you are working with. 1Dmk3, 180 macro, 1/125, f3.5, ISO 800, tripod.

will be and set the focus to that distance. Turn off the auto-focus and use a strip of tape around the lens focusing ring to stop you twisting it inadvertently. Then do a test with the flash gun on manual on any object at the same distance until you have worked out the required power to dial in for correct exposure. Then simply stand and every time a bat flies near enough fire away. It is completely hit and miss but a few photographers have produced some really nice results this way. A variation is to use the ISO range and expose so you record some of the silhouettes and sky to add context and interest to your images.

Seals

In Britain we have two species of seal, the grey and common. Atlantic grey seals are actually more abundant than common seals around our shores. However, the grey is globally a scarcer species. Half of all the planet's grey seals live around the British coast so we have an international duty to protect them. Their numbers have been steadily increasing over the last few decades.

Atlantic grey seal basking on a rock on the Farne Islands. I took this image from the boat so I needed to handhold the camera, use the IS and choose a high enough speed to keep my image sharp. 1Dmk3, 500mm, 1/800, f6.3, ISO 800.

There are a good number of places where you can photograph both species, though the grey usually outnumbers the common at most of the larger seal colonies. In the past Donna Nook in Lincolnshire was the place to get amazing images of seals. The vast majority of photographers arrived at dawn in the October to December pupping period.

Unfortunately the antics of a minority of photographers with virtually no field skills caused a number of problems. The outcome was that a voluntary ban has been imposed that stops members of the public and photographers from walking down to the sea.

Luckily not all the seals pup here so it is possible to get a good range of images of adult and young pups at the top of the beach. Even though you are working from a boardwalk there are fences to limit access and care is still needed.

The seals are used to people but don't rush up or get too close to those that are near the fence. The best approach is to walk along the boardwalk and get a feel for those seals present, then decide which you want to work with. As with all wildlife encounters time invested will usually reap rewards so stick it out all day and wait for that little bit of action or interaction between mums and pups. There will be lots of other people present, especially at weekends, so be patient and considerate.

Grey seals pup in the late autumn in a number of places around the British coastline. Most are secluded beaches and access to them is difficult. A few sites have good potential where greys and the odd common haul out and pup in areas with good access such as in N. Norfolk and the Farne Islands. In most cases these seals are watched and photographed from local boats and you're reliant on the skills and knowledge of local boatmen.

In these situations it is possible to produce images from the boat of seals in the water or on haul-outs which may be rocky islands or sandy beaches. If you photograph from a boat you will probably have to handhold your camera and there will be very little space to set up a tripod (though a beanbag on the boat side may be feasible).

If you do handhold, pay particular attention to your shutter speed (keep it high, such as 1/500+). You will be wobbling a bit and the

A seal pup photographed at dawn from the boardwalk at Donna Nook. 1Dmk4, 500mm, 1/200, f4, ISO 500, tripod.

boat will be moving gently as well. If your lens has IS/VR (image stabilisation) definitely switch it on and use the ISO to get a good high speed. Try shooting at a low f number to create better backgrounds and to keep the speed up. Make sure the servo mode (AFC Nikon) is switched on as the constant movement makes it difficult to get the focus sharp. This is especially true if you're working with seals bobbing up and down in the water. Make sure you check your exposure. Water can be very reflective and you may have to compensate.

If you decide to try to work with grey or common seals at a remote location such as on some of the Scottish or Welsh islands you must adopt good field skills. Females, particularly when they are pupping or suckling and are not used to the close presence of a human, can be nervous. Approach them from downwind and use rocks to disguise your stalk. You should use long lenses. Wide angle shots of females near to their pups can cause them great distress. Many of these beaches may be sheltered by

cliffs and you will be able to view them from the cliff tops, perhaps not the best angle for photography but certainly one that will minimise any disturbance.

Common seals (also known as harbour seals) tend to be a little more solitary than greys but are often found on the same haul outs but in lower numbers. They give birth earlier in the year in June and July.

Many grey seals are very curious and will often come right into harbours or pop up near boats. This bull was photographed from a boat in Norfolk. 1Dmk3, 500mm, 1/1000, f4, ISO 500, IS on, handheld.

Red deer stag roaring during the rut, 1DX, 500mm, 1/250, f4, ISO 1000, stalked. Derbyshire.

Deer

Never has Britain had so many deer. This is certainly true in both the number of species and absolute numbers. Only two of the six 'wild' deer species in Britain today are native, the red and roe. The other four have been introduced at various times though whilst three are relatively recent additions to our islands fallow have been here for a 1000 years. It is widely thought that the Normans introduced fallow deer as another species to populate the first royal deer forests, the hunting preserve of the rich and connected!

Chinese water deer were kept at a number of zoos in the late 1800's but eventually escaped from Whipsnade around 1930. They have a relatively limited distribution in Bedfordshire, Cambridgeshire and Norfolk but they are likely to spread slowly as further reed bed habitats are created.

Muntjac escaped from Woburn and a variety of other animal parks early in the last century and they have also spread across England through deliberate releases. They are now common across much of England and Wales and their range and numbers are increasing still.

Sika deer, which closely resemble red deer and can inter-breed with them, were introduced into Britain in 1860. Their stronghold is in Scotland with smaller populations in Northern England and Dorset.

There are really two approaches to working with deer in Britain - photographing wild animals (which usually will be extra wary because they are often shot or poached) or working in one of the many deer parks that are dotted across the country. Both approaches have their devotees. Not all species are available in a deer park situation. Roe, Chinese water deer and muntjac are rare, mainly due to their more secretive dispositions, so a true wild approach will be necessary. For red and fallow, and to a lesser extent sika, spending your first season working in a deer park and learning as much as possible about the animals is a great way to start. This should pay dividends later, as long as you remember the difference when you try your luck with truly wild animals.

Many photographers, myself included cut their teeth on habituated deer in one of the deer parks in the UK. There are many but not all are ideal. It really depends on the type of images you want to create - those with an urban feel (such as the parks in London) or with a more rural feel. I would suggest that you avoid ones with grass like mown lawns!1Dmk3, 500mm, 1/1000, f4, ISO 400, tripod, -1/3 compensation. Leics.

Red and sika deer

These two species will be discussed together because much of their natural history is very similar. Reds are really woodland animals that live in herds and are distributed across the whole of Britain. However, herds of reds are found on moorlands such as in the Peak District, Exmoor and much of Scotland because sufficient woodland habitat is unavailable. They are actively shot in many places but numbers are rising and they are becoming an increasingly economic and environmental pest, particularly in woodland where they can overgraze young trees. They have no predators in Britain apart from man.

Red deer rut in October, slightly earlier in the south of England (late September) and a little later in Scotland (early November). Large stags attempt to hold a harem of hinds and will fight if bellowing and displaying fails to deter the amorous advances of other males. The stags tend to gather in similar places every year so once you have found a rut one year it shouldn't be too hard to find it the next. The roars can be heard over quite long distances and are the easiest way of finding the rut. The stags can roar at any time of the day though dawn is the best time to hear them (and sound carries further in cooler air). Occasionally you may pick up the clash of antlers when two equally matched stags have a set to. If you can spend some time in a deer park you will quickly pick up the key sounds and remember them. In some situations where reds occur you may also find fallow deer and these tend to rut at similar times. The red's roar is much deeper and prolonged, the fallow's is shorter, sharper and a bit like a cough.

Red deer hinds tend to stick in loose groups around the rut and it is the hinds who make all the decisions such as where and when to go. A good stag looks after his hinds with care whilst younger, less experienced stags can scare them away if they chase them too much. Stags like to wallow in mud during the rut and these wallows can be obvious when searching likely areas. The wallow will have a strong musky smell. Stags also like to urinate over themselves at this time of the year, adding a delightful aromatic touch!

After the rut the stags and hinds tend to assemble in separate herds and browse across their range. In woodlands the herds tend to be smaller than on open moors. Calves are born eight months after the rut in May/June/July. Bambi can make a very attractive image lying cutely in the grass or bracken. However, if you happen across one never attempt to photograph it or touch it. The mother may be watching you and there is a serious risk of her deserting it. Simply move away quickly and carefully.

After the rut stags will lose their antlers and in spring grow a new pair. As the year warms up they shed their winter coat and can look quite 'mangy'.

The majority of photographers only work with reds during the rut or in the winter snows when the stags have good sized antlers. Wild reds like all wild deer are very wary and they have excellent hearing, eyesight and sense of smell.

Once you have located the rut you will have to decide how to get close enough to work it. Camo gear, gloves and face net or balaclava are an advantage. You must work down wind and never break the skyline. The best time to approach is early dawn before first light. On an open moor use any natural valleys to get as close as possible, further advancement will probably mean a belly crawl. Luckily red deer are big animals and with a modern camera and 500 lens you don't need to get really close to catch the drama of the rut.

Red deer print in moorland peat.

Dung of moorland red deer.

Reds in a woodland situation can be very elusive. Look out for dung (black and a bit like sheep's in large pellets, sometimes held together) on paths that resemble big badger tracks. Also look for signs of browsing on the vegetation. During the rut the roaring should provide you with a good clue of where to stalk. Stags also like to bash trees and grasses/bracken with their antlers and this can be a good indication they are present. Take as much care as on the open moor and remember there may be many eyes watching your approach. Use the trees and take your time.

Wild red deer are much harder to work with and you will usually need good stalking skills. I spent over an hour working into position on this large stag during the rut at dawn. 1DX, 500mm, 1/500, f4, ISO 1000, tripod. Sheffield.

An effective alternative to stalking is to approach using a car. This usually means driving around at dawn in prime habitat on back roads and tracks. With luck you can find reds browsing near the road.

Use scrim on the window and approach the animal with the engine idling, or better still turn it off and cruise up. (Though this is a bit of a problem if you need to move again.) Try to have your camera and lens already out as you approach but you will need to hold on to it - you don't want to drop it out of your car window more than once! There are many places in Scotland, particularly in winter, when this approach is ideal. Most deer now come down from the hill and are often fed near roads.

If you know where the deer will be at dawn try to get there early and wait for them. If you find a good area and have access to a four wheel drive ask the landowner if you can stalk the deer on his land using the vehicle. One note of caution though. Many poachers lamp from vehicles so driving slowly around at dusk or dawn will probably raise someone's attention, so please tell locals what you are doing. A quick phone call to the police is a good idea as well.

Red deer in a deer park are obviously easier to work with but if you approach them with an over confident attitude they will quickly move away. You won't need camo gear - it does look a bit of an overkill when you're decked out head to toe in camo gear stalking a deer as a young mother pushing her pram walks by! Approach with caution but don't try to stalk by hiding. This can make the deer quite nervous. Let them see you. Walk quietly and slowly at a diagonal to the animals and take shots as you approach. Don't push your luck but judge carefully how close you can get by watching the animals' reactions at all times. If you see the deer moving slowly you may be able to anticipate where they are going and get ahead of them and wait until they cruise by. You won't need to worry about wind direction, the idea is that the deer can see you and remain relaxed with you there. However, if you can approach downwind do so even though they are well used to the variety of deodorants and scents of folk in the park. Reds will be most active at dawn and dusk. During the day they may lie up and snooze whilst chewing the cud.

Roe deer

The number of roe deer in Britain has risen dramatically in the last 30 years. Roes are primarily woodland animals that graze a wide variety of plant species. Since many woods are small lots of roes leave their sanctuary at dawn and dusk to graze fields and crops. In areas where they feel more secure many now live almost entirely within fields and hedgerows. They are not herd deer and tend to live a solitary existence for much of the year. Bucks will escort females during the rut and breeding season from mid July to mid August. At this time the bucks guard their females aggressively and fights may break out if another buck tries to muscle in. After the rut and into winter females may band together in small groups of 3 or 4. Fawns are born in May to June and twins are quite common. The female will remain with her youngsters for much of the year until the next rut.

Most sightings of roe deer are from roads at dawn with the animals grazing farmers' fields or rough grassland. As the human activity cycle gears up to breakfast these deer generally retreat to the cover and safety of nearby woodlands. Those deer that live much of their life in a field habitat lie up during the day in long vegetation before becoming active again just before dusk. As with red deer, if you find a fawn retreat and leave well alone. Roe deer can easily abandon their youngsters if they think a human has been near them and, like red deer, their sense of smell is acute.

Roes are arguably the most beautiful of our deer. In winter their coat has a distinct grey colour to it but in spring this is shed and the delightful russet summer coat is grown. Bucks have short antlers which they shed in autumn and grow a new set in the spring.

Roe deer are incredibly wary but every now and then a situation develops where wild ones seem to lose their natural shyness. I have only really witnessed this once in the cemetery of a Scottish city where a family of roes lived and bred. This cemetery was right in the heart of a huge urban area and the deer were amazingly confiding. 10D, 500mm, 1/250, f4, ISO 400.

Roe deer leave a number of signs in their territories. Their dung is green-black-brown in colour, smaller than you expect and a bit like a rabbit's in size. It is cylindrical, pointed at one end and concave at the other. It is smaller than reds and since sheep tend not to be found in the same habitat it should be quite distinct. The deer make paths through woods but they will also share these with humans and other animals like badgers and foxes. The big clue is the height of the

Female roe deer are beautiful animals, especially in the summer with their warm russet coats. 1Dmk4, 500mm +1.4, 1/250, f5.6, ISO 800, tripod. Holland.

vegetation above the path. If it's walked by a roe deer it will be much higher than a path used solely by badgers or foxes. Look for grazed leaves as extra clues. If the wood or field has soft earth the deer leave a distinct cloven hoofed footprint.

Roe deer dung (top) and footprints in fresh soil.

Roe deer males will thrash at trees in spring to get rid of the dying velvet from their antlers. Often the same trees are used so look for bits of velvet or skin hanging on them at chest height. If reds share the same wood this may cause confusion. During the day roe deer like to lie up in a scrape which they make by scuffing the surface with their hooves. This can at times be obvious with bare earth showing.

They call at various times of the year, though they don't roar or bellow like reds or fallow deer. Both bucks and hinds have a short, almost bark-like call which may be territorial or an alarm call. It is short in length and a bit like a dog's deep bark or cough. Check out youtube to listen to their barking.

Getting close to roe deer

Getting close to a roe deer is a great challenge and one of the most exciting experiences that the wildlife watcher or photographer can have. Basically there are two methods, stalking them or waiting in a good spot for them to turn up. You can

increase the chance of them turning up and staying a while by laying out some food regularly. The choice of food is varied and often depends on who you talk to. It may be that roes vary in their choice of favourite nibbles around the country or perhaps during the year. Food that has worked includes carrots, parsnips, lettuce, molasses and deer nuts. Cut the vegetables up into small pieces about a 2 or 3cm square. Deer nuts can be bought from many outdoor suppliers or browse the web to find a distributor. Try not to get your scent onto the food at all. It is not the easiest thing to do but is possible. In many cases rabbits will share the roes' woods and fields and tuck into your supply of food. One way to get around this is to hang the food (such as lettuces) on ropes on trees at roe deer head height. It won't deter squirrels but does keep the pesky bunnies away.

Once you have found, or been told of, an area that has roe deer you need to check out their daily activity cycle. Generally they will visit their feeding areas at dawn and just before dusk. This may be in fields or rough grassland near to woodland edges. Wait in a car if possible or hide well downwind of any potential areas before dawn and watch. If you spend a week or two surveying all the likely areas you should quickly pick up where the deer are grazing.

Once you have located the area you want to photograph them in turn up before dawn or dusk and walk to your chosen spot as if they are watching you (which they may be) from the woodland edge. Try to choose a place that offers good cover for you and your lens. Wear camo or browns, greens and greys including gloves and face cover. Be downwind, sit or stand quietly and wait without moving. If you feel you may be too exposed use either a hide or bag hide.

If you use a hide have it in place a week or two before you start photography. Have the camera set to silent mode, Av at it's lowest f number and change the ISO to get a speed that you are confident with to get sharp results. When the roe turns up let it feed for

Roe buck in spring in woodland. 7Dmk2, 500mm, 1/400, f4, ISO 500, handheld. Lancashire.

a while and try one shot. Work from there judging at all times the animal's reaction.

Roe deer have regular paths and by watching over a period of time you can build up a map of where they go during the best times of the day. A reliable method of working with them is to wait near one of their paths, usually sitting with your back to a tree or in deep grass with the camera ready. Try not to sit right on the path because if the deer does come you want it to walk towards you but not straight into you, which would scare it. Always turn your head slowly as you scan the area. If your fieldwork has been carried out well you should have a very good idea where the deer will appear from and where it will walk to. With patience you can get it to come incredibly close. Always try to interpret its body language. Feeding suggests a relaxed deer, ears erect and long stare a nervous one. If it starts to bob up and down and stare hard the chance is that you have blown it and within seconds it will run away. If the deer appears relaxed move your hands slowly to the camera and start photography.

If you spot a roe out in a field or woodland edge feeding and want to stalk it make sure you have read the section on stalking and pay extra care to all aspects of your stalk. If you are successful you have done really well.

Gamekeepers and hunters have a special chair called a high chair which they use to control (a euphemism for shooting) deer, including roes. You may have come across one of these when you have been out in one of your local woods. It's like a mini piece of scaffolding with a platform on top. They are usually situated in rides in woodlands where deer may walk. The idea is quite simple, any human scent will be higher than the deer and blow over them so the deer never realise you are there. They can be very successful for watching and photographing roes.

Not all photographers like using them for the simple reason that their position is higher than the deer's and they like their images taken from a low vantage point. However, they may be worth considering in certain situations such as woodlands. Make sure you are up there before first light or an hour or two before dusk and sit completely still and silently with camo gear or suitable clothing, including gloves and face cover.

Some hunters use special callers to attract roe deer to them. The ethics (photographically) of using these is very similar to using tapes with birds. Some feel it is OK, others don't because you are fooling the animal and possibly getting it to move into an area that it might not want to go to. I would suggest that you don't use these techniques even though they may be encouraged by some wildlife photography authors. It is possible to generate your images in a much more ethical way that does not alter the animal's behaviour.

Fallow deer

Fallow are the most common herd deer of the deer park. They are particularly beautiful with their spatulate shaped antlers and lovely spotted coats. Fallows have been bred for hundreds of years to perfect their colours. The natural colour is a mellow fawn but you can often find black or white deer.

They occur in the wild throughout Britain and stalking them should be carried out in the same way for other deer. They are woodland animals so getting close to truly wild fallows is difficult but not impossible. During most of the year they roam their woods in single sex herds. These can be quite large in some deer parks. The large herd of male fallows at Chatsworth Park is really impressive in late summer before the rut when they have their full sets of antlers.

As the rut approaches in late Sept to October the males and females drift to the traditional rutting stands. It is now that the males are most vocal and impressive. Their necks have muscled up and they now call (like a short bark or burp) repeatedly. They tend to be most active at dawn but during the height of the rut male fallows may defend the stand and call all day. Does and fawns drift in and around the stand rather nonchalantly, often seemingly just to watch.

After the rut the deer disperse again and band up, females with calves and males into various age brackets. Feeding is now voracious as they feast on the autumn fruits of acorns and, if present, their favourites, sweet chestnuts and conkers. In good fallow habitat it's always a sound idea to check out any mature sweet chestnut/oak/conker trees in autumn.

Male fallows rut slightly earlier than reds but the ruts overlap a fair bit. October is the key month in middle England. The buck defends a stand where he barks (almost like a loud cough) to advertise his presence. These stands are used for a number of years and so once you have located one it's a fair bet the deer will be there for the next few weeks and hopefully years ahead. Fights between well matched males are not rare and if you put the hours in you will be able to witness this stunning duel.

Fallow hind running. Always be prepared to switch your camera to a higher speed by adjusting the ISO if any action starts. 1Dmk3, 500mm, 1/1000, f4, ISO 800, tripod. Leicestershire.

Fallow deer leave distinct footprints (p223) and dung around their woods. Their dung is very similar to reds but slightly smaller. If reds share the wood then you need to check carefully, if they don't its fairly obvious. Fallow away from the rut are quiet but it is a good idea to familiarise yourself with their alarm call via youtube. It is similar to that of roe deer, a short bark.

Working with fallow deer in the wild is very similar to working with reds. The best photography tends to be around the rut and since the stands are traditional it is a good idea to locate this one year and then before the rut of the next year prepare a good observation post. This might simply be sitting in a ditch or in some scrub. You could make a place that allows you to hide

The clash of antlers as two fallow bucks challenge each other is one of the highlights of our autumn. 1DX, 500mm, 1/2000, f4, ISO 800, beanbag on a wall. Leicestershire.

with your camera in vegetation. Using a hide, especially a canvas one, can be a problem as the deer will probably rub against it at some time and knock it over. When you plan to photograph arrive at the stand before dawn and pick your spot downwind. Be well dressed - camo gear or browns and greens with gloves and balaclava/face cover. Have your camera low on a tripod, possibly under a bag hide to disguise it a bit. Then wait and use all the caution described earlier for red deer at the rut.

When you decide to leave should be dictated by the deer. You definitely don't want to suddenly pop up and scare them away.

The vast majority of fallow images are taken in one of the numerous deer parks dotted around the country. Here they are usually fairly easy to approach and work with. The secret to working in deer parks is to be early. Most rut and feeding activity is at both ends of the day so dawn starts are the norm. During the day fallow, like most deer, lie up, snooze and chew the cud. The main consideration is to choose a deer park that suits your style of photography. If you like deer on grassy fields that resemble a mown lawn that is fine. However, if you want a more natural, woodland-type image

select a park that has a variety of habitats with bracken and trees. If the weather forecast suggests a particularly cold night and bright morning make every effort to get out there before sunrise and be with the deer as the sun rises. It's now that earlier fieldwork and preparation pays off as you should know exactly where to head for. If you can get into a position to backlight the deer with a clear background their steamy breath can add an incredibly dramatic factor into your images. Experiment with various underexposures and shoot directly into the light for silhouettes and stunning colours.

Getting close to fallows in deer parks is not too difficult, especially if you use a big lens like a 500 on a full frame body. The extra working distance pays dividends because it

A fallow stag bellows on his stand before a group of spectators. Cold, frosty mornings with back-lighting help to show up both the breath of the stag as well as the steam rising from his body. 1Dmk4, 500mm, 1/500, f6.7, ISO 1000, tripod. Leicestershire.

I was waiting tucked into the side of a ride at dawn when this Chinese water deer appeared and walked towards me. Even though I had the camera on silent drive it could hear the shutter and peered at where it thought the noise was coming from. 1DX, 500mm, 1.4 converter, 1/1000, f5.6, ISO 400, hand held. Cambridgeshire.

keeps the animals relaxed and if a fight does kick off it's more likely to happen in front of you.

Chinese water deer

These are a relatively new addition to the UK's deer species. They are, as their name suggests, water-loving and tend to be restricted to reed bed habitats in Cambridgeshire and Norfolk, though as reed beds are being actively planted around the country there is scope for them to spread. They are fairly small, squat deer that some argue resemble teddy bears. They don't have antlers but the bucks do have small tusks that give them an exotic feel.

They are similar to roe deer in their social organisation, mostly living solitary or in pairs. The breeding season (the rut) runs from November/December to April. In places where numbers are high they may form small groups.

Their call is like a short bark. If you are intending to work with this species use the web to listen to their calls to familiarise yourself. In Cambridgeshire and Norfolk muntjac deer are also common so you need to be able to separate the two calls. Chinese water deer have other recognisable calls like screaming when chasing each other or whickering/chittering when males chase other males. Males also whistle and squeak when they court the females.

In ideal habitat the paths that run through it are often muddy so you should see lots of deer footprints. The unfortunate thing is that often muntjac are common in the same area so ultimately spotting the deer is the best way to make sure. If the population is not too small it should only take one early morning walk around any suitable habitat before you spot a few. Look down rides and open areas around the reed beds at dawn.

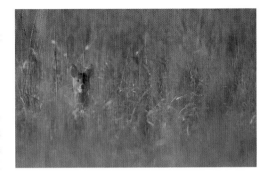

A Chinese water deer amongst reeds at dawn. It is fully aware that I am there and is watching me intently. Even though you can only see its head I do like the light and colours in this image. 7Dmk2, 500mm +1.4 converter, 1/2000, f5.5, ISO 800, handheld, stalked. Cambridgeshire.

75 Chinese water deer can be active throughout the day but most of their time is spent deep in the reed beds so seeing them is not easy, if nigh on impossible. However, they do come out to graze fields and shorter vegetation that adjoin their reed bed home at dawn and dusk. It is here that the best chance of getting images exists. Be up before dawn and hunker downwind of any likely spots and put some time in watching. Once you have worked out where and when they venture out of the reeds you can prepare for photography from either a hide or, using your skills, blending in with the local vegetation.

They can be very skittish and if you show yourself too much may simply run for cover so great care is needed. If you think there might be deer in an opening walk silently along the path or ride and when you get near to the clearing (but are still hidden by vegetation) get down onto your knees or front and crawl slowly into a position where you can get a view.

Muntjac deer

Muntjac are our smallest breed of deer and have spread rapidly across the country in the last few decades. In some areas numbers are so high that they are becoming an environmental and economic pest. Like roe the bucks have short antlers but they are curved slightly. They also have visible canines. The size alone should stop any confusion with our other deer. However, I say this but the last time I saw one I genuinely thought it was a dog. I was photographing red grouse out in the Dark Peak when a medium, dog-sized animal came trotting down the path towards me. I sat in the heather to disguise myself and the animal came towards me unaware I was there. I would have bet money it was a dog until it got close. What threw me was the habitat, we were right out on very open moorland. Muntjac have been nicknamed the 'barking deer' because many think they sound like a dog, a good clue. They don't socialise in herds but large numbers can exist in suitable woody habitat.

Muntjac are small deer that are becoming common across England. This one was photographed in a ride at a nature reserve in Cambridgeshire at dawn. I don't have a lot of experience with muntjac but I did spend some time in fenland working on a nature reserve a few years ago that had a healthy (well, from the warden's perspective too healthy!) population. I found that if I sat at the end of one of the rides the chances were quite good that a muntjac would eventually emerge at dawn. I crept around keeping fairly low and every time I came to a grassy ride I would belly-crawl forward until I could see down it. Often there would be a muntjac out grazing. They were nervous but with a 300/500 lens and converter good images were certainly not too difficult to produce. 1Dmk3, 300mm, 1/800, f5.6, ISO 400, handheld whilst lying down. Lower image, 1Dmk3, 300mm, 1/1000, f6.3, ISO 400, handheld.

Muntjac don't have a defined rut like other deer and can breed almost all year round. They are also getting to become a garden pest and if you are in an area where this is occurring then working with them in this habitat is possible.

They are active all day but like many deer species use the dark to venture out into the open and feed so dawn and dusk are certainly the best times to get to grips with them.

Mountain hare at the end of winter when its coat (pelage) is starting to turn grey-brown. 1Dmk4, 500mm, 1/2000, f5.6, ISO 1600, stalked. Derbyshire.

Hares and rabbits

We have two species of hare and one of rabbit in Britain with only one being a true native, the mountain hare. Brown hares were introduced by the Romans 2000 years ago. There is some debate when rabbits were first brought to Britain. It was either by the Romans or 1000 years later by the Normans. All three species make great photo subjects but they require different field skills to get close to them. All three can overlap in habitat. In the Peak District there are a few moorlands were you can expect to see all three species. However, in most cases you will need to seek out good locations where you can concentrate on one species alone.

Brown hares

Brown hares are distributed fairly extensively across Britain. Their preferred habitat is arable farmland and grasslands, though old abandoned airfields and a few islands can have good, healthy numbers. Hare populations can change almost from one farm to another so you tend to find good areas and others that look suitable but have few hares. Older, more traditional farms tend to have larger hare numbers - small fields with hedges and small woods dotted around are ideal.

A brown hare in its form. 1Dmk4, 500mm 1.4 converter, 1/500, f5.6, ISO 800, stalked, beanbag on mini sledge. Derbyshire.

Before you set to work you need to find a good hare site. This should be done at dawn or dusk when their activity is at its peak in daylight. An ideal way is to drive around in a car at dawn and scan each field with bins. Hares take little notice of cars on roads or on the farm itself. If you are going to check out an area on foot you will need to be careful. Hares have excellent eyesight and hearing so use hedges as cover and try to search fields with your bins from as far away as possible. You should then be able to spot any hares that are running around or out in the field feeding.

The best time of year to start searching is spring. Daylight is getting earlier and any vegetation is still really low so the hares are easier to see. Later, in summer when the vegetation is taller even if the field is full of hares unless one runs down a path you probably won't see any.

A little after dawn, depending on the time of year, any hares that are out feeding tend to make their way to their form. This is a shallow, oval depression, about 30 to 50 cm long in the soil or grass. When the hare prepares for its daily snooze it first tends to sit and have a wash in the form, and then gradually sinks down with its ears flat on its back until it virtually disappears. If the field is bare or with short green grass or crops it is possible to pick up hares in their form with the bins. Check out every brown lump - many will be soil or cow muck but the odd one will be a hare.

The only animal you will likely confuse a hare with is a rabbit. Hares are much larger and have coloured eyes, not black like a rabbits. Both animals run but hares really run. When they do so their much longer legs become obvious. Hares are also browner than rabbits and tend to feed further away from the side of the hedge. Bunnies tend to stick close to their burrows as an escape plan. Hares rely totally on outrunning any predator.

Hares like paths, especially if the vegetation is wet. However, because they feed over a wide area of any field they can wander anywhere. When they run from one field to another you will notice that they have favourite passages through the hedge, often under a gate or through an opening.

Brown hare running across a field in early spring. 1Dmk3, 500mm 1.4 converter, 1/1250, f5.6, ISO 800, beanbag on mini sledge. Derbyshire.

If you disturb a hare it will often sprint across the field and out of sight. It will however make its way back in a huge circle to either the field or the form from which you scared it. This can take an hour or two.

Hares breed from late February right through to September. Each female usually has two leverets which soon split up and stay hidden all day and night. Mum only visits each one every 24 hours to suckle them and she is incredibly nervous when she does so. If you come across a leveret leave it well alone and retreat straight away. Trying to photograph a female hare as she suckles her youngster is very risky. If she suspects any danger she could easily desert her leveret so you should not attempt to photograph this.

Boxing hares is a powerful symbol of spring and March hares are the stuff of folk-lore. Hares do box, this is usually the female refuting the over-amorous advances of a lusty male. Boxing can occur at any time of the year but is more intense in the spring.

Photographing brown hares

There are a number of approaches you can adopt. Probably the easiest way is to use a four wheel drive and slowly cruise around the field looking for a snoozing hare. Better still is to park up in a corner of the field before dawn and watch from there. Clearly you will need the farmer's permission and a four wheel drive. The big disadvantage is that if you want to photograph from the vehicle you are restricted to the angle of view. It's quite high up and many photographers now prefer a much lower view point. If you use this method and spot a snoozing hare you will be able to drive fairly close to it, certainly close enough to photograph it with a 500 lens. If you get too close it will rise up, probably sit for a second or two and then sprint away.

Most photographers prefer to work from ground level. The best method is to get into position an hour or so before dawn. Select a spot that has a bit of cover, say a hedge bottom, from where you can see across the field. Use a groundsheet to lie on - it keeps you a little warmer and drier.

You should wear a camo or green jacket, waterproof overtrousers, gloves and a balaclava to hide your face a bit. Now lie down and put your camera on a beanbag. Next, check to make sure the settings are all OK and the card is empty. Your field work carried out earlier will let you know where and when the sun will rise. Try to be as quiet as possible when you walk to the place you will photograph from but it is not uncommon to see a few hares running away as you approach. Obviously this is not ideal and the perfect spot is one that you can get to unseen but in reality situations like this are rare. Now simply wait. Some mornings you may even have hares feeding too close to focus on, it all depends.

Unfortunately fields, even small ones, are not that small so it may be that the hares are feeding in a different place. If you choose to lie in a hedge bottom you will increase your

The mini sledge and beanbag I use to stalk and photograph brown hares.

chances as hares like to run from one field to the next and often use the hedge side where there is less vegetation to run along. Paths through crops are similar and ideal to set up on. Hares also don't like getting their belly wet. If it has rained or there has been a heavy dew they are far more likely to move around using tracks, so setting up on one of these can be very productive. If the hares are too far away simply carry on waiting.

It is possible to belly crawl up to them particularly if they are distracted with each other but often it's simpler to wait. If the morning is fruitless pack up when the hares have all retreated to their forms. You should try to leave as discreetly as possible and return the next day.

Occasionally you will find one, two or three males distracted by a female. It's now much easier to crawl up and you are likely to get

some good running shots as they chase each other. It can though be a bit soul destroying to spend 30 minutes crawling across a wet field, get close-ish then the female leaves and they all run off. You just need to be philosophical. There's always tomorrow!

Try to use silent mode if they are feeding but switch to servo and a high speed and frame rate if they are running. They never seem to notice the camera's noise until they get really close. Even then they stop and stare at you and lollop around you. It's as if they know something is there but not a human.

Some photographers use a hide which can help a lot if you don't want to lie down. Set it up next to cover like a hedge. Leave it for a week or so before any photography but if it's disguised well you can set it up on the day.

I personally don't use a hide because I want the freedom to move a bit or change the direction of my photography, such as swivelling around 180 degrees if a hare is behind me, which has occurred a number of times.
These two hares met at their form early one morning. 1Dmk3, 500mm, 1/800, f4, ISO 800, stalked. Derbyshire.

There are 2 approaches to stalking hares snoozing in their forms. One seems a bit bizarre. You start by walking towards the hare initially standing up and as you get closer you start to stoop, eventually crouching and then kneeling. The idea is that the hare can see you but as you look the same height all the time it thinks you are not actually getting closer. This only really works when the hare can only see you out of one eye so approach it from the side.

There are few things more exciting than when a hare sprints across a field straight towards you, especially when it has no idea you are there. 1Dmk4, 500mm, 1/1000, f4, ISO 800, Derbyshire.

The other approach is to belly crawl the whole way. Push the lens on a mini sledge ahead of you and crawl using your arms and legs. It's not easy and if the field is wet and muddy not pleasant. Sometimes it works, sometimes not and the hare gets up and sprints away. Once you get close enough you will get shots of it lying in its form. I am never convinced that it does not know I am there. I am sure it does. If you get too close it will rise up (sometimes this can take a second or two) and allow a few images with its ears up. It never stays still long so as soon as it rises take a shot because it will very quickly run away. Personally I am not happy with this approach. I like the idea of photographing hares without disturbing them.

The last method is the old gamekeeper's method of squeaking up a hare. This can be amazingly effective if you are hidden. Using either a car, hide or camo gear get into position. Once you think hares are about (you may see their ears in a crop) try a little squeak by using your mouth on the back of

your wet hand. The idea is that the hare's curiosity is aroused. The hare will usually approach and in some cases come right up to the hide. If you can't get the back of your hand method to work try a commercial squeaker. In some cases though if you don't get it right it will have the reverse effect and the hares simply run further away. In situations where you feel you won't see the hares because of vegetation it's worth a try.

Mountain hares

Mountain hares are our only true native lagomorph and one of the few creatures in Britain with a real arctic feel to them. Originally they were confined to the highlands of Scotland but the Victorians introduced them into Derbyshire 150 years ago which is one of the most southerly global populations of this stunning mammal. Mountain hares turn white in winter and there are few more gorgeous and wild sights than a white hare in a snow field. In Ireland mountain hares are also present but the vast majority do not turn white in winter because of the lack of snow.

Mountain hares can be confused with brown hares in the summer but they are smaller, have more noticeable black tips on their ears and their tail is white on the upper side. In most cases the upland terrain will be a good clue, but not always. It is possible to watch mountain hares grazing seaweed on Mull. You can't get any lower than a beach!

They are most active at dawn and dusk and they use a form to hide up or lie in during the day. The habitat they live in, moorland mostly, is more difficult to work and there are one or two aspects of approaching them that are different to brown hares. Brown hare footprints are difficult to spot most of the time. There is often no suitable substrate for them to leave them on. However, when it has snowed its easy to spot mountain hare footprints, they leave tracks all over the place. Make sure you can separate them from rabbits (see p 223).

A mountain hare runs past my hiding place on its way back to its form in the early morning. 1Dmk4, 500mm 1.4 converter, 1/2000, f5.6, ISO1000, -1/3 under-expose. Derbyshire.

It's not too difficult to find hares in Derbyshire, the areas they occur are not huge. Any of the real upland spots in the Dark Peak like Bleaklow or Kinder have healthy populations. Scotland though is a vast, staggeringly beautiful upland area. The Cairngorms and many of the Monadhliath Mountains have good populations. If you don't want to trek for miles some areas around some of the ski lifts can be productive.

Photographing mountain hares

I have photographed mountain hares in winter in Scotland and during all the seasons in Derbyshire. There is a subtle difference in the vegetation in both places. I have found that the heather in Derbyshire's best hare spots tends to be a bit longer than in Scotland. This may be a general trend or just something that occurs in the places I have worked. I think it is probably to do with the elevation. In Derbyshire I am usually working at a much lower altitude than in Scotland. This difference has seen me adopt slightly different approaches in the two places.

In Scotland you can generally spot hares as they hunker down in their form during the day. In some cases they can be amazingly obvious and stick out like a bright white shape in a sea of brown. If the whole place is covered in snow they are harder to spot but still usually visible with bins. When you spot one you can try to stalk it. You don't need camo gear or white clothing, a sombre green/brown coat and waterproof trousers are ideal. Wear gloves, not to hide your hands but to keep them warm. It's usually freezing! If possible stalk with your lens and camera on the tripod, keeping initially low and looking for cover (usually hillsides) to disguise your approach.

Try not to walk directly towards the hare but take an oblique angle to it and try not to stare at it. The idea is that it thinks you are walking by and not towards it. As you get closer watch the hare all the time to judge its reactions. Once you start to get within 30 to 40 metres approach on your knees and proceed very slowly, taking the odd shot as you progress. If you're quiet and careful you can sometimes get quite close. Now will come the big decision. Just how close do you need to get? One in ten hares will let you can get incredibly close, certainly to be able to fill the frame with its face. Why the hare stays put when you are very close is open to debate. Some think it's because it thinks you can't see it. The other theory is that the hare's main predator is the golden eagle and they have a much better chance of catching the hare when it's bobbing about so it will stay put.

As spring warms up the mountain hares lose their white coats and become a grey-brown colour. 1Dmk4, 500mm, 1/500, f4, ISO 800. Derbyshire.

Unfortunately to find that one hare you will probably flush another eight or nine. Hares in this harsh environment are living on the edge. In severe weather they can starve. If we end up with a stream of photographers flushing hares day in day out we will eventually cause serious problems for them. If you flush the same hare too often it will move to another form or area and you may lose a really good subject.

One warning is needed here. Mountain top Scotland can be a very hazardous place to work. The weather can change rapidly and people die each year on the high tops in winter. Please take all precautions. Tell someone where you are going and when you will be back. Dress properly and for that potential change in weather. Take a freshly charged mobile phone with you and an emergency pack of food and drink. A good idea is to use a handheld satellite tracker to way mark various points to help you find your way back.

There are many really excellent running hare images. To get these you need to find a good

spot for hares and hunker down and take pot luck. Dusk and dawn are the ideal times when hares are active. If you have stalked one and flushed it then you usually only get a few seconds before it runs away but like a brown hare, it will make its way back again so if you are patient, get comfy and wait. Try to be as hidden as possible to increase your chance. If you are sitting in a hollow or lying down the hares won't seem to notice you as they run by.

In Derbyshire I have worked out another approach. In some places you can spot hares snoozing during the day and they can be stalked. (Though there never seem to be any really tame ones like in Scotland). However, in many places the hares' forms are tucked well into the heather and they are virtually impossible to spot. Carry out your initial field work at dawn when they are active. Simply tuck yourself into the heather where you have a really good view of a large expanse of moor and watch. A nice flask of tea always helps. The idea is to watch each hare and see where its form is.

A couple of hours after dawn most start to make their way back to their form after feeding. Usually you spot one ambling along and eventually it works itself into a bank of heather and disappears. That hare will probably use that same form each day for a few weeks. They do tend to shift around the moor during the year so you can't rely on it always being there. Once you have worked out its way back to the form you are now ready for photography.

Mountain hare in white pelage on a snow bank in Scotland. 1Dmk3, 500mm, 1/1000, f4, ISO 400, +2/3 exposure compensation.

Try to arrive the next morning at least an hour before it will return and set yourself up next to the path it will use. Now lie in the heather and have your lens and camera on a tripod nice and low. (Always use a tripod where the legs open fully with no centre column). Now simply wait. If your field work has been accurate eventually the hare will come jogging along the path, or very close to it.

Using servo (AFC on a Nikon) with a good fast shutter speed lock onto the hare as it runs up and press the shutter just before the ideal image size. The chances are it will keep running towards you. It does not know you are there but it will hear the camera. In most cases it will stop (sometimes too close to focus on) and allow some portrait work. Keep still, it knows something is not quite right but it does not know a human is there. In most cases it will retreat a bit and take a slightly different route to the form. Don't take images now but leave it to get home safely knowing that you will have other opportunities with it later.

Another approach is to find a favourite feeding spot. Use the same approach as when looking for the form and in a similar way just get ensconced on the edge of the feeding area and wait at dawn. I suspect that mountain hares can be squeaked up like brown hares but I have never tried it.

Many photographers tend to restrict their hare photography to winter when the hares are white. They are brilliant in this pelage but in spring when they are turning into their grey-blue summer coat they are very attractive. White hares look great but don't ignore the possibilities at other times of the year. One point worth noting is that the hares can shift around during the year. So a good place with lots of hares in winter does not mean it will be the same in summer. You will have to start your fieldwork again.

Rabbits

Rabbits are widely distributed right across Britain and much of Europe. They have even hopped as far as Australia, though with a helping sail from us! Rabbits are classed as vermin and cause a huge economic cost to agriculture. After World War II we quickly realised just how big an impact they were having. It was said that they ate a third of all Britain's crops.

In 1953 myxomatosis, a very efficient virus, was illegally introduced into Britain. It had been previously used in Australia and France where it had dramatically reduced bunny populations. However some rabbits are immune to the disease and the immune percentage rises over time. Today we have millions of rabbits yet we still have myxomatosis. If you spend any time in the field working with rabbits it won't be too long before you come across the distressing sight of a rabbit with the virus.

Rabbits are one of the most wary mammals around. Their eyesight and hearing are acute though their sense of smell is not so hot. They can also feel vibrations on the surface when they are underground.

Rabbits occur in a wide range of habitats though their preferred type is open grassland with hedges or small woods as cover. Most live underground in burrows. If there are enough of these we call it a warren and in some places these can be huge. They are most active at dawn and dusk and often feed overnight.

During the day many retreat underground though usually there is often an odd one about. Finding a rabbit burrow is relatively easy - they are obvious holes with earthen entrances. Well-used ones often have quite a wide, open, earthy area around the entrance. The burrow is too small for a fox or badger to get down so that is the first big clue. The second are the rabbits' pellets (or droppings). These are quite small and there are usually loads of them around the warren or near to the burrow. Many rabbits don't

Rabbit kittens can be very tame as long as you approach them carefully. 1Dmk4, 500mm, 1/600, f4, ISO 800. Shetland.

stray too far from their burrow so the area around it is littered with pellets and has a grazed appearance.

A lot of warrens are in the open but in some areas you will find them in hedgerow bases or woodland edges. A few are even right out on heather moorland. Rabbits also graze road verges. It is amazing just how close a car at 70mph comes to a bunny munching nonchalantly away.

Photographing rabbits

Once you have found the area you want to work decide if you are going to use the dawn or dusk period. In some ways the dusk period is better because you can usually approach unseen. At dawn there are always rabbits sitting around so the chances are they will see you.

Adult rabbits are very wary. They are not impossible to photograph but are difficult. Baby bunnies though can be amazingly tame and make great, cute photographic subjects.

The first thing is to observe the warren or burrows from as far away as possible with your bins. Look for any young ones grazing or sunbathing near a burrow entrance. They tend not to stray too far from it. Adults should also be about.

On the day you want to photograph approach the warren as quietly as possible (though it's not a bad idea to let them know you coming when you're some distance away). Hopefully they will all go below ground though an odd adult may well stay at the burrow's entrance and watch. When you're sure they are all below ground walk as if on eggshells to your chosen point. This will be at the correct distance for your lens and will offer a good view when you're lying down. The big thing is to be really careful with your foot falls, the idea being that the rabbits don't hear or feel any vibrations.

Have your camera and beanbag ready before you start. You don't want to plonk a heavy bag down and start opening noisy zips. Dress appropriately. Camo is good (but not essential) as are gloves. For youngsters these are not really necessary. If you are trying for adults it's not a bad idea to adopt the full camo rig. Lie down silently and get comfy.

Baby bunnies will usually start to come above ground again in 5 or 10 minutes and from the same burrow they use regularly or disappeared down. Let them come right out before starting photography and as always take one shot on silent and watch any reactions. It should only be a matter of a half hour or so before you can take lots of images. If you work carefully you can return on any number of mornings or evenings.

If you are working the adults try to start from further away and use your longest lens with a converter. Many warrens are well walked and the rabbits are used to seeing folk about so approach and let them see you. Another method is to approach during the mid to late afternoon before they come up for their teatime feed. Approach as mentioned before and wait with all your gear set up. You may have to wait longer but

A hide can be used to good effect. Construct it well before you want to photograph and leave it in place with a dummy lens. The best spot is somewhere like a hedge where you can put the hide against it to break up its outline a bit. Use all the same precautions as discussed earlier in this section.

In this colony the rabbits were regularly shot at and so were very nervous. To get this photo of a grazing rabbit I approached before dawn, hunkered down and waited. 1Dmk2, 500mm, 1/250, f4, ISO 500, tripod. Leicstershire.

In most of the UK rabbits are very wary. However, there are a few places where there are no natural ground predators and they are much tamer, such as on the island of Skomer. 1DX, 500mm, 1/1600, f4, ISO 500, beanbag on ground.

if you are lying downwind and at a bit of a distance there is always a good chance of a bunny running towards you or feeding close by. Adults still feed near the warren but at a greater distance then the youngsters.

Rabbit droppings are easliy spotted amongst the grassy areas where they feed. They may accumulate in quite large numbers and are a good clue to the presence of rabbits.

Grey squirrels are often dismissed as good photographic projects because they are so common. However, they are cute and do make great subjects and are widespread across England and Wales now. 1Dmk4, 500mm, 1/500, f4, ISO 400, +1/2/3 exposure compensation, beanbag on ground. Sheffield.

Squirrels

We have two species of squirrel in Britain, the native and drop-dead-gorgeous red and the introduced grey, often referred to as the tree rat. Squirrels' fortunes are ever changing. Once the red reigned supreme across virtually the whole of Britain wherever woods occurred.

Greys were released into Britain in 1876 in Cheshire. Since then they have leapt across great swathes of England, Wales and parts of Scotland. Greys are absent from mainland Europe apart from a small pocket in Italy. Their continual spread in Britain seems unstoppable though there are areas where they are controlled heavily. They are larger than reds, can forage better, feed on a wider range of foods, survive our winters more effectively and carry a deadly disease to reds, squirrel/paravox virus.

Reds are still common in some areas and there has been some success at reintroducing them, such as on Anglesey. Scotland is still their main stronghold having over 75% of Britain's reds. Other areas where they occur include N. Yorkshire, Brownsea Island, Kielder Forest and Formby.

Finding squirrels

Finding locations for greys shouldn't be too hard. If you live in England or Wales (they are not so widespread or abundant in Ireland and Scotland yet!) simply nip down to your local park or wood. It should only be a matter of minutes before you spot them foraging on the ground or scampering about the tree tops. If you ask around you will quickly find people who have them raiding their bird feeders in their gardens. Greys are so abundant that it seems a bit over the top to track them or use clues to find if they are present in an area. However it is worth mentioning food remains.

Greys eat an incredibly wide range of food and often like to have a feed in a favourite place, often at ground level. Piles of stripped fir cones around short stumps in many woodlands are a good clue. These show the central core where the scales have been chewed off. Reds produce fir cones that look exactly the same. If they are eating hazelnuts look for ones split into two halves. If they have holes in the side it will probably be wood mice. Both squirrels produce scat very like rats - long-ish (1.6cm x 4mm), torpedo shaped with variable colour depending on what they are eating at the time.

Since grey squirrels are easy to work with there is great scope to try something a little different as here with a simple silhouette at dusk. 1Dmk4, 300mm, 1/500, f4, ISO 400, -1/2/3 under exposure. Sheffield.

Getting close to squirrels

Locating reds will take a bit of research but you should be able to find locations in Scotland and a few in England where they can be seen easily.

Greys should not pose any real difficulties because they are common and have become very tame in gardens and parks. In many parks people with children often hand feed them so getting close is no problem. To tempt them use either hazelnuts or peanuts.

If you want to get shots of them eating choose hazel nuts because they are a natural food though the ones you buy are much larger than our native ones. If you want authenticity then find some growing hazel nuts and pick as many as you need. Don't take too many though as these are food for a range of wild animals. Another option is to collect a bag of acorns in October and store these in the freezer until March or April when all the local acorns have gone.

Try to choose seasons that add a little something extra - fallen leaves in autumn, snow in winter or a bed of snowdrops in spring all add a little context to the image.

I once used a Canon G11 with the squirrel's nose almost touching the screen, which made for a very dramatic image. It also demonstrated that a moveable screen on the back of the camera can be a great advantage when the camera is on the ground. Many compacts can focus incredibly closely which can create a fresh approach to your images. Grey squirrel photographed with a compact at two cm distance. Canon G11, 1/250, f3.5, ISO 400, handheld on the ground. Sheffield.

When photographing greys look for natural behaviour - when they collect excess food they often run away a bit then, with a wiggle from the bushy tail, bury it in the ground. Greys climb a lot so try some unusual angles like putting your camera tight against the trunk as they descend. This approach can create stunning images if you use a wide angle lens and the squirrel is confident enough to come close. Grey squirrels in parks are possibly the most approachable wild British mammal so you can use this to good effect. Often the ones in your local park are hand fed so you may be able to photograph them on the ground at literally 2cm distance.

A red squirrel in mid-air, IDX, 300mm, 1/2000, f2.8, ISO 3200 (It was dull and I needed the fast speed), hide. Scotland.

Red squirrels

There are a few places where you can adopt similar approaches with red squirrels but on the whole you will have to feed them and get them to come to one spot. Initially you will have to use a bigger lens and a hide. When you have identified the area you want to work in and know that there are reds about choose a spot that gives you a nice background and where the light will be coming from a good position in the early morning. Reds in Scotland tend to be most active and come to feeders in the early morning.

Possibly the best time to work with them is in winter after Christmas because then they have delightful ear tufts and thick, fluffy, red winter coats. Their behaviour may vary from place to place. That is the joy of working with wild animals - you need to do your fieldcraft well to get the best from each situation.

Jumping squirrel images have become very popular and a number of workshops now offer the opportunity to capture this cracking image. It's not too difficult to set one up yourself if you have the right situation and a bit of time. The basic idea is to get the squirrel to jump to a bird table that has a stock of hazel nuts. Don't use peanuts for this because you will end up with a flock of birds hoovering them up instead.

Set up a post that the squirrel can climb up near to the bird table. Start with it only a couple of feet away. It should get the squirrel well used to the idea. You will probably find that the squirrel will often run up the post under the bird table. If it does this too often make an aluminium cone, somewhat like the ones that folk put around a dog's neck when they don't want it nibbling its tail. Put this upside down on to the pole that holds the table This should stop the squirrel from running up the post and get it to use the one you want it to jump from. Don't set up near anything else it can jump from.

Once it's using it regularly move the post a little further away every few days until it's leaping nicely through the air. Don't move it too far away though! You should make sure that the two posts are exactly in the same plane of focus as the front of your hide and consequently the back of your camera. Take time to get this exact. If they are only a few cm out there is a chance the squirrel, or part of it, will be out of focus when it jumps.

When you want to photograph the jumping squirrel put a marker in the ground exactly under the flight path of the squirrel. As long as the bird table is quite thin and long (facing away from the stump) and the stump it jumps from not too wide on the top it really has only one flight path it can choose. When you're in the hide focus on the marker, switch off the auto focus, point the lens to where you think the flight path will be, set an ISO and f number that gives a really good speed (at least 1/2000) and hit your cable release as soon as the squirrel jumps.

Remember it will also jump back so you should get two goes per visit. It takes a bit of practice hitting the cable release at the right

Red squirrel in snow shower. 1DX, 500mm, 1/250, f4, ISO 1000, hide. Scotland.

time and you will probably have to adjust the position of the lens until you constantly catch the squirrel in the place you want it to be. A fast lens (2.8) and a body with as high a frame rate as possible will maximise your chances. When it does work it looks stunning.

Once you have perfected this technique try using the same set up to get head-on shots. This is much harder and more a matter of luck but if the squirrels are visiting every day you will get the shot eventually. You could try a beam cutter device to increase the hit rate but since it's not too hard once you get your eye in it is easier to stick with a simple cable release. You want one that fires the camera instantly, not an electric one or WiFi one that has a time lag built in or may have

a sleep mode. If you have one of this type make sure you try it out first.

A red squirrel visiting a feeder I set up in Dumfries in Scotland during the winter. It didn't take long before they were regularly visiting every morning. 10D, 300mm, 1/125, f6.3, ISO 400, tripod and hide.

A selection of pine cones chewed by a grey squirrel. Cones chewed by reds are very similar.

Wild boar

Wild boar are native to Britain but became extinct roughly 700 years ago. However, a number of escapees and deliberate releases since the 1980/90's have seen some healthy populations establish themselves, particularly in Southern England.

Wild boar are active over a 24 hour period and encounters in daylight are not unusual. If you have a good population nearby, such as in the Forest of Dean, you will almost certainly have heard about it. There are some strong feelings both for and against wild boar re-establishing themselves into the UK. They are an exciting addition to our mega-fauna but not everyone sees wild boar as a positive returnee to our countryside. There is a lot of debate about whether they are beneficial to woodland ecology. They can certainly scuff up fields and gardens with their rubbery snouts as they seek buried roots and insects leaving visible and contentious signs of their presence.

Signs of wild boar should not be hard to find if they are present in good numbers. Their footprints are distinctive, looking roughly like deer prints but with the back toes making a distinctive impression. The other main signs are areas of bare, scuffed up soil which looks like they have been worked over. These could be in open grassy rides, in farmers' fields near to woodlands or in the woodlands themselves. Wild boar droppings are large and fat, about 7 to 10cm long and are initially black. If they dry out after a few days they become grey in colour.

Most sightings of wild boar tend to be when the animals are out foraging and in many cases this is around dusk. Some lone animals can be amazingly tame though these may be recent escapees who have not learnt to be afraid of humans. Generally most encounters are with groups of boar as they are social animals and live in family units.

To watch or photograph wild boar the best place to set up is on a well - used ride or track through woodland where there is a good population. Get set up by mid-afternoon and sit quietly with suitable warm clothing in the side of the ride. Full camo wear is not necessary but you should pay attention to your hands and face with gloves and a hat/balaclava. Use a large lens on a tripod and hope that any boar appears downwind on the path. If you sit quietly and they don't smell you be prepared for a good photo session. As with many mammals set your camera to silent drive, take one shot and judge the reaction.

Hunters who regularly shoot boar use a high chair and you may come across these in some woodlands. The idea is that you are out of both the sight and smell line of the boar. If you can get access to a high chair it is a great and safe way to watch but I personally don't like the angle from this height to work photographically.

Lastly, a serious word of caution. Male wild boar are large, heavy and very powerful animals and it's certainly not unheard of for them to charge at humans on the odd occasion. This is not so rare as to be dismissed so you must be very careful. If you have any worries at all then only try working with them from a high chair.

This wild boar was photographed at a farm in the South West. 1Dmk4, 28-135mm, 1/2000, f8, ISO 400, handheld.

Great spotted woodpecker on a birch branch. The branch has been drilled with small holes filled with a mixture of fat and ground peanuts. 1Dmk3, 500mm, 1/1000, f5.6, ISO 400, tripod and hide. Sheffield.

Photographing birds

Traditionally the vast majority of bird photography was carried out at the nest. Reading some of the classic works by Richard Kearton and Oliver Pike is not only fascinating but gives a great insight into the art of nest photography. If only access to land was as easy now as then!

Today nest photography has become much less popular and fewer wildlife photographers work in this way unless they visit hides set up abroad. The main reason is that so many other alternatives exist. For many photographers the abundance of good hides at nature reserves and the option to buy time in another photographer's set-up has seen a reduction in the use of field skills.

Bigger lenses, digital cameras, access to the web and its huge availability of information have opened up many new possibilities within the scope of bird photography. We now expect images with either action, drama or with a more arty/moody feel to them.

The British list of recorded bird species now stands at 574, though many of these are rare. A large number breed here. Some, such as willow warblers, are summer migrants, others, like fieldfares, winter migrants. Some birds are resident all year round, such as dippers and barn owls. The list is a long one and it can be difficult to know where to start your photography. Some photographers specialise only in iconic species like kingfishers and puffins, others pursue rarities - a bit like twitchers.

The state of Britain's birds is a very mixed one. There are some huge declines (such as corn buntings and turtle doves) yet many of the birds of prey (such as red kites) are booming.

The approach to bird photography can be roughly split into the following categories -

1. Providing the bird with food to come to one place, usually using a hide

2. Working at a drinking pool.

3. Working at the nest with a hide.

4. Working at established sea bird colonies, similar to working at the nest but without a hide.

5. Using recordings of bird calls to attract birds nearer to your camera.

6. Using decoy birds.

7. Working with birds in flight (though this can occur at any of the above as well).

8. Rough walking. Simply walking around an area like a reserve and firing at anything you see.

9. Working at established hides (such as RSPB reserves) and taking pot luck what will be there.

10. Visiting established photography set-ups (such as Gigrin farm for red kites). These may be large, well known places or one of the increasingly common small set-ups run by various photographers selling space in their own hides.

Since this book is primarily concerned with field skills and creating your own projects some of the above methods are self-explanatory.

A good starting point for anyone who is trying to learn the art of bird photography is to work with an established photographer. In many cases this may not be possible so you may need to learn the skills through research and working first with common species that are approachable.

A visit to an established seabird colony (such as Bempton Cliffs or the Farnes) is a great way to get going. Another option is to gain experience with one of the many photographers who advertise workshops or days in their hides. One way to start is to set yourself a project. A good example could be documenting urban pigeons or the bird life of your local park. This may not sound glamorous but it will allow you to build up your skills without causing any real harm to the birds.

Bird behaviour

Once you have decided how you are going to get started or you are an experienced photographer exploring a new approach you must do some research. Working with birds does require you to understand a fair bit about bird behaviour. The first step seems obvious - you must know where to look for and be able to identify them. Both issues should be easily solved but often the information you find won't give you all the details you need. Identifying a bird is far more than simply recognising it from a picture in a book.

Many experienced bird watchers recognise more than 50% of birds from their call, sometimes never even seeing them. Birds have a variety of calls or songs. You need to know all the variations of your chosen species. These should include the male's song used to attract a mate or advertise his territory, the basic alarm call, the contact call it uses to keep in touch and any other specific calls such as the off-nest call and any distress calls. Once you know these you can start to get an understanding of how that species operates in its world. There are sites on the web where you can listen to your chosen species calls or you can buy a set of CDs.

You should find out when it should be around, for example it's no use looking for waxwings in the summer, they are winter visitors. Where can you expect to find the bird? What is its preferred habitat? What does the bird feed on and where will it find this food? Does its food change over the seasons

(such as chaffinches feeding on insects in the spring and beach mast in the autumn)? How and where does it nest? Does it have any specific behavioural characteristics such as the breeding rituals of great-crested grebes? (very photogenic). Does it migrate and if so when? Does it flock up in autumn like many of the tits do?

Gannet, 1DX, 500mm, 1/1000, f5.6, ISO 400, -1 exposure compensation, tripod. Ireland.

A good illustration is the nightingale. This is notoriously difficult to photograph as a rule but there is a way with good fieldcraft. The male arrives in the UK before the female by roughly 10 days. He now sings longer and louder and from a variety of perches. He will bob around his territory and occasionally pop onto a photogenic perch. His song is gorgeous and easy to learn. You will find him by listening to him, not by watching him. He also sings best just before dawn and up to 9.00am.

So your research should tell you how to recognise his song, what he looks like and what sort of habitat you can expect him in (scrubby woods) and if he occurs in your area and if so where. You also need to find out what time is best to photograph him (6-9am) and what date you can expect him to

Nightingale, 1DX, 500mm +1.4 converter, 1/1250, f5.6, ISO 800, tripod. Cambridgeshire.

arrive in April. Once the females arrive he changes behaviour. He sings less, is usually hidden and his song is shorter so he is far more difficult to photograph.

Waxwing, 1Dmk4, 500mm, 1/1000, f4, ISO 800, +2/3 exposure compensation. Sheffield

The best place to start is to get a good bird guide that allows you to identify the bird. More modern ones now talk about the bird's jizz, such as how it walks or flies with visual clues to help id the species, like wagtails wagging their tails. A CD of bird songs will give you the calls. A good bird behaviour book should allow you to be able to predict where and when certain behaviours may occur with details about flocking, feeding

and nesting. Trawling the web and looking at various sites that document or record wildlife will usually give you quite precise locations and dates. There are a number of bird websites that show rarities with locations and dates. All the information you need is there somewhere.

Short-eared owl, 1Dmk3, 500mm, 1/800, f4, ISO 400, beanbag on car window. N Uist.

Attracting birds using food

Redpoll on a perch above a bird table with niger seeds. 1Dmk4, 500mm + 1.4 converter, 1/1000, f5.6, ISO 800, tripod. Finland.

Feeding birds to attract them nearer to your camera is no different from feeding birds in the garden. In many situations you may be bolstering the local population, particularly in hard winters when natural food is in short supply. The birds always have the choice. If they don't like a situation or the food is inappropriate they will avoid it.

The choice of bird food today is huge. Just spend an hour on the web or get a reputable bird food catalogue and see the range available. The choice of food you use will depend on which birds you want to attract. How you present the food is also key to getting the right birds to it. You will find that whilst there are some species that you can rely on across the UK there are a number that seem really fickle. They come regularly in one area, never in another. Birds are also evolving in their tastes and adapting to new foods all the time.

When most people consider feeding birds they think peanuts or seeds and not beyond this as it can be impractical. As a photographer half the skill is thinking up new ways and new foods to work with. The major consideration though is that you work ethically and within the law.

There is a big debate about the use of live food and you should be clear about its legality under the Animal Welfare Act (AWA). Live baiting is considered a none starter unless it's insects or fish and even here the opinions are divided. It is illegal to use live mammals or birds as bait to lure a predator in many countries. Using live mice to attract day hunting owls is morally reprehensible, yet it is done occasionally abroad. If you decide to book an overseas bird photography trip make sure you are fully aware of how the birds will be attracted. Once you know this you can then make an informed decision.

The use of live fish is less emotive. Fishermen can use live bait. The law is clear, you can only put live fish into a river system where you caught them originally. You cannot put fish from one river into a different one unless you have a licence from the Environment Agency (and it would be unlikely for a photographer to be granted one). However using live fish is now becoming contentious as more people are looking in detail at how we operate. Live fish held in captivity are now covered by the AWA. It is also true that many wildlife photographic competitions ask you to state if live bait has been used and may not accept any images when it has.

Mealworms, because they are invertebrates, are less controversial. Many businesses openly sell these as live food. It is probably more convenient for us to store and to use dried mealworms, though they are possibly slightly less nutritious for the birds. The end result is the same, lots of mealworms are bred to feed garden birds.

The use of meat or dead animals is fine but obviously far harder to keep and the food will quickly become rotten. I have two freezers at home, one our normal freezer and the other for my bird food. It's full of road-kill rabbits, squirrels, mountain hares, pheasants and wood pigeons plus anything else that I drive past and I feel I can use. I have a bit of a disgusting habit (well, my partner thinks it is). If I spot a dead rabbit on the road I swiftly jam on the breaks and reverse up to it. A quick glance usually tells me if it has potential (if it's clearly bloated I drive away). If it looks fresh I get out and give it the sniff test. If it smells fresh I pop it into a bag and take it home. Winter is always better. The sniff test may even be unnecessary if it's frozen already!

Where and how you set out your bait will depend on which type of birds you want to attract. The following are broad ideas about types of food plus where and how to set them out. Always be adaptable. Birds change over time in their behaviour. Some times of the year are better for different species.

Seed

There are three ways to use seed - in hanging bird feeders, on a bird table or scattered over the ground. Hanging bird feeders are expensive and cheap plastic ones can be quickly chewed through by your local squirrels. The best I have are homemade from either thick plastic or, even better, aluminium drainpipe. First, saw the pipe into lengths about 30 to 40 cm. Drill holes in the side in sets of 2, one for the seed and one 3 or 4cm below it for a twig to be pushed through for the bird to land on. If you drill them on opposite sides a twig can be pushed right through both holes. Have about 6 sets of holes spaced along the feeder. If the feeder is made of aluminium saw lines into the bottom upwards about 3 cm long. Then tap these over with a hammer to seal the end and use an old can to act as a simple squirrel-proof lid.

For plastic drainpipe feeders I glue a short bean can on the bottom to hold the seed in and a loose one on the top to keep the seed dry and allow me to restock it. They are cheap, durable and oddly don't seem to get stolen! To complete the feeder two small holes near the top are used to thread some wire through to hang it from a bush or tree. If you do buy commercial ones get the ones with thick plastic and aluminium perches. They cost more but are usually squirrel proof. Don't forget to give them a thorough clean every few months to reduce diseases being spread from bird to bird.

Usually you won't want to photograph the birds on the actual feeders so set them up in situations where you can use natural twigs or suspend them from an aluminium pole.

Long-tailed tit on a wire peanut feeder. These are not squirrel proof!

You can then set up another pole with the twig or branch you want to photograph the bird on next to the feeder but out of frame. Try to set up groups of three or four feeders to get the birds coming regularly. When you want a session in your hide take all the feeders down apart from the one you want them

A seed feeder next to a pole with a suitable perch for small birds. The seed feeder is made from a plastic drain pipe and has a bean can glued on the end. It may not look neat and tidy but it is cheap to make and doesn't seem to get stolen when it is used in the field! The perch is taped to the top of an adjustable fisherman's aluminium pole.

to go to. The distance from your twig to the feeder will need some experimentation. For different species it seems to vary. Every time you run a project like this you will find it takes some time to get this right but it does have to be close. It works much better when lots of birds use the feeder because they tend to queue up or wait on the twig for an opening on the feeder.

Placing the feeders is critical. Think about where the sun will be shining when you do your photography. During the day it moves across the sky so decide if you want an early morning session or an afternoon one. The background, as always, is critical. When you place the feeders think hard about what the background will be. Hedges or trees in sun if they are too close in the background won't blur and some leaves like ivy and rhododendron can be annoyingly reflective, creating hot spots in your images.

The main thing is you need a hedge or bush nearby because most small birds don't like feeding in the open. They like to be able to

dart into cover if the alarm for a sparrowhawk rings out.

Choice of perch

One of the most important jobs when photographing at a feeder or anywhere else where you use a perch is to select the best one. One vital factor to consider is scale. You want the perch to look balanced and that means it has to be of a size and width that the birds would choose naturally. Many images are ruined because the perch is too thick. If you are in doubt just spend a bit of time watching your chosen species in the wild and see which thickness of branch or post it chooses.

This bullfinch was coming regularly to a bird table of sunflower seeds with the perch next to the table. Generally they didn't use the perch unless more than one bird arrived at the same time. The choice of perch was aimed at reflecting the natural twigs that the finches used. 1Dmk4, 500mm, 1/500, f5.6, ISO 800, tripod and hide. Sheffield.

Another tip is to look at a range of other photographers' work and get a feel for the type, thickness and style of perch used. The final point is to select a photogenic one. Don't go over the top but look for good colours, lichens and moss or small fungi on your selected twig or post. Try to collect any good posts you come across and store them at home so you know you have always got a few for new projects.

It is not a good idea to use the same perch twice. Once you have used it cut it up or throw it away. You don't want a whole project's work with a set of cracking birds all using the same perch. It gets boring and will be noticed.

Most aspects of siting, running and photographing at a bird table are the same as for a hanging bird feeder. For winter woodland birds try to run both at the same time. The idea of using a bird table or two is that some birds, like robins and chaffinches, don't perch well on a hanging feeder. The main problems are squirrels and wood pigeons (flying Dysons in my vocabulary).

You can deter squirrels by using an aluminium upturned cone-shaped collar to stop them running up the pole that holds the table. Obviously make sure they can't jump on to the table from a nearby bush or tree! Deterring wood pigeons is virtually impossible so I just live with them. They probably don't actually bother your subjects anyway. You just simply shoo them away during your photographic sessions and they are usually far more nervous than the bold tits or robins.

A robin and a long-tailed tit on a home-made bird table. The corners have small gaps to allow rainwater to drain away. This is the small table I use when I photograph the birds. The small size encourages them to use the perches next to to it when they come in to land if there are other birds already on it.

The idea of using a twig to produce your images is the same as before but the bird has a bigger place to land on than the feeder. Again this works best when lots of birds visit as they may then wait on the twig. One way to maximise your chances is to have a pole that you can fit the bird table on. Construct the main bird table with a metal collar that

you simply fit onto the pole. On the days you photograph take this table off and pop on another with the same fixing that is much smaller with less space. If you make your own tables make sure they drain well so rain does not pool up and rot the food. Spilt seed will attract other things - ground feeding birds, squirrels, rats and mice.

Spreading seed on the ground is the third option. You should do this for specific species that don't or won't use a bird table or feeder (yellowhammers being a good example). The main consideration is where you will photograph them from. Many photographers don't like the 45 degree downward angle of looking at birds, they much prefer being on their level.

So, for ground feeders try to create an area that is slightly higher (such as a mound) so the background is improved and use a low hide so you can lie down. If you are going to spend a lot of time doing this then think about digging a big hole to sit in so your camera is level with the ground. You may find an angle finder helps as it saves you getting a cricked neck. The big problem you may run into is that the hole tends to fill with water so you are sitting in cold, wet water - not very comfy!

Choice of food

Most pet shops and supermarkets sell small bags of bird food. However, if you are going to run a feeder for any length of time and it works well you should get through a large amount of food. To save money and time try to buy it in bulk from a reputable dealer (see appendix). They also deliver the food directly to your door which is a great help! Buying from one of these dealers also ensures that you are getting top quality food. It is worth browsing their websites because there are always new foods appearing that may bring different birds to your feeders. When you have bought the food make sure you store it safely away from mice, moths and damp. Plastic dustbins with lids are ideal.

A yellow hammer feeding on mixed seed on farmland in the winter. 1Dmk4, 500mm, f4, 1/500, ISO 800, tripod, low position hide. Sheffield.

Peanuts

Peanuts are loved by the tit family particularly blue, great and cole tits which are usually guaranteed to turn up. Willow and marsh tits are likely if they are occur in your area and you pick the right habitat. Long-tailed tits are variable, coming well in some areas but affecting indifference in others. Great spotted woodpeckers and nuthatches are both possible in woodland situations. Siskins (they used to love the red peanut bags) will also visit peanut feeders in Scotland and in late winter in England. All these species will visit hanging feeders as well as bird tables.

Sunflower seed

Once these were sold only in their coats but now huskless varieties (called hearts) are available which reduces the huge pile of husks that tend to gather beneath the bird table or feeder. Most of the birds that like peanuts also like sunflower seeds, in fact many actually prefer them if they have a choice.

Alongside the birds mentioned above the following species love sunflower seeds - bullfinches, greenfinches, chaffinches (which tend to prefer tables or the ground to feed on), tree and house sparrows, dunnocks (which prefer hearts and tables or the ground), doves, robins and thrushes (because of their size they are not keen on hanging feeders, they prefer tables or even the

ground). Cirl buntings will visit bird tables in the right area (Southern England). Yellow hammers feed primarily on the ground. I have found them virtually impossible to get to land on a post or bird table but they will perch in hedges next to seed spread on the ground. For species like hawfinches that feed in the trees small plastic tubs fitted to branches filled with seed have been known to work.

Cereals

Oats, barley and wheat are not so popular but are ideal if you are running a farm bird project. In winter reed buntings, linnets, greenfinches, tree sparrows, yellowhammers and occasionally skylarks will take them from the ground. If you mix niger and sunflower hearts with the cereals you will increase the attractiveness and the species range of the food. Red-legged and English partridge will also feed from cereals on the ground but both can be very nervous. If you want to concentrate on these two buy a gamekeeper's barrel feeder and stock with barley or wheat. Keep it near cover such as alongside a hedge or a corn crop and run it all winter long with your hide permanently set up. You will find that you have to be in the hide before dawn as the birds come just after sunrise.

Niger seed

These need special hanging feeders with very small holes because the seed is almost like dust. Niger also works well on tables. Redpolls will come in some areas, particularly Scotland. Goldfinches and siskins are the other key species to attract. For goldfinches cut teasels in the early autumn before they go black, dry them out and store them in the dry until the winter. You can then push hollow metal poles into the ground to hold them up without breaking the stems and sprinkle niger seed in the top everyday. Hold a plastic tray below to collect spilt seed when you sprinkle it over the teasels. Once the goldies find them, which usually doesn't take

Crested tits come regularly to peanut feeders in winter if they are placed in the correct habitat in Scotland. 5Dmk3, 500mm +1.4 converter, 1/125, f5.5, ISO 2000, -1/3 exposure compensation.

too long, they will visit all winter as long as you keep the teasels stocked daily. In winter a number of small birds such as snow buntings visit sites along the coast. These birds are seeking small natural seeds in the shingle and will readily take niger seed if it is scattered out for them. In some cases a hide is not necessary, simply lying down in front of the place you scatter the seed is sufficient.

Snow bunting feeding on niger seed sprinkled out on a shingle beach. 1Dmk4, 500mm, 1/1250, f5.6, ISO 400, beanbag. Norfolk.

Mealworms

These can be bought as mini or full sized, either dried, freeze dried or live. If you use dried ones soak them for a while first. The most economical way to buy live worms is in bulk from a dealer (see appendix). If you do buy them in bulk you need to store them in a cool dry place in a large plastic tub (most supermarkets now sell plastic storage boxes that are ideal). You need to feed the worms with bran or oats and supply a few pieces of potato or apple for moisture.

Mealworms can be used on bird tables or small feeders like cups on poles or hanging in bushes. Robins love them in winter as do many of the tits and nuthatches. You will probably find the robin now becomes a bit of a bully and drives many other birds away. Wrens will also eat small mealworms but are often driven away by robins. To counter this hide them in old walls or wood piles but even then the robin does tend to find them. Another approach is to overload the robin by saturating the area with mealworms. It can't defend all the feeders, though it will have a good go!

Dried mealworms. These need a soak in water for ten minutes before you use them.

In summer moorland birds such as wheatears and ring ouzels will take live mealworms. There is one beetle larvae that

Wheatears will feed on mealworms placed out for them. 1Dmk4, 500mm, 1/1000, f4, ISO 1000, Tripod. Scotland.

lives naturally on the moors that ring ouzels love. The last time I photographed a pair at the nest they kept bringing these for the chicks. If I didn't know better I would have sworn they were mealworms. I have seen whinchat, stonechat and bearded reedlings eat mealworms and suspect they will come to them regularly given time. Redstarts certainly love them.

A major problem working with mealworms is that every time it rains the mealworms die unless you can find rainproof, sheltered spots for them.

Feeding birds in summer used to be considered dangerous because it was thought that the birds may try to feed their chicks on mouth-choking peanuts. In rare cases this may be true but the advice now is to feed all year round. Mealworms work well in summer with all the species mentioned before plus some finches and pied/spotted flycatchers.

I spent some time at a farm in Wales where pied flycatchers were feeding chicks in a nest box. The adults fed on the mealworms put out for them but when I was there they never fed the chicks with them, they hunted for caterpillars in the trees instead. There will be many other insect eating birds that will use mealworms. It's just a matter of trying them out. Live ones are better nutritiously and more attractive to the birds.

Fat

Years ago it was easy to go to the butchers and buy chunks of suet, not so now - another victim of Heath and Safety! You can buy ready-made fat and suet balls from bird food suppliers, plus lard from any supermarket. It is easy to make your own fat cake. Grind up a lot of peanuts in a food blender and pop them into a big pan. Then sprinkle liberally with small sunflower hearts and pour molten lard over the lot and stir thoroughly. If it looks too liquid add more ground up peanuts until it's thick. Stir well and ladle it into old margarine tubs to cool for later use.

If you want make fat balls use a small marg tub and a put a bit of wire with a small wooden peg at the end (to stop the fat ball being pulled off) into it. The other end is for wrapping round a branch. Pur the fat/peanut mixture into it and let it cool, Tip it out (warm the tub up slightly in water) when you want to use it. All the tits, great spotted woodpeckers and nuthatches love them. Robins and lots of other birds including dunnocks and blackbirds will also try to feed from them.

A great spotted woodpecker on an oak branch which has been drilled with holes and filled with a fat/peanut mixture. One key point is to make sure any drilled holes can't be seen in the image. The fat has been 'stained' with chocolate to help disguise it a bit. In this image I chose to back-light the bird. 1Dmk3, 500mm, 1/250, f6.7, ISO 500, tripod and hide. Sheffield.

For images with a bit of variety think about pushing fat into old taps, teapot spouts or old fir cones to get blue tits hanging from them. There are lots of objects you can use to try and create images with that little bit of originality.

Fat feeders for woodpeckers and nuthatches

Both great spotted woodpeckers and nuthatches look naturally great on a branch. The trick is to get them to readily use your chosen one. The easiest method is to prepare a number of branches ahead of your photography.

Select one main branch which will be the one that stays out all the time. For this branch choose an old oak branch about 2

metres high. Drill holes with a fairly big drill, about a pencil width in diameter and about ¾ of the way into the branch. Into this squeeze the home-made lard mixture. You need the holes to be quite deep because tits and robins will quickly learn it is there and if they are too shallow they eat up all your food. Fix the branch (with wire or cable ties) to a metal pole hammered into the ground. It is a good idea to have your hide already set up so the birds get used to it. The idea of choosing oak for this branch is because it is very hard and slows down the squirrels chewing the holes open.

Once the peckers and nuthatches are coming readily switch the branch for a more photogenic one, say a nice mossy one or one with attractive bark, such as silver birch. At the end of each session swap back to the oak branch. Try to keep the branch holes filled up everyday. I prepare the fat in the same way as for fat balls but only use ground peanuts. I also add a big blob of chocolate to stain it brown. This is to disguise the fat when the pecker gets some onto its bill - it looks more natural than white fatty blobs.

Earthworms

Earthworms are a great natural food and a classic image is of a thrush or blackbird pulling one out of the ground. You can try to create this image by making a large table-sized unit in a similar way to an infinity pond (p118) but instead of water fill it with cut turf. The base should have many small holes or a fine mesh where the holes are too small for the worms to get out. The grass table is then placed onto an old table or aquarium stand to get it off ground level.

You can feed blackbirds on here with raisins (they love them) to get them into the habit of visiting regularly. If you put enough large earthworms on they tend to burrow into the soil but because it's shallow they can't get too deep. Eventually a blackbird will find one and, if you're lucky, it will be facing the right way for your image. Digging up worms can be a bit of a chore but luckily many bird food or fishing shops sell them.

Feeding cuckoos

This cuckoo picked up the caterpillar from the branch when it landed on it. 1DX, 500mm, 1/2500, f5.6, ISO 400. Scotland.

Cuckoos feed on hairy caterpillars like those of the eggar and fox moths. In some years they can be really abundant and seem to be crawling all over the moors. It is possible to set up a post or find one that a cuckoo regularly perches on and pop the caterpillars on to it. They will cling to it and hopefully if a cuckoo lands it will find one and eat it.

Raisins/Sultanas

Raisins and sultanas are both good, high sugar foods for blackbirds and other thrushes. Sprinkle onto the area you want to work, especially in winter when the weather makes worms and other natural foods difficult to find.

Apples

Fallen apples and pears in old orchards can be a mecca for winter thrushes. The problem is that there are not many old orchards anymore so the trick is to supply your own fruit. Many greengrocers will happily give or sell you bruised apples at a cheap price. The best time to use them is during a really hard spell of frost. The longer the better because any winter thrushes like fieldfares, redwings, mistle thrushes and blackbirds will switch to these when the berries in the trees run short and the frozen ground stops them eating invertebrates. It tends to work better the later in winter/early spring you do it i.e. February to March because the natural world's larder is running short. Try to pick an area with no rabbits. You will just end up feeding dozens of them everyday.

Acorns / Beech mast

Foods such as acorns and beech mast are always the best to use if you want natural looking shots, such as a jay carrying that iconic acorn. In bumper years gather up a few big carrier bags of both and freeze them (especially acorns because they tend to dry out and die and the jays seem to be able to spot this and refuse to eat them). Start the project in late winter, around February. The idea is that any fallen, natural acorns have long gone and the jays are struggling for food and looking for buried ones. To conserve your acorns set up a nice branch with channels chiselled out and fill these with peanuts.

Jay collecting acorns from a prepared stump. 10D, 500mm, 1/1500, f4, ISO 400, tripod, hide. Sheffield.

Once the jay is coming regularly and is used to your hide use your thawed out acorns. The jay needs to swallow about five or six before its crop is full. It is the last acorn that it will carry in its bill. You will find that they tend to swallow them really quickly and fly off so you need to keep them stocked up. They are basically doing what they do in autumn, collecting as many as they can and burying them for later. You will be amazed at just how fast they can get through a few carrier bags' worth.

Fieldfare feeding on apples placed out in a field during a long period of snow. 1Dmk4, 500mm, 1/1600, f5.6, ISO 500, +11/3 over exposure, tripod, low hide. Derbyshire.

You can use beech mast for bramblings and chaffinches in winter. If you find flocks naturally feeding on them try a low level hide but if you want to prepare in advance set up an area in woodland and get the birds coming regularly using sunflower hearts. Once this is happening switch to the beech mast on the day you photograph. It looks a 100% better in the bill than a black sunflower seed!

Meat + Road kill animals

Meat and road kills are not for the squeamish but their use attracts another group of birds to your camera - birds of prey and corvids. Many birds of prey think nothing of eating dead animals, some actually specialise in them, such as red kites and buzzards. One main consideration is to keep the prey and bird as natural as possible. Obviously if the bird is an opportunistic scavenger like a buzzard it will probably tuck into any dead animal like a sheep, deer, badger or rabbit. Many buzzards, now they are far more common, are killed by cars because they have learnt to work road verges for potential meals. In some cases it might be easier to get

the bird coming regularly using a different, more easily available food source you can buy like dead chicks or mice. Both are sold in reptile pet shops.

You will probably find that using dead animals is very much hit and miss. There are areas in Wales where you can set up a hide at dawn, stake out a dead rabbit and within two hours have a number of buzzards all vying with each other to tuck into it.

In other areas of the UK it may take months before a buzzard starts to feed and then it may remain incredibly nervous. The only way is to try it and see. If you plan to do this you need to select an area where your chosen bird is abundant. Have the hide up for a few weeks or longer if possible before you place the bait out. Use rabbits for buzzards and secure them to the ground with four or five tent pegs, long ones driven in at different angles. There is nothing more frustrating than to watch the buzzard land then drag away, or even fly off with, the rabbit before you have even taken a shot.

Opening up the rabbit and showing the white belly fur and some red meat increases your chances. Try to take the guts away so it stays fresh a little longer. You may find that

This buzzard is trying to feed on the dead rabbit staked out for it. The crow hopes that by being a nuisance it will drive the buzzard away. This rarely happens but I guess it's great fun for the crow. EOS 3, 500mm, 1/800, f4, ISO 100 (slide film), hide and tripod. Wales.

A red deer carcass used as bait for buzzards. The camera, flash and 16-35mm lens are placed into one end of the carcass (in a plastic bag) and are fired using a remote device from a hide 50m away. 1Dmk4, 1/160, f13, ISO 400. Derbyshire.

the rabbit disappears every night - you might even spot the fat fox! Stake out a rabbit every few days. You don't need to do it everyday. You will find that crows and magpies become a massive problem but if a buzzard does come it can hold its own, even though they will tease it endlessly.

As a rule place your hide next to a hedge and have the bait out in short, natural grassland about 30 metres from the hedge. Don't forget to garden any long bits of vegetation out of the way and make sure the background is good. In areas with lots of red kites you are likely to get one of these down as well.

Using larger carcasses, such as sheep, works well but unfortunately under the law these have to be removed from any field within 24 hours so it's unlikely you will come across one. A decade or so ago this was not the case and I wonder how many ravens and buzzards suffered when we removed a good supply of food, especially in hard winters.

Using red or roe deer is not subject to the same regulations as they are wild animals so if you come across a road kill, or know where they are being culled and can get your hands on one, they can be staked out. Again remove the guts to keep flies down and allow it to stay fresh longer.

For a very dramatic image it is possible to set up a camera with a wide angle lens inside a dead deer. The camera can be fired remote-

ly from a hide. A small fill-in flash to light the inside of the deer will probably be needed. If you try this you may have to wait for a while and use several carcasses because if it's new many birds view it with suspicion until they get used to it. This is especially true if you use a dead deer in a place where they may never have seen one before. As buzzard and kite populations rocket the chances of success will increase. A hard winter will boost success even further.

It is possible to work with golden and sea eagles in a similar manner. Golden eagles are very wary and I would hesitate before I recommend anyone to try this. The main thing is to get a permanent hide into place and possibly leave it there for a year or more. A small stone-built structure erected in summer which blends into the landscape is a good starting point. Scotland is about the only place possible in the UK and you really need to live there to do it justice. Read Mike Tomkies book 'Golden Eagle Years' for advice.

Golden eagle feeding on a road kill fox. 5Dmk3, 500mm, 1/80, f4, ISO 160, tripod and hide. Finland. The choice of low ISO and speed may seem odd but the idea was to get some blur into the falling snow.

During a good, snowy, hard winter you have to place a deer carcass in front of your established hide. I have worked with golden and sea eagles at bait in Finland and Poland and the challenges to complete a successful project are big, but not impossible. You need to be in the hide in the dark in the morning, so how far you have to walk is an issue. You also can't leave the hide until a good hour after dark in the evening.

The Finnish eagles come all winter but they live in an area where natural food is hard to come by and the weather is sub-zero and snowy virtually all winter. Of all the birds I have photographed I would rate golden eagles as one of the most wary. We had to wait until the birds had landed and were feeding. Any camera noise or lens movement before then and they would be off and not return for at least 24 hours.

The food has to be staked down really firmly as well. Eagles are very strong and can drag quite large carcasses out of camera shot. For long term projects a large concrete block can be sunk into the ground in summer with one or two metal hoops firmly attached. The bait is well tethered to this the following winter. A good read about the workings of a successful golden eagle project in Scotland is Laurie Campbell's 'Golden Eagle'.

Sea or white-tailed eagles are much easier to work with. They are becoming fairly abundant in some parts of Europe and are increasing in the UK. They are natural scavengers and take a wide variety of dead food, including pork and fish. I have worked with them in Poland and whilst, like golden eagles, they were nervous initially once they started feeding they quickly settled down. The main issue with both eagles in the UK is sensitivity - it may be hard to persuade all the groups and individuals concerned to allow you to work on such a project.

Running a winter sea eagle feeding station in the UK would not be too difficult if you can get the landowner's permission and have the option to construct a permanent hide in good sea eagle territory. Baiting every few days from late autumn will let the eagles know food is there. Feed every day when the weather gets hard and keep the project running all winter. If you repeat this every subsequent winter it will only take a few years be-

White-tailed eagles fighting over bait put out for them in the winter in Poland. 1DX, 500mm, 1/1600, f5.6, ISO 1000, tripod and hide.

fore you start to get good numbers of eagles visiting regularly.

Probably one of the most impressive shots of a sea eagle is it barrelling down out of the sky and plucking a fish from the surface of the sea. Once nigh on impossible now it is very easy to get such a shot. A number of habituated sea eagles now reside in Scotland, some on Mull and others near Skye. Local boatmen will take you out and throw dead fish behind the boat. You simply have to be able to focus and follow the eagle down as it takes the fish. Dramatic and spectacular.

To set this up yourself would be possible but time consuming and expensive so in this case it's much easier and cheaper to pay the boatman and take your chance. Norwegian sea eagles offer much the same. You get far more goes with your camera but you need a strong bank balance to pay for it!

On a similar note, getting a shot of an osprey diving into a lake and emerging with a fish with water droplets glistening like diamonds in the sun was once incredibly difficult. I spent a week in Finland six years

A white-tailed eagle just after it snatched a dead fish from the sea. 1Dmk2, 300mm, 1/3200, f4, ISO 400, handheld from a boat. Norway.

ago on such a project and loved the whole experience. However, today it's now a much easier image to add to your portfolio as more places are offering diving osprey hides, the latest being a set of fishing ponds near Rutland Water. There is also the established set up at the Rothiemurchus fish farm in Speyside.

Several of our smaller hawks and falcons such as sparrowhawk, goshawk and kestrel can be lured to dead food. There are always a few birds in every area that will feed this way. Kestrels are fairly easy to get to come to dead mice though the biggest problem in some areas will be magpies. Once they realise there is an easy meal they will usually

An osprey fishing for trout in Finland . 1Dmk3, 300mm, 1/5000, f4, ISO 400, beanbag + hide.

beat the kestrel to it. The main thing is to secure the dead mouse firmly to the post or they simply grab it and fly away. Try to use brown or grey mice as they may have never seen a white one before.

The hide should be up for a while before you start photography. To increase the authenticity of your image use dead wood mice or voles on the day you choose to get images. It is fairly easy to get a steady supply of these. Just simply ask around until you find someone whose cat is bringing home dead wood mice and bank voles as presents. Ask them to bag each one up and pop it into their freezer. Wild kestrels will also come to dead day old chicks.

Sparrowhawks can be photographed in a similar way though the only set-up at the moment where they are coming regularly uses dead mice as bait - great to keep the hawk coming regularly but if the mouse is in the image not a natural shot. It is good idea to collect road kill small birds so you can generate a more natural image. The area where this project is running has the advantage of no magpies competing for the food.

Goshawks can be baited in the same way - staking out a dead wood pigeon on a prominent stump in good goshawk woodland habitat. Unlike working with kestrels or sparrowhawks it is imperative you are in the hide in the dark in the morning. When I did this many years ago the goshawk would arrive at dawn to feed, often when light levels were too low for slide film. Working in woods that are keepered can have the advantage of reducing magpie issues but there are not many keepers who will want to see you encouraging goshawks. However, a good counter argument is that every dead wood pigeon they eat is one less pheasant.

It is possible to photograph sparrowhawks on their natural plucking posts in summer. When the pair has chicks in the nest the male is the primary hunter. Once he has caught a bird he will often fly to one of a number of established plucking posts in the breeding wood. You have to spend a fair bit of time walking the wood to find them all. They don't always have lots of feathers lying around but look for small feathers stuck to a branch or post. It does work but you do need to find the most photogenic plucking post and he will probably only come once a day because he tends to rotate around them.

This male kestrel was coming regularly to this stump because it was baited with a dead mouse. The mouse is hidden in the hollow centre of the stump. 1Dmk4, 500mm, 1/400, f8, ISO 1600, tripod and hide. Worcstershire.

It is not impossible to get hen harriers to come to dead food set out for them, such as quail and rats. This could form part of a project (as has been done in the past) to try to get hen harriers back onto English moorlands. You never know you may be lucky enough to be involved.

A rather unexpected bird that will come occasionally to dead bait is the water rail. This only really happens in periods of long-lasting, frozen ground. During such frosts the water rails cannot feed by probing the hard mud for worms. They are basically starving so any food set out may be a real lifeline. You can feed them with both mealworms and maggot castors. Mealworms have the disadvantage of showing up more in the image and robins finding them quickly. Maggot castors are readily available from fishing shops and are dark in colour. Sprinkle a load out in an open area on the edge of the reed bed. It won't take long before the water rail finds them. It only seems to work in hard

weather. Once the frost has gone they don't bother with them anymore. A long time ago I remember seeing an image of a water rail tucking into a dead moorhen, rather bizarre but the bird was probably starving.

Both barn owls and tawny owls will come to dead bait. Some tawny owls will regularly come to dead chicks that have been staked out on a stump in woodland. If you try this you may have to use flash as they tend to be fairly nocturnal. Barn owls are more likely to be around on the margins of the day and photographable in daylight.

Little owl, EOS 10D, 500mm, 1/500, f4, ISO 100, tripod and hide. Derbyshire.

Little owls can very easily be tempted to live mealworms. The starting point is to locate a pair. Luckily they are crepuscular i.e. they come out at both dawn and dusk in fairly good light. Little owls have a very distinctive call so are easy to pick up in the breeding season. They are also usually faithful to their breeding place (a hole in a tree, wall or building) so baiting them can be a long term project·

During a very cold spell a few years ago I visited a nature reserve where I knew a stream wouldn't have frozen over. All the still water such as the local ponds and lakes were locked solid with ice and the kingfishers larder was firmly closed. I didn't have long to wait until this female showed up. 1Dmk3, 500mm + 1.4 converter, 1/250, f5.6, ISO 320, tripod from a hide. Yorkshire.

Once you have located a pair place a few small bowls of mealworms around their local territory on gate posts, walls etc. As with all fieldwork watch before you start photography and see which are their favourite posts and perches and concentrate here. You can always put up a post with the bowl nailed very close to the top. Once you get them coming it's a simple matter of changing the post to create variety in your images.

Fish

Dead fish as bait are a bit smelly but work well with a number of birds. Herons have become quite common urban birds and will take readily to a dead fish. As always the winter increases your chances. One way to get dramatic shots is to put a plank of wood just below the surface of a pond or lake. It takes a bit of effort to get it there but the idea is to get it just below the surface of the lake.

Herons will quickly find it if you bait it with dead fish which can be bought from your fishmonger.

The sunken plank creates images that are very clean with the heron standing out in what looks like shallow water. Obviously the best image is with a freshwater fish like a roach, eel or pike. It is possible to come across these - they can even be bought and stored in your freezer. Use cheap mackerel to get the herons used to the idea and switch to the dead eel or pike when you carry out your photography. As in most cases have the hide up permanently and in advance so the herons get used to it.

In many urban areas herons have become incredibly tame and will respond really well to a few dead fish left out for them. Try not to do this in too public a place and think carefully about the composition of your final image when deciding where to place the fish.

In periods of severe frost bitterns and herons really struggle and both will soon learn to feed from a frozen lake surface. A few years ago a local nature reserve froze over for some weeks and one bittern was feeding every day on sprats thrown out onto the ice.

An urban heron that has become used to humans. Some of the herons in London's parks are ridiculously tame. 1DX, 500mm, 1/250, f5.6, ISO 800, tripod. Nottinghamshire.

The trick is to keep the fish close to the edge of the reeds so the bittern does not have to venture out too far, but far enough for your images. If you intend to do this the chances are it will be on a nature reserve so make sure you have spoken to the wardens and have their permission.

This bittern was clearly struggling in the long, frozen period in 2010. A few bird watchers fed it sprats on the ice and it would leave the reed beds every morning to stock up on the much needed food. 1Dmk3, 500mm, 1/800, f5.6, ISO 800, +2/3 exposure compensation. S. Yorkshire.

Kingfishers

There are now quite a few pay-as-you-go set-ups where you can photograph kingfishers, either as portraits on branches or reed heads or, more dramatically, diving into a pool. All of these use live fish as bait to entice the kingfisher to one spot where it will perch before diving into a pool or tub. I visited one of these a couple of years ago and the images it produced were fantastic. However, the aim of this book is to show you that you can generate your own images using your own field skills.

If you intend to set up your own project using live fish you must read through the Animal Welfare Act (AWA) 2006 and familiarise yourself with the relevant sections. The most important part concerns keeping animals in captivity. 'Any vertebrate that is kept in captivity (permanently or temporary) is a protected animal and whilst in captivity must not suffer unnecessary mental or physical suffering'. There are exceptions to this and licences can be granted but it is unlikely that one would be for wildlife photography.

The Wildlife and Countryside Act also tells you that it is illegal (without a licence) to put any fish into a river that do not originate from that river.

However, it's not impossible to create your own project and produce good images of kingfishers without using captive fish but this requires a few prerequisites. First, the river or lake has to have kingfishers on it. This is more likely if there are small fish around (like roach or minnows) and most lakes and streams are now clean enough for good fish populations.

Check out your chosen river or lake and learn to identify the high-pitched, sharp, call of the male kingfisher. Once you are sure they are regular on your chosen place then you need to seek out a spot to carry out your project.

The best place is where there are no natural perches for the birds to use and there is good light. This is often the main sticking point. Many streams have kingfishers but for the majority of their length they are shaded by trees.

The simplest method to getting close to a kingfisher is to adopt the 'wait and see' technique. Select an area of the river or stream where the water flows slowly and there are no natural perches or trees overhead. Choose an appropriate perch. It could be a natural branch or a 'no-fishing' sign. Set it

I took this image of a male kingfisher carrying a small brown trout on a river near to where I live. I used the 'wait and see' approach. I set up a perch over the river where I thought a kingfisher might land. It did take quite a few hours before it arrived but when it did my heart rate definitely went up! 1Dmk2, 500mm, 1/1000, f6.3, ISO 200, tripod and hide. Derbyshire.

of small fish gather to feed. Kingfishers will learn quickly where such situations exist. Similarly minnows will shoal in warm shallow water and again this would provide an excellent place to introduce a perch.

You can increase your chances to attract the birds even further by using groundbait bought from a fishing shop and create your own shoals of fish. You will have to experiment a bit before you get it right but I have seen it work well in the past.

Creating images of diving kingfishers is very difficult and time consuming, however not impossible. I have read of one photographer who attracted shoals of fish to an area of a river where a kingfisher was fishing regularly. He used a dark board with a hole cut into it into which the kingfisher dived. He now had a specific place to focus on. In this case he used flash to get sufficient light to freeze the bird. However, with a set-up in the right place and using your camera set to auto ISO and a speed of 1/2500 at a low f number it should be possible to freeze the action as the kingfisher erupts from the hole with a fish. Getting your camera at water level on a tripod and firing with a long cable release will eliminate any bits of the board.

In hard winters when ponds and lakes freeze over feeding opportunities for kingfishers are severely reduced. In really hard winters their population can take an appalling drop. However they have the ability to breed rapidly and will bounce back over the next few years.

If you experience such a winter go on the hunt for ponds or lakes where there are still a few areas of open water. These are often created and maintained by ducks. It is quite likely that a kingfisher may now be using the same hole and may be able to provide you with some photographic opportunities.

If no holes exist think about creating one and maintaining it over the freezing period. A bit of ground bait sprinkled into the water may attract small fish and it shouldn't take too long before the electric blue flash finds

out in the stream at about 1 to 2 metres high. The best places are where it overlooks a natural pool within the stream where small fish may shelter or hide. Set up a hide that allows a good vantage point for photography, with a clean background and the light in a favourable direction. Then simply sit and wait. Have all your camera gear set up and ready to fire a shot if and when a kingfisher lands. I would estimate that at least 50% of the time I have done this a bird lands within 4 or 5 hours so it's definitely worth doing. On some occasions the kingfisher may fish from your perch and return to it with its catch. This is far less likely but it does happen.

You can increase the possibility of a kingfisher actually fishing from your perch if you can site it over an area where fish naturally gather. On some of the industrial canals in Sheffield warm, organic waste water is discharged and where this happens large shoals and fishes your ice hole. It may seem that you are exploiting the bird in the severe conditions but it could be argued that in fact you are helping it through this difficult time. It is the same as putting extra food out for our garden birds to help them survive cold periods of winter.

Many years ago I thought I would produce a book called 'Wildlife on a Bicycle'. I started the project by buying an old bike which seemed to have character and placing it propped up in an industrial stream in Sheffield. I set up my hide on the stream bank and waited. A kingfisher actually landed on several different parts including the photogenic seat. EOS 1, 500mm, 1/250, f5.6, ISO 100 (slide film) tripod. Sheffield.

Coastal waders

A classic image is of a sanderling, its twinkling feet suspended in the air, racing across flat, wet sand. The main problem is trying to keep the birds close to you - they usually work around you or dart by on those dainty, rapidly moving legs. A good food source and one that is natural that works really well are prawn shells. Whenever you have prawns with their 'coats' on and have to peel them collect up all the skins (exoskeletons) and store them in a plastic container in the freezer.

The idea is to be lying down on the sand well ahead of the sanderlings, close to the shoreline where they feed. Sprinkle out your prawn bits close to the sea, where you anticipate in a few minutes the birds and waves will meet, and wait. They tend to come much closer to you because you are low and they are approaching you, not the other way

round. Once they find the bait they will mill around for a good few minutes tucking in. You may find turnstones and knot will also eat the same food.

Fully opened razor shells also work really well with godwits, redshank and turnstones. One major problem is the tide is never still. An incoming tide is better if you can judge the speed of the tide and the birds so they both meet near you at the same time.

One issue worth considering when working on sandy or muddy beaches is your tripod's reaction to sand and seawater. Many photographers today use carbon fibre tripods with leg screw joints. These can be very prone to getting sand and sea water in the joints and they are a nightmare to clean every time this happens. If you choose not to clean them you run the risk of the joint becoming seized up. For beach and sea work it's a good idea to use an old aluminium tripod that has simple leg extenders, not screw ones. Once you get home you simply pop it in the shower and wash it clean in seconds.

I worked with this redshank on the shoreline. Unfortunately my tripod was flat on the sand and the joints became full of salty, sandy water. A beanbag on my mini sledge would probably have been a better idea. 1Dmk4, 500mm, 1/2500, f5.6, ISO 500. Yorkshire coast.

An alternative is to fix your tripod head to a type of mini-sledge. You can buy commercial ones now that look like large saucers. If the sand is incredibly flat and smooth an old skateboard with a beanbag on it is ideal. It is really easy to slowly push this ahead of you when you're belly-crawling along the beach.

A sanderling sprints along the tide line. 1Dmk3, 500mm, 1/2500, f8, ISO 500 +2/3 exposure compensation, tripod flat on the sand. Lincolnshire.

These two redshanks were fighting over food dug for them on the beach. 20D, 500mm, 1/2000, f4, ISO 400, tripod. Yorkshire coast.

In areas where fishermen dig for bait redshank and turnstones sometimes work over the dug piles of sand right next to the bait digger. Using your own spade it's no problem to dig a few holes and see if any of the beach waders show an interest. It only occasionally works but when it does it can be very productive.

Many ducks are easily attracted to food. Bread is often used but wild bird seed is nutritionally much better. Many of us have seen the eiders at Seahouses being fed bread and chips! A much better choice is to buy a big bag of mussels if you can't collect your own. If you want to work with eiders it's far better to go early in the year before the Farne Island boats start for the season when it's nice and quiet.

Sprinkle a bit of bread (to get them interested and because they are used to it) and the mussels on the shore line. With perseverance you can work for a good few hours and produce a great range of images of eiders on the shore or calling at sea and hopefully with a mussel, their natural food, in their bill.

This knot is feeding on small shrimp bits that I had scattered on the tideline. I was lying on the sand with my camera and lens on a beanbag on my mini sledge. 1Dmk4, 500mm, 1/2000, f5.6, ISO 500. Yorkshire coast.

Non-food attractants

During the breeding season many birds are seeking out nesting material. Lots of small birds use wool, feathers or hair to line their grass or twig-based nests. Long-tailed tits use thousands of feathers in their incredible dome - shaped nests. The idea is to set out a variety of materials in prominent photogenic spots and hope for a bit of luck. Most birds build early in the morning, have a rest around midday and have another concentrated effort in the late afternoon. Placing the material needs a bit of thought. As always make sure the background is nice and clean. You will have to place or lightly stick the material on a natural prop. A strand of rusty barbed wire is great to wrap a bit of wool or horse hair round (get a bag from your local stables). Feathers can be stuck to brambles with a dab of mud.

Timing is important. You obviously have to have the project running and be in the hide when the birds are lining their nests. This technique can be a bit unreliable but it does work. You just have to experiment and give it time. You can repeat it in a variety of habitats to try for different species. Yellow hammers will take hair (as do bullfinches and dunnocks) and chiffchaffs have been photographed collecting feathers set out for them. Long-tailed tits need lots of feathers and they collect the majority from dead corpses, probably as a labour saving strategy. You could try setting out a dead wood pigeon which are easily found as road casualties.

It is possible to take this further and put out feathers for sparrows, sand martins and swallows. There have been some fabulous images of swallows plucking feathers from puddles and small pools. The basic idea is to anchor the feather loosely to a stick which is just below the water's surface. The bird, with luck, will fly down and pluck the feather whilst in flight. Fast speeds are needed, at least 2000+, but because the feather is not blowing across the water it is possible to pre-focus on it and turn the auto-focus off. F8 is a good starting depth of field and the birds

should keep returning if you can coincide your feathers with the time they are lining their nests.

This female linnet was collecting nesting material I had placed out for her. I had spent some time watching the linnets which were nesting in a colony amongst the gorse in one of my local patches in Sheffield. I had noticed that the linnets were collecting fluff from thistle seed heads. I simply collected some myself and positioned it amongst the gorse. It didn't take long before the linnets starting collecting the material from where I had placed it.
1DX, 500mm +1.4 converter, f5.6, 1/1000, ISO 800, tripod. Sheffield.

It is possible to get images of rooks collecting sticks. Generally the rooks will have lots of choice but as with many birds they will always take the path of least resistance. All you need to do is to set out an area near to the rookery with a good selection of twigs. The best rookeries to choose will be ones where the birds are familiar with people so you won't need a hide. Rooks can become very tame when they are used to people but are incredibly wary if a situation changes.

Drinking pools

This male bullfinch is perched on the end of a reflection pool I constructed in my local woods. 1Dmk4, 500mm, 1/1600, f4, ISO 250, tripod and hide. Sheffield.

All birds will drink and most love a good bathe in clean water. Providing a supply of drinking water is a simple method to attract a number of birds. How elaborate you want to make it is entirely up to you.

The most basic design is a simple plastic container, like a bin lid or drip tray. Sink it into the ground and make the edges blend in with the natural surroundings. Keep it topped up with water and it can be amazing just what will arrive. The trick is to know where and when to use a pool. Sandy soils drain well so naturally standing water is often in short supply, similarly in dry summers. Any pool that allows birds to drink and bathe will usually result in a hive of activity.

Think about how the birds will approach and have some natural cover nearby, say a bush/tree or in fields by the edge of a hedge. Make sure the background and direction of the sun are taken into account. Try to have your hide up at the same time you start your pool.

If you want something a little more permanent or larger then dig a hole and use a pond liner. A couple of things need consideration. Blend in the edges with the local ground cover - moss and leaves in woodland or bare soil in a field. Make sure the sides slope very gradually in. Most birds don't like any deep water so provide a stone or rock in the middle that is a 1/2cm or so below the surface for the birds to use. Make the sides you don't want to photograph on less attractive, say with a low board or long vegetation, so the birds will drink where you want them to.

It has always been thought that water dripping into the pond increases its attractiveness. You can suspend barrels of water above the pond on a mini scaffold and allow it to drip in every day. Another trick is to use a cheap solar water pump which creates a spray of water into the pond.

One, if not the biggest, problem is keeping it full with water. You will be staggered at just how fast it evaporates in hot, sunny

Birds visit ponds not only to drink but to bathe as well. Robin, 1Dmk4, 500mm, 1/250, f5.6, ISO 400, tripod and hide. Sheffield.

weather. A nearby source is a real bonus - like a standpipe in a set of allotments or a local stream. If this is not possible you will have to carry your water in. Then you will realise how much the pond uses and how heavy water actually is! You could fashion an old golf trolley to carry a big water container to make the job easier. It really helps and the trolleys can be cheap. Its big wheels are also great over rough ground. (You can also use this arrangement to carry heavy gear over sand and mud estuaries as well). If you can site your pond as near to a track as possible you may be able to drive fairly close.

The longer you run the pond the better. Some ponds work well and others fail miserably. Be prepared for a lack of interest and if it's not working try another area. Ponds in the ground keep the water cooler and a big deep area in the middle helps. If the pond is shallow it warms up quickly in sunny weather and many birds do not like warm water.

A variation of this to attract nest-building swallows and house martins is to create a permanent area of damp mud. This is very effective when it's a dry early summer and the martins and swallows are nest building. Simply create a puddle with a shallow liner and have soil all around so that it absorbs the water. Keep it topped up every day. It won't take long before you have a number of birds visiting to collect mud. Obviously choose a farm or area where there are nesting birds.

Reflection or infinity pools

These have become very popular in the last ten years or so and do produce dramatic images with lovely reflections and clean backgrounds. The trick is to build the pool above ground so you can site your lens along it at literally water-level. If the pool is on the ground then you would have to dig a hole for you and your gear. Many people use wood and create a frame. They then use boards for the base of the pool and shallow wooden laths down all the sides. The pool is then lined with a pond liner to hold the water. The far end, where you will photograph the birds, is very shallow.

One factor that needs some thought is the colour of the water. This will be exactly what is reflected into the water as you look along it in the direction you will photograph. If it reflects the sky the water will be either blue or murky grey, not too good. If you can get trees reflected then it will be green. Some pools are built with a painted backboard on stilts about 2 metres behind the pool to create the desired water colour.

To attract birds to drink you can add a cheap, solar pump to create a small water jet at one end. This does work and it should increase the number of birds but performs only on sunny days. Obviously you need to site the pool where you are not going to get it vandalised or stolen.

One problem you may have is the middle may sag a bit making the ends too shallow. To fix this put a wooden beam across and under the middle and use an old car jack to push it back up again.

Top two - hide and reflection pool. Third down - solar water pump. Bottom - adapted golf trolley with five gallon water container.

I built my reflection pool using old scaffolding with the base being a set of 8 foot planks. I used 5cm high, long laths down all 4 sides with a pond liner inside to create the pool. The one I built was about 1 metre wide and 2.5 metres long though I have seen slightly shorter ones. I positioned mine for morning light with the sun behind me.

My pool was in a set of abandoned allotments in Sheffield next to an infrequently walked path. If any walkers glanced across they could see it. I ran it for 2 years with no problems but the whole lot was stolen in its third year when the allotment had got a bit overgrown.

Occasionally birds will foul the water so about once every other week simply tilt the pond up a bit and swill all the old water out and after a quick clean add fresh. Keeping the pond topped up needs serious thought. When the weather is warm you may have to top it up every other day with at least 5 gallons of water!

Some reflection pools are never totally successful. You will get a number of birds drinking from it and you may find the local squirrels also come for a sip. However, you may sit there for days with garden warblers, blackcaps and willow tits all singing around the pond yet in warm, dry weather they never visit. They must be getting a drink from somewhere further away than your pond. The problem may be they feel too exposed or the water is too warm.

In an attempt to solve this you can try using the pond more in winter and actually feed the birds on the far end where you want to photograph them. You can create sets of twigs with glued-on leaves or moss to run across the back end of the pond. The idea is the birds will perch on these when you want to photograph them. You can hide the food in small holes in the moss or leaves. It is also worth experimenting with sinking food such as sunflower hearts in the shallow end. This may work to some extent though you might be able to see the pale seed under the water. The main problem with feeding the birds, particularly bullfinches, is that they drop

Another problem you will certainly run into is keeping the water scrupulously clean. Any floating leaves, small twigs or dandelion fluff show up in the images really badly. To solve this keep a small pond net handy and every time you work at the pool sweep the surface clear.

seed bits onto the perch or into the water so you will be forever nipping out and cleaning up. Some birds like nuthatches, don't feed but simply collect the food and leave. Blue, great and cole tits tend to do this as well. However, you will notice that quite a few birds now drink from the pool.

A lot of people run reflection pools and one issue that is very noticeable is that many don't pay enough attention to the back of the pool where the birds perch. You can often see the pond liner in the images. It always pays to take that extra bit of attention to get the look just right.

Nuthatch at an infinity pool. The colour behind the bird is diffused woodland. 1Dmk4, 500mm, 1/2500, f5.6, ISO 500, tripod and hide. Sheffield.

The most successful pools are probably permanent ones that are deep at one end and sunk into the ground. They will keep naturally cool but your hide also needs to be sunk into the ground as well. This is a long-term project with higher costs but hopefully would produce good images over the years.

Photographing small birds in flight

Getting sharp, well-lit images of blue tits or nuthatches in flight is challenging at the best of times. It is very difficult to auto-focus and track them with servo because they are small and move quickly. It is though quite easy, if a bit fiddly, to get really great images of them using bird feeders.

A blue tit flying to the feeder. 1Dmk3, 300mm, 1/2000, f8, ISO 800, tripod and hide. Even at 1/2000 the wing tips are blurred. To freeze these you will need speeds around 1/3000. However, the blur in the wings does convey the sense of motion. Sheffield.

To start the project set up one feeder on the side of a bush or small tree on the edge of woodland in winter. Once it is running well with lots of birds visiting it you can start to think about photography. The use of a chair hide is ideal and you can put it up on the day - most small birds are not in the slightest bit bothered about a hide appearing. They can get tame so quickly that in some cases you can work without one. However, if you think the birds are a bit nervous leave the hide out for a few days first.

The next step is to move the feeder about 2 or 3 metres out from the edge of the wood using a pole to suspend it. It should now be out in the open with a good background and the sun in your chosen position (for either front or back lighting). To increase your success rate set up the feeder with only one hole (with seed that they can feed from) and one perch for the birds to land on. Simply block all the others up. You need to make sure that the tree or bush has one prominent branch that sticks out further than the rest. You should have had the feeder running on this branch to get the birds used to visiting it. You need this branch because you want the birds to fly to the feeder in its new position on the pole from this branch only.

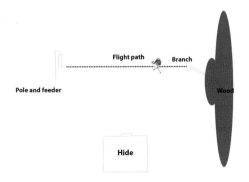

A plan to show the position of the hide, feeder and branch when working on small birds in flight.

Once the feeder is set up position the hide so it faces exactly the line from the branch to the perch on the feeder. (You want the back of your camera to be in this exact plane). You can set up a twig on the ground exactly below and in the middle of the flight path from the branch to the feeder. In your hide prefocus on this and switch the auto focus off. Next set a high speed - at least 1/2000 or even higher if the light is good. If you want to make sure it remains on this speed at your chosen f number (say f8) use auto ISO. Move the camera so it is looking at the middle of the flight path and tighten the tripod.

Every time a bird flies to the feeder use a cable release to fire the camera (which should be set to its highest frame rate). After a few goes review the images. You can now see where the birds are in the frame and if they are in focus. You will tend to find that different species fly using slightly different flight paths. Many dip down and fly up as they approach the feeder, some curve slightly forward or further away. Adjust your focus by looking at which part of the bird is sharp. If it's the near wing then focus a little further away and so on. You will also need to reposition where the camera is pointing once you can see where the flight path is.

A nuthatch in flight. 1Dmk3, 300mm, 1/2000, f8, ISO 800, tripod and hide. Sheffield.

It is much easier to work on one species at a time, say nuthatches, until you are confident of getting sharp images. Then use another session to work only on blue tits. A good choice of lens is either a 300 or 70-200. You can increase your hit rate if the bird is smaller in the frame, then crop back a bit. The most reliable place is just before they land on the feeder so you may have to clone out the feeder in quite a few images. If you have the background a nice neutral blur this only takes a minute or so later on the computer.

The mini-fan

Some birds are certainly more curious than others. It may be that they are exploring for potential food or seeing if another bird is around. A simple device that often works well is a small hand-held battery fan. You can buy a couple for a few pounds and adapt them by added a long wire (about 20 metres) with a switch so you can switch the fan on from your hide. However, you may find that it doesn't work because the batteries are not strong enough to send the current all the way to the fan. The solution is to remove them (usually 2 AA's) and make a simple holder and wire in 4 batteries.

Paint a white blob on the end of each of the blades (there are 2). Barn owls will fly over and hover above as will kestrels and skylarks. Most birds just hover over it and never land. Use servo (AFC) and a high frame rate. If you think you will need to exposure compensate because you may be shooting into the sky, experiment and get it right before you start.

The mini-fan with extension cable.
I have tried it on a few birds and I suspect it will work on other species as well. I set up a hide, put the fan out in grassland and run the wire back to my hide. Once the camera and lens is set up I wait until my intended bird is near and then give the fan a few bursts. I don't leave it on, just fire short bursts of a few seconds. It sometimes seems more effective if one of the blades catches a bit of grass so that it makes a noise.

Prefocusing at the correct distance you anticipate the bird to be will also allow the camera to lock on quicker and not go hunting. You may only get one chance so try not to waggle the lens all over the place. Once their curiosity is fired keep giving it the odd burst, don't leave it whirring away. Less is best. You will probably find that it often only works well once. If you want to try again you will need to work in a new area with different birds.

A skylark hovers above the mini-fan for a quick look. 7Dmk2, 500mm, 1/5000, f5.6, ISO 640, +2/3 exposure compensation, hide and tripod. Sheffield.

Working at high tide roosts

Spectacular images have been generated over the years at high tide roosts in winter. Snettisham, before the storms and in certain years, has produced stunning photos. The best were created from the low level photographer's hide. Unfortunately this is no longer available due to some photographers abusing the trust of the RSPB and demonstrating poor field skills. There are not that many areas now where you can run a good high tide roost project but as we explore more of our coastline new sites will be found.

The trick is to spend a lot of time watching and making sure you have good access to accurate tide timetables. Once you are sure you know exactly where the birds roost at high tide, and how far the tide will come in, then construct a permanent hide in summer, or if you use a canvas one have it up for a week or so. A dexion frame which can be used to anchor it down and hold the hide above water level will help.

The hide will almost certainly get wet and depending on where you site it possibly get washed by high tides so make sure it's really secure. Shorelines are often flat and very windy so make sure it is staked down well. The key is to know where the birds will roost at the highest part of the tide and then you select those tides (say spring ones) that work well for your hide.

Remember that the height of the tide changes every day with a couple of very high tides each month. This means you must use tide timetables and site your hide according to the height of the tide on the days you want to work . If you don't you may find the tide races past your hide and half submerges it or the sea stops a long way before it reaches you.

You should be in the hide at least two hours before the highest part of the tide. Only leave after it has turned and every bird has

Knot at a high tide roost on the Wash. 1Dmk3, 500mm, 1/1000, f8, ISO 400, tripod, low level hide. Norfolk.

flown away. It is essential that you are safe and comfortable because you will be there for at least 6 hours. If you miscalculate and the tide is far higher than you imagined then you must abandon the hide. Don't sit it out and panic!

It's a good idea to have the hide near the top of the shore and not out on a mud flat. Any miscalculation here can spell a real life - threatening disaster. As with any potential danger make sure you have your mobile charged and you can get a signal. Also ensure someone knows where you are and what you're doing.

Bird flocks

In winter starlings gather at a select few places around the UK. Some are well known and easy to find. Others are slightly more ephemeral and are only good in the odd year. You don't really need any field skills here apart from common sense. Arrive an hour or so before dusk and set up with a mid-sized zoom lens such as a 70-200 or 28-135mm.

These are ideal because you have the option to go tighter with your framing or pull back if the flock comes closer or opens up.

The last time I photographed a starling murmuration (the correct term for the winter roosts) I visited the site over 30 times and worked at creating slower shutter speed images at about 1/10 to 1/30 second. The spectacle is only really good when the whole flock is present in the air together and they form tight and amazing patterns. More modern SLRs with their higher ISO ranges are certainly an advantage when the light is poor.

As a rule the tight patterns occur if a bird of prey like a peregrine visits the site. They tend to ignore sparrowhawks and buzzards. If no bird of prey disrupts the birds the flock goes to roost in dribs and drabs so repeated visits are definitely the way to go.

Very few people watch the following morning when the huge flock leaves. They don't create the patterns of the previous evening but do allow a different image to be produced. Arrive an hour before first light and have your camera and lens set up on a tripod. When they go they won't give you very long to experiment so be prepared.

Starlings flocking above Gretna Green train station. 1Dmk4, 70-200, 1/320, f3.2, ISO 2500, handheld. Scotland.

Barnacle geese at Caerlavarock. 1Dmk3, 500mm, 1/2500, f5.6, ISO 400, tripod and public hide. Scotland.

Similarly, geese leave their winter roosts out on the mud flats just before dawn. A few mornings spent watching should give you an idea where they fly to and where from. You can then plan which type of images you want and choose mornings where the sun will rise as a burning orange ball for those dramatic silhouettes. If you want good silhouettes and intense colours under-expose by a stop or two and set your white balance to 7000 or even higher.

Wide angle work

Images of wildlife taken with a wide angle lens offer something a little unusual and require a different set of skills to produce. When nest photography was popular many photographers built a number of sound-proof boxes to house their SLR and lens. These were wooden boxes lined with polystyrene and cork with a double-glazed, picture glass front. Originally the camera was triggered with a very long (50m) cable which worked well but was a bit cumbersome. Today infra red remote/wireless triggers are far easier and more flexible to use. These can be fairly cheap to buy if you shop around.

A dummy box (same size and colour with glass front) is used to move into position over a week, exactly like you would a hide. Unlike a hide however this has to be really close to the bird. A small spirit level on top is useful to make sure the horizons are level. When you are ready and feel the bird is relaxed you switch the dummy box for the real one and fire the camera from a hide 50m away. You have to obey all the rules of normal hide work when taking the first shot because whilst the box is small it is very close to the bird. It certainly helps to do a trial run with a model bird the same size as the one you are working with. This allows you to set the correct depth of field and choice of zoom on the lens to create the image you want.

A sound-proof box built to house a SLR camera and wide angle lens.

Little-ringed plover incubating in an old quarry floor. EOS 5 in sound proof box, 24mm, 1/60, f16, ISO 100 (Sensia slide film), remote trigger from a hide 100m away, licence. Derbyshire.

I remember one situation many years ago when a kestrel nested on a ledge of an old quarry. I thought that a wide angle image might work well so I bought a Ricoh compact (film) camera with a 28mm lens and had it adapted to take a cable release. Again I made a dummy box and placed this on a branch that I actually glued to the cliff face just above the ledge. It did work well. The main thing was the Ricoh was very quiet. I also used this camera and lens on a mini floating hide that I introduced over a couple of days to a little grebe's nest. This image was taken over 20 years ago and today a kestrel still uses the same ledge in most years. Ricoh G compact camera with 28mm lens, adapted to run a cable release. 1/125, f16, ISO 100 (Sensia slide film), hide at 100m.

Today there are a number of good compacts that shoot in RAW and can be used with remote triggers. I have used my Canon G11 a number of times for this type of work. It does not need a silent box (no film winder or mirror, so it's really quiet) and it focuses down to almost 1cm so I can get it really close.

It is possible to experiment such as putting it out on a small stick (p125) in a field where waders or geese roost. You never know what you will get but occasionally you get some really unusual images. Another idea to try is to have its back flat on the ground, lens facing upwards and get a group of ducks to feed around it. Unfortunately, they may walk all over it though it shouldn't suffer too much. An improvement is to dig a small hole and use a bit of glass over this to get that really weird angle of a duck's world from below.

The potential for wide angle images is vast. If you see a favourite spot that a dipper or heron uses a small compact on a stick will go unnoticed and if fired from a distance, because it's silent, almost certainly won't disturb the bird. Always use a small hot shoe mounted spirit level to get the horizon level and fire a few test shots to check for dof, speed and if you need any exposure compensation. If you are worried about splashes or rain fix a plastic bag around it and cut a hole for the lens. One thing you will have to do is turn the save energy mode off so it does not go to sleep. Check if this is possible and if you can fire it remotely before you buy one.

A set of 'sticks' to hold the camera can be made from old plastic tent pegs. Drill down the top and thread a short length of 1/4-20 or 3/8-16 bolt thread into the hole (The same thread size that the camera screws onto a tripod - check which size you have.) You can now screw a mini ball + socket to this to hold the camera. The peg is light, easy to push into the ground and very versatile.

Tent peg with 3/8 thread and ball + socket.

If you are thinking about doing wide angle work in a river then use an old sturdy tripod to hold the camera. The bird will simply think it's a set of twigs.

Working at the nest with a hide

For anyone contemplating hide work at the nest in the UK a review of the Wildlife and Countryside Act, the licence system and the RPS's Wildlife Photographer's Code of Conduct is a good starting point (p 215).

It is often said that we can learn nothing new about nesting birds and that all the images we could ever want of a bird incubating its eggs or feeding its chicks has been taken. It is certainly true that working with birds at the nest has fallen out of favour and has become a bit non pc. However, there is still lots to learn about nesting birds and bird photographers who keep accurate notes have a vital part to play. It is also probably true that as new camera specifications increase the demand for nesting bird images will rise in the future as the 'old stock' starts to look jaded and dated.

I remember a gamekeeper who was helping me work at a merlin's nest on the moors. He was sceptical about what the merlins were feeding their chicks on, even after I had shown him my notes. I encouraged him to spend a day in the hide and he saw first hand that all the food taken that day were meadow pipits. I didn't see the merlins ever bring a grouse chick back. To this day that gamekeeper is now a strong supporter of breeding merlins.

If you do this type of work please make sure you join the nest record scheme run by the British Trust for Ornithology (BTO). It is one of the longest running and possibly the most important wildlife/environmental survey not only in the UK but globally.

Woodlark, 20D, 500mm, 1/160, f8, ISO 200, hide, tripod, licence. Nottinghamshire.

Before you decide to work at the nest you must be sure you can get help from another experienced photographer. Most nest work requires two people for the majority of the time so it's not something you should really take on as an individual.

The first step is to decide on what species you want to work with and then check if it is on Schedule 1 (p220) which would mean you require a licence. Initially you should only work with common species. Rare ones are under enough threat as it is without photographers adding unnecessary pressure.

Research should provide you with the likely dates that your chosen species breeds and how and where to look for its nest. It is beyond the scope of this book to provide such information, it is vast. Unfortunately no new books or websites can adequately provide it. There are a couple of books, now long out of print that are excellent sources of this information (See appendix p224).

Once the nest is found where it is will give you a clue as to what type of hide to use. If it's high up in a tree then scaffolding will be necessary. If it's in a bush then some form of short scaffolding or a Dexion tower may be sufficient. In an extreme situation you may even resort to using a cherry picker to erect a hide near to a tree nest.

One major consideration is to decide when you start hide work. There is no simple answer. For some species, like waders, you will have to photograph them when they are incubating because the chicks walk away from the nest hours after hatching.

For birds that have chicks that stay in the nest then the ideal time is to start just before the eggs hatch. If you know when they were laid then it is easy to calculate when they will hatch but if they were being incubated when you found the nest then it's harder to do so. In this case you should err on the side of caution and start your work when the eggs are starring (or on the hatch). For waders the ideal time is to start about halfway through incubation.

The first position of the hide should be at some distance from the nest if that is practical, such as with a ground nesting bird. Obviously if it's up a tree you put the scaffolding and hide up in stages starting with the bottom layer. You should time yourself with each visit and keep the time to

Twite chicks in the nest. These are only a day or two away from leaving it. It is now far too late to start any hide work as the chicks may explode from the nest and scatter before they are ready to leave naturally. Only start your hide work when the chicks are very young. Yorkshire.

a minimum, say 15 or 30 minutes depending on the species and size of eggs. Never do any work in rainy weather as the chance of the eggs cooling is too great. Similarly don't do any work in the evening before the birds go to roost because they may struggle to return before dark. If the situation allows it you could place a wool hat over the nest and eggs to keep them warm when you're moving a hide closer.

A hide set up on a reed bunting's nest. The nest is in one of the sedge clumps. I didn't actually photograph the bird at the nest but on its way back to it when it was returning with food. Nottinghamshire.

Once the hide has been put up at half height you must retire to watch the bird's reaction. (You must do this every time you move the hide). Hopefully it will go straight back to the nest, though be aware that some species naturally take their time, such as many of the waders. Leave the hide for at least one day before you make the next move towards the nest, again the hide should be at half height. Observe and act accordingly. Over the next few days move the hide closer and eventually up to its full height. A good idea is to keep an old bottle pointing out of the lens hole to get the birds used to seeing a 'lens'. The major consideration is the welfare of the birds. If they look slightly nervous and keep trying to return but keep veering away from the nest then take the hide down and stop immediately. There will be other situations to try on other days.

I started the hide on this ringed plover's nest on May 30th. The eggs were in the second week of incubation. They take 24/25 days to hatch. The hide was started 50 metres from the nest at half height and I spent 15 minutes putting it up. I retreated to some cover and watched the bird go back to the nest. It took 10 minutes to return, running its characteristic zigzag way back.

I had watched the birds at the nest previously and noticed they generally took 10 to 15 mins when they were disturbed. The next day I moved the hide up 10 metres, again at half height. The bird returned in roughly the same amount of time.

The next day another 10 metres so I was now 20 metres from the nest with the hide at half height. The following day it went to full height. Every time I watched the bird back to its nest. I left the hide for another day then was walked into it with my gear by a friend. When I had set up the camera and tripod (which took 15 minutes) and I was sure I was ready he walked away.

The idea is that the birds think the hide is empty. I sat and waited. The bird returned in 20 mins. I took my first shot after an hour. This was before I had silent drive so I had wrapped a jumper around the camera to help reduce the noise. The bird looked up but didn't leave the nest. I waited another 30 minutes and took a second shot.

By day three of photography the birds didn't take any notice of any camera noise at all. When the agreed time was up my friend walked in to relieve me. I took the hide down after the chicks had hatched and left.

In situations where we needed to keep in contact we used a walkie-talkie or we would text. I could then ask him to relieve me earlier or later depending on the bird's behaviour and how my photography was progressing.
1Dmk2, 500mm, 1/250, f4, ISO 500. Sheffield.

The possible scenarios are numerous. Many birds such as willow warblers are very tolerant of hides at the nest and react without blinking an eye. Others can be very nervous and never really settle down. Meadow and tree pipits can be very tricky and you should always take twice as long as normal. Individuals within a species can react very differently. I remember working with a lapwing one year that was its normal nervous self and I took 2 weeks to move the hide up. The following year I worked with another lapwing that never blinked an eye at the hide.

Male reed bunting returning to its nest with food. EOS3, 500mm, 1/250, f4, ISO 100 (slide film).

Watching, usually from a concealed place at a distance with binoculars, is vital to read how the birds react. Always remember that many birds nest as a pair and share feeding and incubation so you have to be aware that you include both sexes when moving a hide to the nest. In some cases it's virtually impossible to tell the sexes apart so you may have to wait for a nest changeover when the birds swap at the nest to check reactions. Some birds, such as woodcock, where only the female incubates can be tricky as she will try and sit it out as you work the hide in so you have to really take your time. She leaves the nest every 3 hours or so for a feed and you may have to wait until she does this to check she returns and accepts the hide.

A hide set up in its final position at a stone cur-lew's nest in Norfolk.
During 15 years of active nest work I have only had the odd nest predated and never one deserted (well below the statistical average of natural nest failures). In many cases I believe the hide actually increased the chances of the nest being successful. I have even been asked a couple of times by wildlife organisations to work at a specific nest because they were worried it may be targeted by certain individuals and the presence of myself and the hide would act as an effective deterrent.

With birds that you feel may be frightened by the camera going off for the first time use a tape recorder with a timer. Record your camera's shutter noise on a tape and leave the tape recorder/player in the hide playing the sound of the camera intermittently during the daylight hours. As the hide gets closer the bird starts to hear the camera and gets used to it before the hide is at a working distance.

One dilemma that often arises when working with nests is dense foliage, such as a snipe's nest in a tuft of grass or a yellowhammer's in a thick hedge. You will have to decide if it is possible to open up the vegetation blocking your view of the nest to see it through the camera. Clearly this will also allow any predators to see it as well.

Garden warbler's nest in dense foliage. Opening this nest up so I could photograph would have been very irresponsible so I chose to photograph the birds on the way back to their nest when they perched on plant stems. However, they did this so infrequently that I only got one decent image in 3 days of photography. The vast majority of the time they approached the nest hidden in the dense foliage. Sheffield.

The rule is that you cut nothing away - you bend grass over using tent pegs and any branches are gently bent back with string or clips. As soon as you finish your session you return the vegetation back to its original position. If you ever feel that the amount of vegetation you have to move is too excessive then leave that nest and look for another. Remember the welfare of the bird is more important than your images.

One criticism that is occasionally raised is that hides attract predators to birds' nests with the subsequent loss of the eggs or chicks. Many photographers' experience is actually the complete reverse. They find that any crows, magpies or foxes keep well away from the vicinity of the hide. They view it with the upmost suspicion.

Another couple of issues need consideration. You must have the landowner's permission, even if you are working under licence. The second is the

Stone curlews at their nest during the change-over when one incubating bird relieves the other. I took this image some years ago from the hide on p128. If I had the opportunity to do this again I would try to use a much lower hide to get a lower POV of the birds. Stone curlews are on Schedule 1 so I had a licence to work at this nest. 1Dmk 2, 300mm, 1/500, f8, ISO 500. Norfolk.

visibility of the hide to other humans. You do not want to attract anyone to its vicinity. Even the mildly curious who do not understand its context may inadvertently step on the eggs.

If you have any doubts about your ability to disguise your hide do not work that nest. If you think there is a small chance of people walking by then use scrim and cut vegetation to completely disguise the hide. I did this once when I was working with a pair of merlins in the Peak District (p21). The hide was in the middle of a very isolated moor with no footpaths anywhere near it. None the less I used scrim and heather.

One afternoon I was in the hide with the female merlin near the nest having a break. I noticed in the distance a white 'blob.' A quick peak through the lens showed it to be a naked bloke with leather cowboy hat, walking boots and rucksack! He was walking directly towards the hide. I was unsure what to do. Would he notice the hide or even

attempt a conversation? As he got closer I kept quiet. I could see that he wouldn't walk over the nest so there was no risk to the chicks.

The female merlin screamed a bit and he glanced at it but carried on walking straight towards me. In the end he passed by the hide 5 metres away and walked on. He didn't even glance at it. To this day I am not sure what I would have done if he had stopped for a chat - or even if he had actually seen the hide at all!

If all goes well the birds accept the hide and react completely naturally. That same female merlin used to perch on my hide every day after she fed her chicks and every time she returned to the nest. Her claws actually pierced the canvas and I could see them poking through only inches above my head - an amazing experience!

Opportunities will arise when you may be working at a nest without a hide. Generally this is when a bird nests in a public place and is habituated to humans. The most common examples are water birds such as coots and swans that nest a short distance away from a well walked path. Generally you shouldn't cause a problem but field skills should still be employed.

Using recorded bird song

This is one of the more contentious areas of bird photography. When I wrote this book I considered whether I should include it at all. In the end I decided I would discuss it because it is still carried out by some photographers and bird watchers.

If anyone ever goes on a bird watcher's trip abroad you will come across it. (Quite extensively in some countries). Some birdwatchers in the UK use their mobile phones and play a call when they see a bird they want a better view of. So it is something that does happen even if now some feel it is out-dated and inappropriate.

A corncrake calling in N Uist. Corncrakes will respond to a fingernail drawn over a comb that mimics their harsh 'crex crex' call. There is a very fine line between 'fooling' a bird or using good field skills to get closer to it and attracting it to your camera. Ultimately the emphasis is on what you personally feel comfortable with and is within the letter of the law and the RPS's code of ethics (p215). 1Dmk3, 500mm + 1.4, 1/1000, f5.6, ISO 400, beanbag on car window.

The main criticism is that when it's done too extensively it may cause the bird distress. The problem is that it is often carried out in the breeding season when the male birds have established their territories. So when they hear another male singing they investigate and want to drive it out. If the tape is too loud and played for too long because they can't find the bird they may become distressed.

Many country people had great skills in calling up birds. It is fairly easy to use a comb to attract a corncrake into a better photographic position and some people can entice tawny owls by imitating their call by blowing into their hands. I have tried to summon male cuckoos by imitating their call but I am nothing like as effective as a tape. (Many images of cuckoos are produced by playing either the male or female's call when they first arrive back in May).

Pishing is a bird watcher's trick. The idea is to make a sound very like 'pishing' or 'pish pish'. The hope is that any small birds lurking in scrub will move up and towards the edge so you get a better view. Why they do this is a mystery but since so many birdwatchers do it, it obviously has some levels of success.

A recent article in Wild Planet Photo Magazine (June 2015) discussed using tapes and reached no firm conclusion as to whether it caused a problem or not. The author suggests not playing it for more than a minute and never on reserves or in public places. When I discuss bird photography techniques I find some people I speak to think using tapes a step too far. It may cause distress and since the aim of this book is not to do so my advice is that you don't consider using tapes.

Decoy birds

The shooting fraternity has been using decoys for centuries. Gun shops often sell plastic crows, wood pigeons, owls and ducks. The basic idea is to put a decoy out and a wild bird will fly down to inspect it. It does work occasionally but it is very hit and miss. It also has a similar criticism to using bird calls, it is fooling the bird. I have used dummy birds that I made from papier mache and painted to resemble life-like birds.

Many photographers believe that the birds come to no harm. Usually they pop down, have a look, realise that it is not real and leave. In those few moments you hope to get your image. Different birds around the country respond in different ways so it may work well in one area and not another.

Some birds are certainly more willing to investigate. Others never give them a glance. It's really trial and error. Many don't believe that the use of a decoy bird is as potentially harmful as the use of tape but it is up to you to only work with what you are comfortable with.

A few random notes

Barn owls

Barn owls hunt primarily at both ends of the day. In summer when they have chicks in June to September (if there is a second or late brood) they can be out a little earlier than usual and your chance of flight shots increases. Most owls struggle to hunt well when it's windy and/or raining and they may not even hunt at all. The day after bad weather often sees the owls out much earlier than usual and they may hunt almost to mid morning. The same applies in cold weather in winter when the days are short.

Nightjars

Nightjars are one of the most enigmatic of our summer migrants. Even if I don't spend time photographing them I love to spend a summer evening just sitting and listening to the fern owl churring away. Most images over the years have been taken at the nest but it is possible to work with them away from it as well. The male nightjar has white flashes on his wings. It's the easiest way to tell the pair apart in the dim evening light when they fly. He is curious so a white hanky waved a few times often raises his interest.

If you stand still, or better sit, and do this a few times just after he appears in the evening (when it starts to get dim, usually around 10.15 in late June or early July) he will often fly quite close to you for a quick look. To photograph him you can use a flash on your camera and a torch held onto the lens with a thick rubber band and hope it locks on as he hovers in front of you. You will only get one shot but it is possible. The best lens is probably a 70-200 2.8 because he will be close and you will need a fast lens in the low light levels.

Rivers with weirs

Male goosander fishing at the base of a weir. 1Dmk3, 500mm, 1/200, f4, ISO 1000 (it was a dull day). Scotland.

Many rivers have large weirs and sometimes fish gather around the base as they are washed over or are trying to get back up river. In one or two places goosanders work hard in the turbulent waters to catch fish. A hide placed alongside the weir allows for some really dramatic images. If you try this make sure you get the exposure compensation adjusted correctly and use servo (or AFC) with only the centre focus sensor on. It's difficult but with a good speed certainly possible.

Landfill tips

Never ignore what is all around you or might at first glance seem ugly. Gulls that feed on landfill tips make great subjects. The main problem you will come across is the onerous mantle of Health and Safety. I eventually managed to get permission on my local landfill but it took ages and I had to ac-

Gulls on a landfill tip in Sheffield. 1Dmk4, 500mm, 1/800, f16, ISO 400, tripod.

tually go on a training course, sign all sorts of forms, wear a high vis vest and so on. We all understand why it has to be done but it takes a fair bit of perseverance to simply be able to stand near a tip to photograph some gulls. However, if you do make the effort, the photography can be superb!

Building your own nest box

Many small birds will take readily to a nest box. Unfortunately many that are put up are not ideal for photography. Some birds, like pied flycatchers and redstarts, will often perch on a convenient branch on the way into the box. By making your own and siting it with the branch already in position you can increase the chances of the birds using it regularly. The best way is to put a selection of boxes out, each at a height that is ideal and where the light falls nicely onto the branch/perch.

The cost can be kept to a minimum if you make the boxes yourself (p222). Old skirting boards are ideal. It only takes minutes to saw them up and nail together. Make sure the lid has a hinge so you can clean it out each year. The lid should slope gently forward to stop rain pooling up and a bit of old inner tube nailed across the join helps to keep it watertight. The size of the entry hole is critical for each species and you can buy circular drill bits of each size. Leave the back board longer than the box so you can nail it to the tree and don't site the box in full sun or in windy situations.

Entry hole sizes: 25mm - blue tits, 28mm - great tits, pied flycatchers and redstarts, 38mm - tree sparrows, 45mm - starlings.

Male pied flycatcher at one of my home made skirting board nest boxes. 1Dmk2, 500mm, 1/200, f5.6, ISO 400, fill-in flash, hide. Derbyshire.

Birds at the Lek

Some grouse species display by gathering at a lek. This is a place where a number of male birds gather (usually at dawn in the spring) and display to each other. In Britain we have two species that do this, black grouse and capercaillie. Many photographers in the past (including myself) have worked from hides at capercaillie leks in Britain. However, nowadays this is not possible. Capers are rare birds and are now protected under the law so can't be photographed at the lek without a licence in the UK.

Black grouse, whilst not as rare, have declined alarmingly in the past few decades and people are urged not to disturb them at the lek. They can seem robust at the lek but repeated disturbance can see them abandon old leks or leave before first light. There are excellent opportunities abroad to work with both these species where they are far more common.

Toads in their breeding pond. Split level, neutral density filter, underwater bag, 5Dmk3, 16-35mm, 1/250, f20, ISO 2000, -1/3 exposure compensation. Derbyshire.

Reptiles, amphibians and fish

We are not overly blessed with a wide range of reptiles and amphibians (herptiles) in the UK. Ireland has even less. The main reason for this was the separation of Britain and Ireland from mainland Europe as sea levels rose hundreds of thousands of years ago. Basically, not many herptiles made it here fast enough. Our other problem is that we are too far north and we are not really warm enough for these cold blooded animals to thrive here in numbers.

As native species we have three snakes (adder, grass and smooth) and three lizards (the common or viviparous, sand and the slow worm). Amphibians are represented by one frog (common), two toads (common and natterjack) and three newts (common or smooth, great-crested and palmate).

Keeping herptiles as pets has been popular for decades now and over the last 80 years a number have escaped or been deliberately released so our native herptiles now have a number of European and N. American cousins to compete with.

European non-native species now residing wild in the UK include aesculapian snake, common wall lizard, Italian wall lizard, green lizard, alpine newt, Italian crested newt, European tree frog, edible frog, marsh frog, pool frog, midwife toad and yellow-bellied toad. From North America we have red-eared terrapins and American bullfrogs.

The pool frog is an interesting species in that there is now evidence that it is in fact a native species occurring in Norfolk. There is also some evidence that clawed toads from South America are living wild in the UK.

Most of the non-indigenous species pose no threat to our natives and many feel add greatly to our island's indigenous herptiles. Most have a distinct southern bias due to the warmer summers and milder winters. Every now and then we get the occasional

hard winter and this can check or even eliminate some populations. Only a couple of our newbie's pose a threat - Italian crested newts (because they may interbreed with our great-crested ones), red-eared terrapins (because they can be a problem for small, young water birds) and bullfrogs (because of their size and competitiveness).

Of our native species, four are protected under Schedule 5 so if you want to work with them you will need a licence. They are great-crested newt, natterjack toad, sand lizard and smooth snake. It is not illegal to photograph them in the wild as long as you don't touch, pick up, move or interfere with them in any way. Personally I would not try to photograph them without a licence because you have to be so close that it is debatable whether you are interfering with them. Three of these are protected because they are rare and restricted to a few sites dotted across the UK. Great-crested newts however are common but protected because Britain has a significant proportion of Europe's total.

Common toad photographed in my garden.
1Dmk3, 180 macro, 1/250, f8, ISO 200, beanbag. Sheffield.

Frogs and toads

Both common frogs and common toads are abundant across the whole of mainland Britain. Many of us are familiar with frogs and their spawn in garden ponds in spring and they are one of the most accessible and photogenic species to work with. Toads are equally common but have a distinctly more rural life and are far more choosy and traditional in their choice of breeding ponds.

Natterjack toads are on Schedule 5 of the Wildlife and Countryside act so a licence is needed to photograph them. 1Dmk4, 180 macro, 1/1250, f7.1, ISO 400, beanbag. Lincolnshire.

Finding either is not hard during the spring. Later, when they leave the ponds they are more difficult. If you want to locate a frog or toad to work with later in the year choose warm, wet evenings, especially after it has rained during the day. Use a torch and search likely areas - garden lawns and flower beds, old, un-mown, grassy fields and woodland.

Both species are abundant and ubiquitous so you can expect to come across them by chance almost anywhere. Frogs will spend time back in their ponds during drier weather. Both species fall victim to our road drainage systems unfortunately. A few years ago a set of new roads was constructed in a country park. The drains were literally full of toads, a few frogs and wood mice. The latter drowned quickly but the toads and frogs were rescued every few days. It does make you wonder just how many frogs and toads must die annually in Britain this way.

When you choose to work with either species you will have to decide if it's in the pond during the breeding season or on dry land later in the year. One thing you should be very careful about is handling them because their skin is sensitive and absorbent, unlike reptiles. The best advice is to rinse your hands in some rain butt water or water from a pond or stream to get rid of any chemicals such as soap.

Frogs are frisky and slippery so it's easy to damage them. Be careful and handle them as infrequently as possible. If you are going to contain one for a short while be aware that frogs jump a lot and can damage themselves so use something like a plastic dustbin with moss in the bottom. Toads are easier to handle – they are drier and tend not to jump as much. They are much more docile so a small tank with damp moss to hide under is great for an hour or two.

There are a number of approaches to working with both species in their breeding ponds. You can work from the bank photographing them as they sit with their noses out of the water, work with them underwater or catch them and photograph them in a tank. Obviously the last option is the most invasive and needs the most care from the animal's point of view.

Working with them at the surface is the easiest approach. When you walk up to the pond the chances are they will all dive for cover at the bottom. You should now lie down using an old sleeping mat to keep dry and protect your clothes (or wear ones you don't mind getting muddy). If you do lie down make sure you don't flatten bank-side plant life. Use a beanbag for your camera and choose a medium range lens like a 180 macro or 200/300 with extension tubes. Be sure the sun is where you want it and before you start check the water colour (which is whatever is reflected in it). Sometimes by moving you can change the surface colour.

Common frogs in a pond in spring. 5Dmk3, 180 macro, 1/500, f7.1, ISO 800, +1/3 exposure compensation, beanbag on pond side. Sheffield.

Other things to look for are reflections in the water and hot spots from shiny objects like leaves. Once you're down and comfy take one image and check your exposure, adjust your ISO if you need to and set any exposure compensation. You can also check the image for any obvious distractions you didn't spot initially. Now simply lie and wait for the frogs to pop up again. It shouldn't take more than five or ten minutes.

If you move the camera do it gently and slowly. The same goes for moving your hands (gloves may help to make them a little less noticeable). You should now be able to experience a few delightful hours photographing the frogs as they move around showing their heads. Look for interesting compositions with two or more frogs, or out of focus ones in the background.

Once you have a nice set of well lit portraits you can switch to a wide angle lens and try for 'animal in the landscape' style images. The issue here is that the front of the lens will have to be close to the frog. Make sure you move the camera slowly over the water surface towards the frog. Choose auto-focus because you will probably be unable to see through the viewfinder. Try to keep it level (harder than you think) and take shots as the camera gets closer to the frog. Silent drive helps. It takes a bit of practice but it does produce lovely images with a bit more of a story. You can take this further by trying it in the evening if the house lights are on and a dab of fill-in flash to create more moody, nocturnal images. The scope is very wide and is only limited by your imagination.

Split level images with an underwater camera bag

I must admit I love this type of image, part of its attraction being that it is not widely carried out so the images still have a degree of originality.

The first consideration is to buy a bag that suits your pocket and your camera and lens combination. There are a number on the market that run from approx £20 to over £300. If you want to take underwater photography further you may decide to look at camera housings. These are very expensive (£1000+) and generally made for a specific body and lens combo. When you buy the bag choose one that will take your preferred body and lens such as a DSLR and 16-35 zoom.

For split level images you will need to buy a split level neutral density filter to balance the big difference between light levels above and below the water. This simply screws onto the front of the lens. You then screw the lens holder for the bag to this. This holds the lens secure behind the glass port the camera looks through. The lens is obviously not actually touching this. It's a

Common frog in a garden pond photographed using an underwater bag. Keeping the horizons level is very difficult. A small spirit level on the hot shoe really helps. 5Dmk3, 16-35, 1/500, f8, ISO 2000, -1/3 exposure compensation. Sheffield.

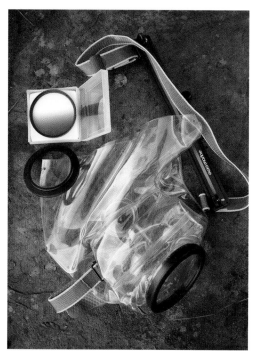

I chose the EWA marine range for my underwater bag. It has proved very reliable. One issue that I have struggled with is firing the camera when I have manouvered it close to a frog or toad. I leave the top undone and run a cable release from the camera. I use this to fire the camera but it is a bit risky because if I don't pay attention water may flood into the bag, which has happened once. The top of the bag fastens with a long bar. The image on the left also shows the split level neutral density filter which is needed to balance the dark underwater part of the image with the brighter sky above.

bit further behind the port so you tend to get a circular image like a fish-eye within the normal rectangular format. You simply crop on the computer within the circle to get the more normal format when you process the images. The more zoom you use the less circular effect.

Using the bag is tricky and will need a bit of practice. There are a couple of issues that need concentration. The first is that it is amazingly easy to tilt the bag, even when you are convinced it's perfectly horizontal. Many of your images will have a tilt, some at such a degree you won't believe you didn't notice it when taking the pictures. The solution is to use a small hot-shoe mounted spirit level. This helps greatly. The second issue is the depth you submerge the front glass. For split shots one half is in the air, the bottom below water. Unfortunately if you sink it a little too much then raise it again the water leaves a wet smear on the glass which creates an area of blur. You will probably find that you need a kitchen roll with you and will be forever wiping the glass dry. One trick is to clean the front glass with some water with vinegar in it which does reduce the smearing somewhat. Obviously don't let vinegar get into the pond!

Underwater bag with 5D camera. Note the red tape to stop the lens focus and zoom rings turning when the camera is put in the bag. A cable release is attached to the camera to make it easier to take the shots.

The next area to work on is the distance to your subject and focussing. Auto-focus is incredibly unreliable underwater. A better method is to decide what size you want the frog or toad in the frame and what distance at 16mm (or your preferred lens size) it would be by experimenting with the camera out of the bag.

To do this choose an object the size of a frog, focus on it to get roughly the size you want then switch the auto-focus off. It's worth remembering that the size won't be exactly the same when the camera is in the bag because the lens is a little way behind the glass, but it's close enough. Then, using a stick, place one end next to the front of the camera and by looking through the camera

fix a bit of tape onto the stick at exactly the spot it's focused on.

You now have a guide you can use to judge the distance to any frog or toad when you're operating the camera. You simply hold the stick with the red tape to the front of the camera bag and now know what distance you need to move the bag up to so you can hopefully get reliably sharp images. Set the camera to f16 to get a good depth of field. This also helps with the part of the image above water.

Tape the focus ring with electrician's tape on the lens once you have set its focus distance and switched off the auto-focus. This stops you accidentally moving the focus when you put the camera into the bag, which is easily done. Next, take a test shot with the bag in the water at the correct depth and look at the speed it gives at f16 on AV. Then adjust the ISO to get a reasonable speed, somewhere around a 1/60 or higher.

You are now set to have a go. Simply lie as described before on the side of the pond and, holding the bag and cable release (which you can tape to the top of the bag), sink it to the correct depth with approximately half the glass above the water. Keep glancing at the spirit level and checking with the stick so you know the rough distance you have to be from the frog or toad.

When they are above water and relaxed slowly move the bag towards them and take shots as you get closer and keep taking them for as long as possible. Then slowly move the bag back and take the bag out to have a check for exposure, focus etc before you repeat the process. It does take a while but you should find that if you approach the frogs and toads with the bag slowly they are not the slightest bit bothered by it or the camera's shutter noise. Their minds are on other things!!

The choice of pond you will be working at is critical. The water should be as clear as possible. There is nothing you can do about this but if it's too murky look for another pond. Many small garden ponds with frogs have clear looking water but you will be surprised how murky it looks in the images.

You may also find that sunlight makes a huge difference. It should help to pick the toads out below water - in dull light they can be virtually impossible to see in the images. The other consideration is the view above the water. Flat open skies can be boring so look for buildings for urban images or trees in rural ones.

Toads in amplexus in their breeding pond in spring. 5Dmk3, 16-35, 1/320, f16, ISO 1600, underwater bag, +2/3 exposure compensation. Derbyshire.

Once you have mastered the use of an underwater bag you may want to explore further. Wide angle images of frogs and toads taken from below water looking up at the sky can be very impressive. One way is to sink the bag and camera completely and place it lens up facing the surface of the pond. You will have to anchor it down and getting it level is difficult. The problem here is how to fire the camera when a frog or toad swims across. One of the newer, infrared remotes that are available from a number of companies such as Hahnel (roughly £20) do work when the camera is underwater.

Many modern cameras now have Wi-Fi capability and this can be an excellent way to fire the camera using your mobile phone. You can also review the image and in some cases make adjustments (such as exposure) without having to move the camera.

Again, water clarity is an issue. One approach you could try is to buy a plastic garden pond (about £60) and build a wooden frame to hold it up. Fill it with clean rainwater from your garden water butts. If you don't have any it's always worth setting up a couple - the ready availability of clean, natural water is really handy. A few bits of washed weed add a realistic feel. You then place the camera on the bottom of the pond and anchor it down. You could build a small frame to hold it level as well. Then it's a simple matter of placing a frog or toad in and waiting until it swims around. Remember to replace the frog or toad where you found it and don't use any during the main breeding season.

Photographing underwater animals using small tanks

When I started photography I used a number of small tanks to get images of frogs, newts and pond invertebrates. I originally started by using bought fish tanks but found that they didn't deliver what I was after in terms of image quality. I then explored designing and building my own tanks and eventually settled on a number of different options.

I keep the tanks small and always use the best picture glass (2mm) for the piece that I will take the images through (usually the front). The rest is built with thicker window glass (3 or 4mm).

For tanks where you intend to shoot through the front a good design has the back longer than the front so that the back two corners are less likely to show up in your image as straight lines.

The size you build will depend on what it is you hope to photograph. Some can be built up to 45 cm long (for small fish) but smaller ones for invertebrates/tadpoles etc can be roughly 20cm to 30cm long on the front with the back at 30cm for a 20cm front (see plan).

A mini tank used to photograph small animals such as newt larvae. The tape is simply a method of reducing cut fingers!

Tank set up to photograph newt larvae.

Smooth newt larvae photographed in a tank using natural light. 1Dmk4, 180 macro with extension tube, 1/1000, f8, ISO 500, tripod. Sheffield.

A height of 15cm works well. It is a good idea to keep them quite shallow, roughly 10cm or 12cm wide. This keeps the animal active in quite a small area and easier to work with. For small pond invertebrates you can create them smaller - 15cm front length, 20cm back and about 10cm tall and 8cm deep.

To get the exact measurement simply draw out the front and back lines on paper at the desired distance apart (the width) and join the two ends with straight lines. Measure the length of all 4 sides and choose an appropriate height. Get the base cut larger by a cm or two all around, it's easier to glue to this. You can keep the sides sharp until its all glued then use some wet and dry to rub the exposed edges to remove the sharpness. If you don't you end up cutting your fingers all the time. You can run a thin bit of tape or a strip of wood over these sharp edges to protect yourself even more if you want. Make sure you use aquarium silicon sealant (the clear stuff) and never one from a hardware store that may have anti-mould chemicals built in which will kill your subjects!

Gluing the sides together is a bit fiddly. Start by running sealant along two edges of one piece then stick it to the next side and base and hold up loosely with blocks/bricks or books. You then repeat for all the sides. Once you get all 4 sides done it tends to stay up but the use of sticky tape to hold it all in position helps greatly. Be careful not to slide the edges too far as you get sealant onto the glass surface and it's a nightmare to get off. Once it has dried run a bead of sealant along all the internal joints and flatten into the joint with a knife. The main thing is to get the tank water tight and the front glass completely clean. Leave it to dry thoroughly for 48 hours before testing. If it leaks dry it out and dab some sealant where the leak is.

A sheet of card or plastic behind the tank can be used to create the background colour you want. Greens and browns work well. The only problem is that they tend to produce too even a colour with an unnatural feel to the background. Another option is to build another tank, rectangular this time, slightly longer than the back edge but the same height as the tank you are working with. Keep this tank quite thin (about 8cm) and use it for weed and murky pond water. This tank is the backdrop for the main tank. Because you will probably tend to shoot mainly at low f numbers with a shallow depth of field this tank's contents will blur nicely. You can vary how far it is away behind the main tank to get different effects.

Mini tank plan

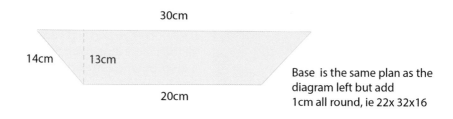

30cm

14cm   13cm

20cm

Base is the same plan as the diagram left but add 1cm all round, ie 22x 32x16

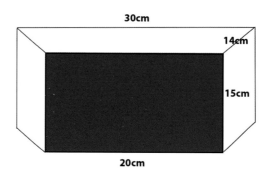

30cm

14cm

15cm

20cm

Once you have the tanks ready you need to consider the water you will use. The best is obviously from the same pond the animals come from but usually rain butt water is fine. If you do use water from the pond collect a few gallons more than you need and let it settle for 48 hours. Then, using a long plastic tube, decant the majority into a clean container.

Hopefully it is now clean. If it is not run an aquarium pump and filter in it for a day or 2 to take out as much of the muck as possible. Before you add any water to the tank make sure it's scrupulously clean, then decant the filtered water into your aquarium. Give it a day or so to settle. You may get air bubbles forming on the glass. Use a thin, clean stick to brush these off. If you want to add any props to the tank like gravel, stones, weed or dead leaves make sure they are thoroughly washed first. A point worth considering is to keep all the props as natural as possible. Don't use aquarium gravel. It's a dead giveaway. Try to collect any gravel from your local river. It takes ages to clean but it does look natural.

In some cases the gravel may contain small stones and lots of shale, a common rock. This may be almost impossible to keep clean. It seems to be continually disintegrating. One solution is add the gravel dry to the tank and arrange it into the shape you want then carefully pour matt varnish over the whole base, swilling it round very carefully so as not to disturb the gravel. If you heat up the varnish initially it will become runnier. When it dries it looks completely natural and keeps the water clean. It does mean though that this tank is now only available for use with this gravel. You wont be able to get it out!

Set the tank and background tank on a table outside in natural light (bright overcast days being best). Now you can introduce your subjects. You can pop these into an intermediate tank with clean water to get them dirt-free before you put them into the main photographic tank. Many whizz about for a bit, some just settle on the bottom. It will all depend on their natural behaviour.

Once they are in it's a matter of waiting for them to swim or move into the middle of the tank to get shots. Auto-focus works well unless it's for very small invertebrates like water boatmen when you may have to manually focus. One thing to be aware of is reflections in the glass. Wearing black gloves helps to reduce these as does altering the angle of the camera slightly. You need to be careful here though because if you shoot at any slight angle to the front of the glass the images can start to distort a bit.

Shoal of small roach photographed in a tank. 5Dmk2, 180 macro, 1/80, f3.5, ISO 1000, tripod. Sheffield.

Bullhead on river gravel which has been varnished to keep it clean. 1Dmk2, 180 macro, 1/125, f16, ISO 400. Derbyshire.

You can try suspending black velvet in front of the tank with a hole cut for the lens. It does stop reflections but it can be a nightmare to work with. You just now need to be patient and experiment with your f numbers. Try to have your lens on a tripod for stability and so you can have a cuppa without it losing its position.

These tanks are ideal for photographing small fish like sticklebacks, perch, tench and roach (only use small ones, larger ones tend to get stressed) plus newts, frogs (and taddies) and a variety of water inverts like diving beetles, water boatmen and dragonfly larvae.

In pre-digital days many photographers would have used flash. This added lots of light when you were confined to a maximum of ISO 100. However, there is some debate about the effect of such harsh light on delicate eyes (many of these animals live in low light environments) and it does show up

every speck of dirt in the water. As it is, using natural light you will get specks but far less than using flash. If you want to add a bit of light onto a subject then use a small torch.

The sizes and styles of tanks you can make are potentially vast. You can experiment with any number of other designs. Square, shallow ones can be used to photograph bottom dwelling animals, like bullheads, from above. Another option is to make a square one but with picture glass as its base and use this to photograph from below. If you have the time and energy you can fashion an old table with a cut-out square slightly smaller than the tank. Use a bit of beading around the square so the tank does not slip to either side. You now have space to lie below the table and photograph directly upwards. One thing you will need to think about is what is above the tank. It's best done outdoors using the sky - blue, with

Shanny photographed on the shore in a small tank. I caught this fish in a rock pool. Fish caught in rock pools experience naturally quite high temperature changes, especially in summer. However, whilst it was in the tank I kept it in the shade and made sure the temperature only rose a few degrees. 5Dmk3, 180 macro, 1/500, f4, ISO 1000. Yorkshire coast.

Water boatman suspended from the surface of the water in a mini-tank. 180 macro, 1/100, f8, ISO 800, tripod. Sheffield

fluffy white clouds looks good. You have to juggle with the lighting to illuminate the undersides of the fish, frogs or newts. A desk lamp or torch is ideal to produce the lighting you want.

It is easy to work with British sea life using these tanks as well. The main consideration here is that many fish don't experience large temperature changes in their natural environment unless they are regular rock pool dwellers. If you work with small fish that are caught beyond the rock pool zone

Tub gunard photographed in a small tank. 5Dmk2, 180 macro, 1/50, f8, ISO 1600, tripod. Lincolnshire.

you may need to devise a system to regulate the temperature of the water.

For species that live in rock pools you can take your tanks, filters and a table onto the shore and worked directly there. Try to collect some seawater the day before in large five gallon containers. Overnight the sand and sediment settles. A quick run through a filter in the morning will further improve its clarity . You don't need to be so worried about temperature changes in the aquarium because rock pool inhabitants will naturally experience quite large temperature changes, particularly in summer on sunny days.

Newts

Newts are brilliant for tank work. Spring is when their colours are best and they have crests (male smooth newts and great-cresteds, palmates don't) which they use in the pond as part of their display ritual. As with all tank work make sure the water is clean and has the same chemistry as their pond water. Try to have everything set up and running before you catch the newts. Smooth newts are very common. The easiest way to catch them is to use a small net and a torch at dusk when they come to the surface far more and are easier to spot.

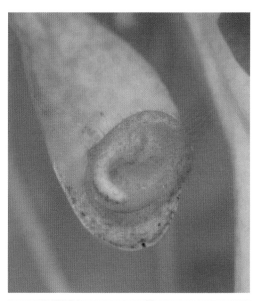

Frogs, toads and newts out of the water

The easiest species to work with is the common toad because it's far more tractable. Frogs are jumpy and they can damage themselves if confined to a tank. Among our newts you can only work with common and palmate newts without a licence. They are very delicate, dry and dull coloured out of water. It is difficult to produce good images bar head shots in damp leaf litter or moss.

Toads offer lots of scope. A great source of shots with a good conservation story attached can be found at a toad crossing in the spring. These are traditional places where toads cross busy roads. Without assistance a lot end up very flat and very dead. Toad lovers gather at dusk and carry the toads across the road in buckets. Using a torch or fill-in flash you can usually help out and get a great series of images in the twilight hours.

A large variety of images can be produced such as shots of toads on the road silhouetted with car lights in the background. Lying down creates that low position of view that

Developing egg of a palmate newt. 5Dmk2, 180 macro plus extension tube, 1/50, f11, ISO 400. Sheffield.

If you can find a few eggs on pond weed these can be photographed in the tank. As long as the tank is in the shade and is large enough you can follow the egg's development to create a series of images. Newt eggs are laid singly, unlike toad spawn (in strings) or frog spawn (in large clumps). The egg is stuck to a small leaf of pond weed that is half folded over. Once you get your eye in they are easy to spot.

Toad at a toad crossing in Sheffield. 5Dmk2, 180 macro, 1/125, f5, ISO 1000, beanbag.

Frog and plant pot, a typical garden image. 1Dmk2, 180 macro, 1/250, f8, ISO 400, beanbag. Sheffield.

adds a degree of intimacy. Shots of toads being picked up, in the bucket and later in their breeding pond can create a great conservation story.

Other images could be simple garden ones either with a normal zoom, 70-200mm or wide angle (16-35mm) to add background

Male midwife toad carrying a batch of eggs. I am lucky that we have a colony of this delightful, introduced species fairly near to where I live. 1Dmk2, 180 macro, 1/200, f10, ISO 400, beanbag. Sheffield.

Yellow bellied toad, 5Dmk3, 180 macro, 1/750, f8, ISO 400, tripod. Bulgaria.

and context. The big advantage with toads is that they tend to stay put for a few minutes so getting your shots is not too difficult. If you want to create a garden story prepare the year before by creating a set of photogenic props like moss-covered terracotta plant pots. If you can't get moss to grow naturally in your garden find a secluded place in a wood that is very mossy and set out a series of old plant pots, garden tools etc where they won't get found. Within a year or two they should be naturally covered in moss. You can try gluing moss to plant pots but they never seem to look quite right.

When working with a toad try to handle it the bare minimum of time possible. You can keep the toad in a plastic aquarium with some damp moss or leaf litter and take it out and place it where you want when everything is set up. Make sure you have done a test shot to get all your camera settings and the depth of field correct first. It does help to have someone else as well to guide the toad a bit. If it gets wilful and starts to look stressed or you have been using it for more than 5 minutes pop it back into the tank and give it a rest. Once you have your shots let it go at dusk exactly where you found it.

Midwife and yellow bellied toads are both very photogenic. Midwife toad males carry their eggs on their back until they are nearly hatching then they drop them into their breeding pond. They are out of water the whole time they carry the eggs. If you know where they occur and you want this shot be careful. Find your toad (which will be hiding under stones, logs etc during the day) and handle it with extreme care. Only work with it for a few minutes then put it back where you found it. If it was under a stone let it crawl under by itself, don't pop a stone back on top of it. Care is needed because the males will drop the eggs if they get stressed. Yellow-bellied toads are similar in size to midwife but have a stunning belly. They are more water loving and make a great subject for tank work.

Male great-crested newt during the breeding season photographed in a tank. I needed a licence for this work because these newts are on Schedule 5. It is difficult to get the image to look natural so I always try to get the props, weed and dead leaves from the actual pond the newts are breeding in. 1Dmk3, 180 macro, 1/60, f16, ISO 400, tripod. Derbyshire.

Frogs

Frogs are the hardest species to work with. They jump and can damage themselves. As with toads create the set first and then wait for a warm, dank evening. If you intend to keep a frog for a few hours keep it in a large dustbin with lots of leaf litter. Working with another person makes life easier, particularly trying to get it to pose where you want it, which is never easy. Try to select smaller frogs as they are easier to handle.

It is possible to produce images of jumping frogs. You simply pop the frog between two long boards of wood (about 60cm long and a frog's width apart). Then pre-focus on the line extending from the boards (camera on a tripod) and place the frog between the boards on the ground. Make sure you do this on a nice soft lawn or have the pond near the end of the boards. Often the frog will jump when it reaches the end of the boards. When it does hit your cable release and hope the motor drive catches the frog midair. There is no real way to do this without some form of control and the ability to predict the plane of focus the frog will jump through. If you have frogs in your garden then have the set permanently out and every time you come across a frog take a couple of shots before releasing it.

The snakes

Britain has three native snakes - the grass snake, adder and smooth snake. The latter is very rare, restricted to southern England and on Schedule 5 so a licence would be needed if you want to work with it.

Grass snakes and adders are fairly generally distributed across England and Wales. Adders occur right up to the North of Scotland but grass snakes are only really found as far as the SW. Both do occur in the same area but generally are found in different habitats. Grass snakes tend to prefer lower altitudes and one nickname, the water snake, is a good clue. Gardens with ponds, brown field sites, farmland, woods and some coastal areas are all potential grass snake habitats.

Adder sunbathing in a mossy part of the colony. 5Dmk2, 180 macro + 1.4 converrter, 1/1000, f5, ISO 400, stalked. Derbyshire.

Adders prefer drier, rougher areas but not exclusively. They can be found on commons, moors, woodlands, coastal areas and even railway verges. Grass snakes tend to wander a bit more and are found in a lot of places but adders are usually more conservative and stick to well known colonies, so once found tend to be in the same area year after year.

One serious issue (which should be common knowledge) is that adders are POISONOUS. Most bites won't kill but there is a chance so act with every precaution if you want to work with them. Always wear good boots that protect your ankles and thick trousers if you intend to kneel down.

Finding either species should not be too difficult. The best way is to join your local natural history group or even better, if one exists, a local reptile and amphibian group. Be open and say what you would like to do and hopefully they will let you know where the nearest or best places are. Helping with surveys and supplying images will go a long way to improving communication and getting them to trust you.

Try to work with both species in the early spring. Adders and grass snakes hibernate and once the first warm days start to appear they will pop up for a sunbathe on the surface above their hibernation place (hibernacula). Adders tend to come out earlier. In my area (Yorkshire) early March is when I start to look for them. I tend to see my first grass snakes in April. Obviously the further south you are the earlier the date and the opposite for further north.

Adders

When you are looking for adders choose sunny days with cold air in spring. Afternoons are often best. The idea is that the cold air keeps them cool but they are up and sunbathing. Adders like all reptiles are cold blooded. This does not mean they have cold blood but that they can't regulate their internal body temperature by their metabolism like we can. They have to warm up by sunbathing. When they are cool they tend to sit out and will allow a closer approach than when they are warm. Usually at the first sign of danger when they are warm all you hear and see is a rustle in the grass as they slither away.

Once you have found an area that adders use pick your day and wander very slowly around, paying attention to any spots the sun warms on the edges or within vegetation. Often south facing banks are popular. They generally won't be lying out in the open. They are difficult to spot so wander really slowly, taking a couple of paces trying not to cast your shadow on the area you are scanning. Stop and look carefully all the time.

Use your binoculars to check anything that looks possibly like an adder. It does take time but with patience you will find a few. The good thing is that they will tend to be in the same area for a few weeks when the weather is sunny. They also will be there year after year.

Once you spot one withdraw slowly and get your camera ready, unless it's already slung around your neck. Try to use a 180 macro lens (or 70-200 or 300 with extension tubes) and handhold it. It is difficult to mess about with a tripod and the chances are you will scare the snake anyway. Adjust the ISO to get a good speed (1/250+) after deciding what f number you want. Then approach slowly until you are a couple of steps away, making sure your shadow does not fall on the adder. You may be able to kneel down as well. Take a couple of shots and note the reaction. If you have approached correctly it will stay put. The chances are there will be annoying bits of vegetation in the way. You can slowly lean in and adjust your position to try to get as clean an image as you can. If the vegetation is a problem there are two approaches you can use.

Always carry a stick, on the end of which you have taped a small half hook. You can use this to gently move any vegetation that is above the snake and blocking your view. If you move slowly it is possible to bend quite a few nuisance bits out of the way without the snake slithering off. The key is to study the vegetation carefully and only work on bits that don't touch the snake. If you bend a bit of bracken away that the snake is lying on then the chances are it will be off.

These three images are of the same adder which reguarly sunbathed in the same grassy spot in spring. By learning where and when it sunbathed I was eventually able to manage a shot of the head with a clean background. I removed a few of the more obtrusive grass stalks to increase my chances but even after a number of visits over three years I only managed a few 'clean' images. Most were like the top two images with a lot of distracting grass in the way. 1Dmk2-3, 180 macro +1.4, 1/400, f5.6, 1/400, 1/640, ISO 400-1000, stalked and kneeling down. Derbyshire.

The second approach is to return on a dull, cold day when the snakes are unlikely to be out. Now you can prepare the spot by arranging any nuisance bits out of the way. Don't remove lots of vegetation or it probably won't use that spot again. Try to leave a few big bits over the top so it

This adder sunbathed every sunny day in roughly the same spot in a mossy area. It was usually below a number of bracken fronds which I was able to bend slowly out of the way before I took my shot. The adder was aware that I was there but because I moved slowly it carried on sunbathing. 5Dmk2, 180 macro, 1/160, f16, ISO 500, handheld, stalked. Derbyshire.

provides some cover but allows the sun to hit the ground. Then when you return for photography these bits are easily moved away using the stick. Always replace them when you leave.

Many photographers today like images taken in the animal's world i.e. at ground level. If the spot is on a bank it is possible to prepare it beforehand to allow you to get clean head shots. You can do this with adders sunbathing on the flat but you will have to lie down and you must make very sure there are no adders anywhere near where you lie.

If you stick to the rules outlined it is possible to get really nice adder images. If you go early in the year you will be working with the smaller males. Females (fatter/squatter and usually browner) tend to come out a week or two later. Keep visiting when the weather is ideal so you produce a range of images. If you are lucky you may come across the adder's 'dance' when two males are fighting to mate with a female. Whilst this is great to watch, it is difficult to photograph and the chances are you will disturb the snakes as they are very active and move around a lot.

A few notes about their behaviour should help you perfect your approach to them. When they are cool they are sluggish so will generally stay put. The snake does know you

are there. It's about trust and the snake's decision about how close it will let you get. If you scare it below ground you have failed. If you get too close it will either slither off or puff up a bit like it's breathing heavily. It's now switching to defence mode. It may also hiss and if it does retreat slowly. You are too close. An image of an adder striking at your camera with its mouth open may be dramatic but is very irresponsible.

Some photographers move adders to better, more photogenic spots. Many of the images we see of clear head shots or bodies with clean backgrounds are produced like this. I have done this in the past and as long as the snake is replaced exactly where you found it within a few minutes of you moving it then I believe no harm is done at all. However, it is not permissible to do this on nature reserves without permission and it has become a bit of an issue so I would encourage you not to do it. The problem lies with the volume of photographers today. Try to work in an area that will cause the least problem to your subjects and not one that has become popular where the reptiles might be placed under stress by lots of photographers and wildlife watchers.

Grass snakes

Grass snakes are often faithful to an area in early spring so, picking similar weather and working in exactly the same way as with adders, search edges of vegetation for them sunbathing. However, you may find they are less likely to stay put so be more cautious.

Another approach is to watch ponds or canals in good grass snake habitat. You may spot one swimming and as long as your camera is out and ready you may get a shot or two before it disappears into cover. It is possible to work with grass snakes in the pond by lying on the edge and getting a shot with its head sticking out. It is worth noting that a lot of close-up grass snake images are produced by catching the snake for a few minutes. If you do this it is unlikely to bite but it will probably void its bottom and produce a real stink from its anal gland. This takes days to wear off. It may also play dead where it goes limp and lets its mouth flop open. It's not dead but is a neat strategy to get the predator to drop it.

The best photography will always be with wild subjects in wild situations so it is best not to catch snakes but watch, learn and photograph them during their normal daily lives. It should also be far more satisfying.

Grass snake playing 'dead'. 5Dmk2, 1/500, f8, ISO 800, hand held. Oxfordshire.

Many snakes and lizards love metal sheets to snooze under. They offer security and in sunny weather are delightfully warm. If you come across an area with a few clearly set out leave them alone, they are probably part of a survey project. However, there is nothing to stop you setting up a few in your own area. Don't put them where others will interfere. Choose quiet, secret places. Sheets of old metal like corrugated tin roofs are great. Lay them out in spots where the sun will catch them during the day, or part of it at least. Leave them for a while to flatten the vegetation below and to bed in. Then inspect them whenever you want, especially during/after sunny weather in spring/autumn when it's cool. You should come across a wide range of reptiles and amphibians if they occur in that area. Always let the tin settle back gently when you replace it.

Lizards

Our three indigenous lizards are the common (viviparous), sand lizard and slow worm. Sand lizards, particularly the males in spring, are stunning but they are a Schedule 5 species. Common lizards are widespread

This grass snake often sunbathed in a local abandoned churchyard. To create this shot I popped a large ice cream tub over it so it would settle down and and I could set my camera and tripod up. Once I was ready a friend lifted the tub and I quickly took my shot. The snake continued to use the same area and often the same spot to sunbathe over the following weeks and years. EOS 5, 28-135mm, 1/250, f16, ISO 100 (slide film). Sheffield.

and abundant, occurring in a variety of habitats across the UK. Like the adder it is a very northern species and gives birth to live young. In a way this is a bit misleading because whilst it is true the young still develop in an egg they are just retained in the adult female until they hatch. The idea is that the sun's warmth is at a premium this far north so they don't take the risk of laying the eggs in one place. Keeping them in the female means she can be constantly moving into new sunny spots to help them develop.

Common lizards are very variable in their colour. The traditional type is brown with lighter markings but black, green and even blue varieties occur in different areas, just like the adder. They hibernate from late autumn to March/April so working with

A large adult grass snake hiding in an area of weed on the side of a pond. 1Dmk2, 180 macro, 1/500, f8, ISO 400, beanbag. Derbyshire.

them is a spring and summer activity. They love sunbathing, particularly if the air is cool, and will have favourite spots.

A typical brown common lizard sunbathing. 1Dmk3, 180 macro, 1/500, f4.5, ISO 400, stalked. Derbyshire.

To find them choose a cool spring day with good sunshine. Walk around the area you suspect they live in and look for bits of wood or sunny spots that are close to vegetation. If the lizards are on moorland search banks of south facing heather looking into areas that are sundrenched within the heather or on its edge.

They will often sunbathe on path edges and on wooden boardwalks. Once you

have found one (and if it's in a photogenic spot) crouch down slowly and inch forward. Handhold your camera and lens (180 macro or 200/300 with extension tubes) and take shots as you get closer. If you take your time you can easily get frame filling images. The main thing is to be low - your profile against the sky must seem huge to a small lizard and it's easy for it to detect any movement of a shape against the sky.

Common lizards are abundant on the moors near where I live. Most are the brown variety but occasionaly I come across green ones. 5Dmk2, 180 + 1.4, 1/100, f13, ISO 400, hand held. Derbyshire.

You could wait until the lizard moves away and prepare the spot by removing any untidy vegetation and grass stalks. Then return early on a day that you hope it will be sunbathing with cool air and long sunny spells. You then

I found this slow worm under an old roof tile at the base of a hedgerow at a wildlife centre in Devon. I placed it on this prop of birch bark and placed a plastic tub over it. I took the image immediately I lifted the tub. I then replaced the slow worm back under its roof tile. 5Dmk2, 180 mm, 1/400, f10, ISO 1600, tripod.

Photographing slow worms needs preparation. The best approach is to find a centre that has a few captive ones that they will allow you to work with. Prepare your props before you arrive and have an idea of what type of image you want.

simply sit in position and this time a tripod is fine because it's set up before the lizard gets there. Make sure your shadow won't be over the spot and wait. It does not always work but at least 50% of the time it does. Wait until the lizard is settled then take one shot, observe its reactions and take more accordingly.

Slow worms are common, more so in the south but can be found in Scotland as well as England and Wales. They are rarely seen sunbathing or moving around in the open because the vast majority of their lives is spent underground. If you do want to work with them you will have to either catch one or borrow a captive one.

Metal sheets in an ideal habitat will usually prove fruitful eventually. They can either be photographed side on to get head shots (using a macro lens) or placed on a photogenic surface and photographed from above.

A lot of my slow worm images were taken at a wildlife centre in the south of England. I had collected a range of props such as flat, lichen crusted rocks and bracken. I found that the slow worm would generally try to get underneath the prop so I popped a margarine tub over it and left it to settle for 5 minutes. If you find a wild one and work with it for a short while make sure you place it back exactly where you found it. 1Dmk3, 180 macro, 1/125, f8, ISO 250, -1/3 exposure compensation, tripod. Devon.

Male orange tip roosting on a bluebell bud, backlit at dawn. 5Dmk3, 180 macro, 1/1000, f8, ISO 1000, -12/3 exposure compensation. Sheffield.

The Invertebrates

is to embrace this stunning and accessible kingdom with our cameras.

The number of invertebrate species inhabiting Britain is vast, running into tens of thousands. They literally occur everywhere. Certain groups (such as butterflies and dragonflies) are ever popular with wildlife photographers. Others (such as spiders), perhaps due to irrational childhood fears, are seldom photographed.

So many wildlife photographers overlook the incredible beauty and diversity of our invertebrates. It's far too easy to fall into the trap of working with species that everyone else does. There are now millions of images of all the big iconic animals - why not break the mould a bit and be different? Many competition judges have become image weary when they are confronted with dozens of pictures of similar species from honey pot sites. So perhaps one way to move forward

Your garden can provide you with such a stunning variety that you could simply photograph there for a year and with a little imagination produce an incredible portfolio of great beauty.

The number of potential subjects is huge. Britain has 59 species of butterfly, 2400 moths, 4000 beetles, 2000 bugs and over 500 species of spiders - and that's not mentioning slugs, snails, crustaceans and flies! Invertebrates occur in ponds as well as all terrestrial habitats so you won't have far to look to get started.

There are many approaches to finding and working with invertebrates. Many involve using traps (such as moth traps) because the chance of finding them otherwise is very low.

There is one technique that has been around for decades and is still used but is considered by many photographers to be unethical and that is cooling insects down artificially. Temperatures usually vary greatly in the UK between day and night and inverts are adapted to this. Many just become torpid during the cold hours by roosting and going into mini-hibernation. They may be unable to move or fly well but are probably aware of your presence.

As temperatures decline in the late afternoon they seek a place to roost and slowly cool down as the night rolls in. The key point is *slowly cool down*. It might take a few hours to drop by 5 or 10° C. In the morning, just before dawn, they will probably be at their lowest body temperature and, for many, completely inactive. Now is a good time to work with many groups like butterflies.

Others, such as moths, are active during the cooler night so you need to work with them when they roost during the day. In the past, and still today to a lesser extent, some photographers exploit this cold torpor

This caddis fly was found near my pond in my garden in Sheffield. 5Dmk3, 180 macro, 1/25, f20, ISO 1600, torch for extra light, -1 exposure compensation.

This red admiral was feeding on ivy late in the summer. 5Dmk3, 1/800, f8, ISO 1600, +1 exposure compensation, backlit, handheld. Sheffield.

by artificially cooling the insect. They may simply pop it into a fridge or ice box in the field. A spray has now been produced that you can use to cool the insect.

Many photographers now have some very serious misgivings about this practice. When I started insect photography 30 years ago it was common and I did it a few times in my first years. However, I was never satisfied with the results. Some of the butterflies looked distinctly unnatural and I quickly came to realise that there were other ways to work with cool insects naturally. The main issue is that the insect is cooled down by 10/15°C in a matter of minutes, something that would never naturally happen. Then, when it's placed out into the full sun to photograph it warms up by the same temperature range in even less time. It is hard to believe that this does not damage the insect even if, as is usually claimed, 'it flies away none the worse from the encounter'.

Some may argue for the use of artificial cooling but I would implore you not to do it. You may decide you want to take your photography further afield and book a macro trip abroad. If you do, please check if any insects will be cooled this way and decide if you are comfortable with this or not.

Butterflies

Whilst we do not have the range of butterflies that our southern European neighbours have we do have 59 species which breed in the UK. Our butterflies are on the wing dominantly in spring to early autumn, though with the odd warm spell in winter it is possible to come across a few species in any month of the year. The first consideration is to decide which species you want to work with. Each has its own season. A quick glance through one of the suggested texts in the appendix should allow you to discover the correct month plus a few good locations to visit.

Butterflies in the UK are suffering hugely due to a number of serious threats - habitat loss and fragmentation, the over-use of agricultural chemicals and changing climate. Of our 62 species - four are extinct (though the large blue has been successfully re-introduced), two are critically endangered (large blue and high-brown fritillary), eight

Nickerl's fritillary roosting on a flower head at dawn in Bulgaria. The wildlife skills learnt in your own country should be transferable to any other country when working with many butterfly species. 5Dmk3, 180 macro, 1/500, f5.6, ISO 500, handheld.

The following species are all either, nationally threatened, vulnerable or endangered. However, in the right situation they can be added to your list of potential species.

White-letter Hairstreak, Heath Fritillary, Dingy Skipper, Grizzled Skipper, Silver-studded Blue, Northern Brown Argus, Marsh Fritillary, Grayling, Swallowtail, Small Blue, Chalkhill Blue, Adonis Blue, Purple Emperor, Small Pearl-bordered Fritillary, Wall, Mountain Ringlet and Small Heath.

Once you have mastered the various approaches with the more common species you can start to include those that are under some form of threat as listed above.

The basic approach is one of two methods - working with them when they are naturally cool and working with them when they are warm. Each approach has its own methodology.

Butterflies will roost every evening and cool overnight as the temperatures fall. As the sun slowly warms the air the following day they become active again. Different species of butterfly roost in different places. Probably the best places to find a variety of butterflies are wildflower meadows. Many species will roost, wings closed, on the side of a grass head or (with luck) on a flower.

This common blue was roosting on this dead seed head in the early evening on a cool day. I bent a couple of distracting stalks out of the way so they didn't show in the background. 5Dmk3, 180mm, , 1/100, f4, ISO 1000, tripod. Derbyshire.

are endangered, 9 are vulnerable, 11 are near threatened and 28 are of least concern.

(Butterfly conservation/JNCC report 2010.)

Clearly, as wildlife photographers we do not want to be added to the list of threats so it would be best if you restricted yourself to the 28 species of least concern initially. Some of the endangered and near threatened may be locally abundant and potential subjects but it is your responsibility to check which species this might apply to and act accordingly.

If you are an inexperienced butterfly photographer the following list is a good place to start.

Green-veined White, Large White, Small White, Large Skipper, Small Skipper, Meadow Brown, Ringlet, Gate Keeper, Marbled White, Common Blue, Holly Blue, Brown Argus, Small Tortoishell, Red Admiral, Peacock, Painted Lady, Dark Green Fritillary, Speckled Wood, Comma, Brimstone, Orange-tip, Green Hairstreak and Small Copper.

If there has been dew overnight the butterfly may be covered in water droplets and make a fantastic subject. The hardest part is to find them if numbers are low. Start at dawn and walk very slowly through the field scanning constantly all the vegetation as you progress. Keep kneeling down every few paces and look across at grass head height. You are looking for any shape that seems a bit out of place. It does take a while to get your eye in and it is easier to perfect the technique with a species that occurs in good numbers.

A good starting point would be a colony of silver-studded blues. In some UK colonies the butterflies can number in the thousands. Once you get the idea, in the right habitat and the right month you should be able to find a variety of blues (common, silver-studded, chalkhill, adonis, brown argus), skippers (large and small), marbled whites, browns (meadow and ringlet), small heath and a number of fritillaries.

I photographed this backlit marbled white on a cool day with sunny spells. I watched the butterfly go to roost when it clouded over. By moving in very carefully I was able to work with it when the sun came out again. 5Dmk3, 180mm +1.4, 1/500, f4, ISO 800, -12/3 under exposure, handheld. Yorkshire.

An alternative method is to visit a meadow in the late afternoon. Use binoculars and watch the butterflies as they flit about. You will soon learn which are hanging around a certain area. Common blues are a good species to work with in this way. Eventually you will see them fly into a patch of vegetation and not leave. They are probably preparing to roost. Don't go charging in as they will still be able to fly. Mark the spot (a bit of wool tied to a nearby bush or prominent flower a few metres away from the butterfly works well) and then return the following morning and search the area. You may find that some species roost semi-colonially. In some areas common blues certainly do, so if you spot one be aware there may be others close by.

Once you have spotted a potential subject you need to assess the situation. As with all wildlife photography the background is just as important as the subject. In a grass field this will usually mean a variety of stalks in the way. Use a stick with an open hook to subtly bend any grasses out of the way. Long tent pegs can be used to hold them in position. If none are to hand sharpened twigs can be improvised and work well.

Many books may suggest that you set up using a tripod. There are some definite advantages - it helps to fine tune composition as you move distracting grasses out of the way and it will allow you to use slow speeds and reduce camera shake. Setting up the tripod though can be difficult and it may damage a fair bit of vegetation alongside scaring the butterfly away. You will flatten some plants anyway just by simply being there but you should be keeping this to a minimum.

Today many wildlife photographers are starting to modify their techniques for two reasons. Modern DSLRs with high ISOs mean that you don't need to use slow speeds anymore and digital means every image is free. There is no film cost so you can risk experimenting more and take more images. If placing a tripod looks like it will cause too much disturbance an alternative technique is to hand hold the camera and use servo mode (Canon, AFC in Nikon which is predictive auto-focus) and a fast frame rate. Set an

ISO that gives a good speed (say 1/125+) and hand hold the camera and macro lens. Then lean in gently and take bursts of images as you get closer until you're at the correct distance. This is far less intrusive and allows fine tuning of the composition without moving the tripod and risking knocking the stalk the butterfly is roosting on.

The most important consideration is that you must get the plane of the back of your camera exactly the same as that of the butterfly's wings. The idea is to have the hairs on the tips of its wings sharp as well as its eyes. This is far harder to do than you might think. You will probably be using a low f number to keep the background blurred, f4 or f5.6 are ideal. At f16 or above the grasses in the distance start to show up as lines and can be very distracting. If you're not sure take a burst at each f number and check which gives the best compromise between background and depth of field.

Once you have taken a burst lean back slowly and review your images for sharpness across the wings. If you have not got it right try again, perhaps increasing the f number slightly. If you struggle get someone to stand at the side of you and watch the plane of the back of your camera and the plane of the butterfly's wings so they can advise you.

Using servo mode can be great but it tends to be less accurate if you want to put the butterfly to one side of the frame. The sensors furthest from the centre can be quite inaccurate and struggle to lock on. Another technique is to set the lens to manual focus when you're roughly in position. Then stop focusing and rock back and forwards slightly and slowly. As you see the butterfly come into focus take a burst of frames. If you do this four or five times you will get a few where the butterfly is sharp.

Once you have found a butterfly and taken a series of images wait till the sun comes up and, with luck, as it catches the insect you should be able to get a few images before it warms up and flies away. It usually takes about 5 minutes if the sun is warm. The

quality of the light now is fantastic. Just be careful with your shadow. If the day is dull you can add a bit of warmth by using a torch to brush the butterfly with light. The old filament bulb ones are the best - some of the neon style bulbs can be a little blue. Many photographers now prefer not to use full flash for the reasons given earlier (p18) but fill-in flash should not cause any harm.

Skippers often hold their wings at an angle and it is difficult to get them sharp across the whole wing unless you choose a large DOF. 5Dmk3, 180mm, 1/250, f16, ISO 1600, handheld. Yorkshire.

If the situation allows it use your tripod. The key point is to be careful where you place the legs and not to knock the plant the butterfly is roosting on. The big advantage is that you can set the camera up and then garden the background and keep checking in the camera to see your results without the camera moving.

Many cameras have a depth of field preview button. Very few photographers seem aware of this let alone use it. The depth of field preview button is often a small black button near the lens mount. Once you have selected your approximate f number you press the button and see exactly what the image looks like.

When a camera is focussing it is never at the f number you set. It's always at the lense's minimum f number to let the maximum amount of light in. It only goes to the correct f number once you take the picture. The button allows you to see exactly how the background looks but be aware, it will look darker than the final image because the camera uses the speed to adjust the light to get the correct exposure.

Another option is to use live view. You can see the real image and have the option to zoom in for very fine focussing on the exact point you want sharp. The main problem with live view is that it's only really viable when the camera is on a tripod and if it's sunny or bright it can be hard to see the screen well.

This ringlet was resting between sunny spells. It is was very active so I had to approach very cautiously. I chose to experiment with my DOF because it stayed in situ for a good two minutes. Top, 5Dmk3, 180mm, 1/200, f8, ISO 1250. Bottom, 5Dmk3, 180mm, 1/1000, f3.5, ISO 1250, handheld. Yorkshire.

There are a number of hoods you can buy to shade the screen and you may find one of these suits your style of photography.

The other method of working with butterflies is when they are active and flying around. Once you get a little experience you will quickly find some species are definitely easier than others. Some, like dark-green fritillaries, are strong fliers and never seem to settle - making for a very challenging day's work! Others may be seeking nectar and frequently visiting flowers. In mid to late summer plants like knapweed, thistles and teasels can be powerful magnets for butterflies. Brambles in sunny woodlands can be equally good for a variety of species.

Once you have identified a number of plants that are being visited you have two approaches. Stalk the butterflies or sit and wait. Stalking butterflies has the same basic rules as stalking birds or mammals. However, they are often only present in one spot for minutes feeding on one flower so you won't have the luxury of spending 20 minutes working into position. Start by staying low and try to avoid making a big shape against the skyline. Move slowly into position and try to be at the same height as the butterfly. The main thing to watch is your shadow. Don't let that fall onto the butterfly.

The bigger the macro lens you can afford the better. A 150/180mm is ideal. You may even be able to add a 1.4 converter. This allows a respectable distance between you and the butterfly. For an image the same size you have to be half that distance away with a 90/100mm and half as close again with a 60mm macro. By now you are so close most butterflies are flitting away. A good alternative is a 200 or 300mm with an extension tube.

As you get close move in slowly and lean forward, taking images all the time. With patience and practice it is fairly easy to get close to many butterflies. The best days are when the air is cool with the sun out and the butterflies active. As it gets hotter they become more skittish.

When you are close you have to think about the background and composition. Many butterflies hold their wings at an angle so getting the whole insect sharp is a real challenge. You can try high f numbers like 16, 22 or 32 but the background may become intrusive as you go higher. Try to bear this in mind and select angles that hopefully allow the background to be as far away as possible to reduce distracting lines.

Another approach is to try head-on images with shallow depths of field (f4 say) and just keep the eyes and head sharp. The forward edges of the wings can be used as compositional lines to add impact to the image.

If you want flat, open wings, which usually occurs when the butterflies are sunbathing, you will have to get your camera's back in exactly the same plane as the open wings. This can be tricky because your shadow may inadvertently creep across the insect and scare it away. Always carefully watch your shadow as you move into position and try to keep it just to the side of the butterfly.

During some summers we are invaded by thousands of beautiful painted ladies which love nothing better than visiting knapweed flowers. I sat next to this clump of flowers and let the butterflies come to me. 1Dmk4, 180mm, 1/800, f8, ISO 500. Derbyshire.

The number of individual flowers that offer nectar is often the factor that decides your approach. If there are limited flowers and butterflies are visiting these regularly it is a far better policy to get into position first. You can now try to tidy up the background a bit by removing or bending away any obvious distracting twigs or grasses. Then sit comfortably and wait. If the situation merits the use of your tripod then use it. It saves

aching arm muscles a bit and helps to keep the camera in position. However, usually there are various plants/flowers for the butterflies to settle on so you may end up hand holding your camera and lens. Simply lean forward when a butterfly lands. This method has real advantages for a number of reasons. It's very relaxing and you won't get hot under the collar chasing fast flying butterflies all over the place. Secondly, you can improve the background and lastly the butterflies behave completely naturally and tend to stay longer than when you stalk them because you are there when they first land.

Once you have become familiar with the more common species you may want to try to work with our two largest and most showy species. Both are protected and now so popular with photographers that it is easy to find sites where they exist.

Swallowtail, 1Dmk3, 180mm +1.4, 1/250, f5.6, ISO 800, stalked. France.

The swallowtail is arguably our most gorgeous butterfly, though there are quite a few who would claim that His Worship, the emperor, holds that accolade. Sites for both species are now well advertised on the web.

Swallowtails are a spring species that are very common across a lot of mainland Europe and are now photographable at a couple of East England reserves, such as Strumpshaw Fen, in June. The king of British butterflies though (in my opinion) is the purple emperor. The male, with his metallic purple wings, is an object of stunning beauty that would grace any rainforest glade. The unfortunate thing is that he tends to patrol his favourite oak tree in late June at quite a high elevation which gives little chance to get a good view without binoculars and a cricked neck.

However, he does have a weak spot in his armour. He likes nothing better than descending to the ground for a sip of a heady brew which naturally would have been from animal dung. Butterfly collectors for centuries have exploited this with a wide variety of attractants such as a dead, pungent rabbit; fresh, steaming horse's dung or smelly brews. His Majesty can also be tempted down with a white sheet. Today butterfly enthusiasts annually gather at a number of woods in Southern England to watch this stunning insect and spread their own brews out to entice him down from his lofty, oak perch.

Purple emperor male feeding on fresh, damp horse's dung and resting amongst oak leaves. 1Dmk2, 180mm +1.4, top 1/200, f8, ISO 400, bottom, 1/400, f8, ISO 500. Wiltshire.

Photographing emerging butterflies

There are few things more beautiful than the emergence of a butterfly from its pupa. As a child I remember the first time I watched a cabbage white that I had found in my garden emerge. The splitting of the pupa followed by the unfurling of the delicate wings fascinated me then as it still does now. It is not too difficult to photograph or video this stunning transformation with a little forward planning.

The first thing is to decide where you are going to find your pupae. Probably the best place to start is to buy a painted lady kit and work with the pupae as they develop. They are readily available from many suppliers easily found on the web (p 224). To produce the best pictures you need to have the pupae on something natural, such as a nettle stem.

There are two ways to achieve this. The best is to put a variety of nettle stems in the unit you keep the caterpillars in when they are about to pupate. Luckily the supplier will provide a care sheet that helps you work out when this is. The use of a few dead woody nettle stems that you have prepared earlier is ideal and natural. Painted lady pupa hang down from one end which is stuck by a sticky pad to the object the caterpillar chooses to pupate on.

Often though they do not pupate on the stem you want to photograph them on. If this happens wait a week or two by which time the pupa will have hardened and using a very sharp scalpel or craft knife carefully cut it off. Make sure you do not cut the pupa, just through the pad that glues it on. Be aware that the pupa is alive and may wriggle a bit. Be extra careful if you hold it, don't squeeze it. It is safer to do the whole operation over a soft towel in case the pupa falls. Then use a small dab of super glue on the nettle stem and gently place the pad on the end of the pupa onto the super glue. Only use a drop of glue so you won't see it in your final image. When you do this have the pupa lying on its

A small tortoiseshell emerging. The whole process took five minutes from the first opening of the pupa to the butterfly's wings being fully pumped up. When I worked with ten small tortoiseshell pupae I found that 80% emerged at first light or within an hour or two of it. The occasional one chose a more civilised time in the morning! I don't know why they emerge so early, though I could hazard a guess – they need enough time for the wings to dry and be able to fly away before the potentially chilly night. If they do not emerge by 2pm they almost certainly won't until the following day.
5Dmk2, 180mm, 1/125, f14, -2/3 exposure compensation, ISO 800, tripod, natural light. Sheffield.

side on the towel and introduce the twig and glue to it. Then leave it for ten minutes or so to harden. Next lift it carefully up and let it dangle as if it had pupated there in the first place.

This method should be used as a last resort. The best plan is to get the caterpillar to pupate on the stems you want to work with. If you have these set up in the middle of the unit, not touching the top, with the caterpillars feeding around them hopefully they will choose your twigs.

The next thing is to work out when they will emerge. The care sheet will tell you an approximate length of pupation time. You then set up the stem and pupa in a clamp and stand. (An old school lab clamp, boss and stand makes a fantastic photographic aid). A day or two before the butterfly emerges the pupa will colour up. You will see the colour of the wings appear. Once this happens the butterfly will emerge the following day or the one after. Generally they emerge early in the morning so a dawn start is needed.

When the pupa is ready to emerge put the vegetation it is stuck on in a clamp. Once you have everything set up stay put, do not pop out for a cuppa or loo break - stick it out because it can be very quick! Use a macro lens with the camera on a tripod and a cable release. It is easier to fine tune the focus in live view and make sure you choose a high f number such as f16. If your background is not ideal consider hanging a sheet somewhere behind the pupa. Black velvet is great to create black backgrounds. Other colours can work well but may be too uniform and create an unrealistic effect. Another option is to print out a couple of A3 prints of out-of-focus vegetation and use these. Have all this trialled weeks before you start. You don't want to be flapping around on the morning looking for a good background.

Once you have everything set up to photograph the pupa and have checked all the camera settings it's simply a waiting game. You have to watch carefully for the back of the pupa to start splitting. As soon as it does take images of each stage. You will probably take over a 100 images over the next ten minutes or so. Several stages can be quick, particularly when the butterfly pulls itself free of the pupae. Take lots of shots now. Once it's pulled free the crumpled wings hang down and slowly pump up. Hopefully the butterfly is in the plane of focus you want. It's now that having the whole set-up on a clamp can be an advantage as it's easy to slowly rotate it. Try not to move the camera and lens during your photography. This will help you to edit the images into a time lapse sequence later which will look odd if the size or position changes.

A big question will obviously now arise. What do you do with the live butterfly? Strictly speaking it is illegal to release it because it has been raised in captivity. Most of the care sheets suggest you keep the butterflies alive in captivity and feed them until they die a natural death. (They will live a week or two). In reality many of them end up released which, since the painted lady is a migratory species, probably does no harm to wild populations.

Once you have mastered the technique you can move on to trying other native species. It is possible to buy many live pupae, eggs and caterpillars from entomological suppliers (see appendix) or you can find your own. This technique is only really feasible with species whose pupae hang down or are stuck on the side of a twig, such as orange tips. Some species' caterpillars bury themselves when they pupate so are not really suitable.

Finding your own pupae or caterpillars can be great fun. You will need to learn a bit about each species and where and when to find them. The following species would make great projects - green-veined, small and large whites, red admiral, peacock, small tortoiseshell, painted lady, orange tip, speckled wood, meadow brown, ringlet, brimstone and comma. All are fairly common, are well distributed across Britain, are large (so are easy to work with) and form obvious pupae.

Collecting pupae from the wild is not easy. You will need a fair bit of practice and skill. Collecting caterpillars is easier, especially ones that form colonies such as peacocks and small tortoiseshells in nettles, which can often be spotted from a distance. Be aware that a great many wild caterpillars are parasitised. These pupae never colour up and butterflies don't emerge. You find a small wasp will pop out. For grassland species choose areas where the butterflies are abundant and learn what the pupae look like. It may take many hours crawling in a field before you start to find caterpillars or pupae. Many are very well camouflaged. Occasionally you may find large numbers. A few years ago I was working in some local meadows and there must have been thousands of very easily spotted burnet moth pupae glued onto the grass stems.

Another option is to prepare your garden by planting out suitable food plants. A row of cabbages will quickly attract whites and once the caterpillars appear sleeve the whole plant by surrounding it with a large bag of fine muslin (available from many entomological suppliers) to stop parasites from infecting the caterpillars. A corner planted up with a big bunch of nettles may attract small tortoiseshells or peacocks.

Producing a series of images of the whole life-cycle can make a fascinating project. To start you need to decide which species you want to work with and have a ready source of food plants growing. Next, you need to either find or buy the eggs. When they are on the food plant sleeve it up with a loose muslin bag. Good research should tell you roughly when the eggs will hatch and how long the caterpillars live before pupating. Make sure you don't overcrowd the larvae as many can turn cannibal or disease may spread. If you buy the eggs you should ask for specific rearing details. Your research will tell you if the pupae will emerge in a few weeks or if they overwinter. If it's the latter place them in a plastic container in a shed outside so they experience a natural winter. Don't forget they are there and get them ready at the right time the following year.

Butterflies have always attracted wildlife photographers. It's not too hard to work out why - their visibility and beauty makes them well known but moths are far more varied, just as stunning, yet very under represented photographically. The main problem is that most species are nocturnal, though not all. Diurnal species like cinnabar, burnet and latticed heath can be worked in the same way as butterflies but the vast majority that love the dark hours need special techniques.

Angle shades moth. 5Dmk2, 180 mm, 1/13, f16, ISO 1250, live view, tripod. Sheffield.

The number of moth species and individuals in the UK far outweighs those of butterflies but getting to grips with them is a bit more challenging. We are all familiar with the way many moths gather around lights at night and some of you may have been on moth nights run by your local natural history group. If you haven't it's a great way to start. The most reliable way to find and work with a variety of species of moths is to attract them to you. There are two main ways to do this, use a light trap or entice them to a sweet meal called sugaring.

Light traps are exactly that - a type of bulb that attracts the moths and a box that collects them until the following morning. There are a number of basic designs. The Skinner, Robinson and Heath trap are the best known and have been well tried and tested over the years. All these can be bought commercially and range in price from £130 up to £300+. It is however possible to

I have run a number of different light traps in my garden over the last ten years but two years ago I made a major effort to run one for most of the spring, summer and early autumn. I caught over 140 different species in that time yet if I searched my garden during the day I probably would only have found the odd moth. Many of these moths are incredibly beautiful. Some are large and showy, others more subtle. Identifying them is not easy and I spend hours on my computer and looking through books before I am 90% sure I know their names, and even then there are a few I am really guessing at!

Grey dagger. I caught this moth in my trap and placed it on this old fence post which was chosen to complement the grey colour of the moth. 5Dmk3, 1/100, f16, ISO 800, live view, tripod. Sheffield.

build your own box and just buy the electrics for a fraction of the cost.

Skinner traps are a large wooden box, Robinson traps are generally metal or plastic and circular and Heath traps are square but smaller than Skinner traps. I personally use a home made Skinner with bought electrics.

Building a Skinner moth trap

Start with 4 pieces of good quality plywood of size 51cm x 38cm. Use the plans (p167)

to see where to cut two 19cm grooves into each of the longest sides. The groove's width needs to be the same width as the ply as they form the points where you slide the sides together to form the box. On the 38cm sides, flush on the edge, screw on a 38 cm length of 2cm x 2cm wood. You now have the four sides of the box.

Use a jigsaw to make the 4 pieces that you will screw onto two of the sides. Use 2cm thick wood to make these. The two pieces labelled A are to hold the cross member that will have the electrics. You screw these onto two of the facing sides at the top in the middle.

The two pieces labelled B are also 2cm thick and are used to hold the sheets of perspex. These are screwed to the same sides as part A, in the middle but lower down with the bottom edge of B 4cm from the bottom edge of the side.

You now need the cross strut, this is piece of 5x2cm wood 47cm long. You will attach the bulb holder and small shower cover to this.

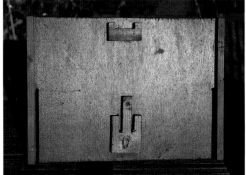

My home made Skinner light trap set up in my garden. The lower image shows the side with the wooden pieces used to hold the electrics and the two long pieces of perspex.

The perspex can be cut at home or you can order it to size. You need 2 long pieces 47x5cm and 2 pieces 38x47cm. Glue 2 pieces of 2x2cm wood on the edges of the 38cm side of each large sheet.

The base is any piece of wood that is larger than the assembled box, say 60x60cm. Check it all assembles correctly and when you're sure its all OK varnish it to protect it from rain.

To assemble fix the 4 sides together using the grooves to lock into place. Slide the two long, thin bits of perspex into the two grooves in part B. Fill the bottom of the box with a number of old egg cartons for the moths to hide amongst then slide the two large perspex pieces sloping from the top to rest on the two long pieces. Use the photos to help. The long wooden piece with the electrics rests across the top in the groove in piece A.

This image shows the two long pieces of perspex and one of the two large pieces fitted into the wooden piece B.

Mercury vapour box and timer switch with leads that run to the mains and to the light trap.

The choice of electrics is determined by a number of factors. Basically there are two types of bulb commonly used, mercury vapour (MV) and a neon tube called actinic. Both work well though MV set-ups attract a far greater number of both species and individuals. MV bulbs need a control box and work from mains electricity so you need to be near a mains supply. The bulbs are usually 125w and emit a lot of light and get hot so may burst if it rains on them.

Actinic bulbs can be run from the mains or a 12v battery. The latter set up makes it far more portable since you only need a good powerful 12v battery, like a car battery or a lithium battery. They remain fairly cool and are not as bright as a MV.

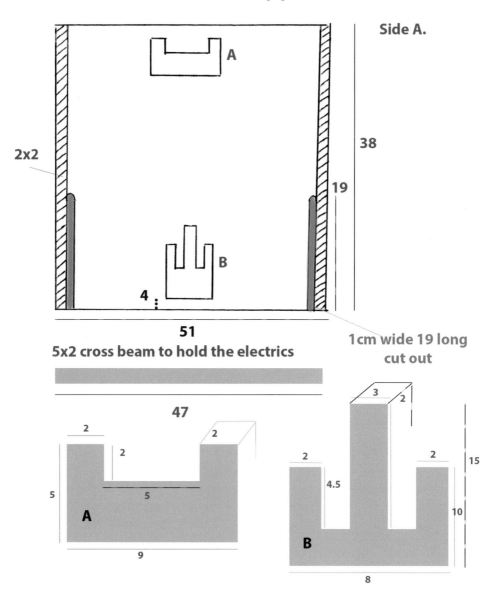

Skinner moth trap plan

167

Side A.

2x2

38

19

4

51

5x2 cross beam to hold the electrics

1cm wide 19 long cut out

47

3
2

2
2

2
5

2

15

2
4.5

2

A
5

B
10

9

8

All measurements are in cm.

Where to place the trap needs a bit of care. One major issue is if your garden is overlooked by other houses. They may object to the bright light all night so if you're not sure just ask or try to shield it a bit. The second issue is rain. When you build your trap you need to construct a small perspex shield above the bulb. Strips of aluminium with a rain cover bolted to the cross strut work well. This is fine in light rain but not brilliant in a heavy shower. You have two choices, only run it on nights you're sure it won't rain or run it under a large umbrella. My trap is on our garden table which has a large brolly so it's ideal if it rains. It also keeps the electrics dry! I plug the control box in the greenhouse but you can run it from your house with the cable going out through an open window.

Once you get into mothing (which is great fun) you will quickly work out that warm, muggy nights are best. The trap will provide a good range of species from April to September. Each month has its own assemblage of moths so you are constantly finding new species as you progress through the year. Don't forget to keep a log of what you catch as well. All your records (especially moths) are an important part of your area's natural history and since moths are very under-recorded any records you get will be gratefully received by your local natural history group or Wildlife Trust. You never know but you may come across some great rarities or 'firsts' for your area which could be vital for future conservation projects and help understand moth distribution.

Once you have run the trap you need to empty it each morning. Don't place the trap where it will be in morning sunlight or you will bake the moths and make them very lively. Have a set of small plastic pots handy. The ones that your local Indian supplies full of yoghurt for bhajis are ideal! Some moths will quietly wait until you coax them into the tubs, others tend to rapidly fly away as you open the trap. With care many can be persuaded into your tubs. If you are not going to photograph them simply id them and let them go. Oddly even this will need a bit of care. Many birds in your garden may

work out that a protein rich titbit is readily available every morning!

One group of moths are known as the thorns and these rest with their wings folded like butterflies. When I photograph moths I spend a lot of time selecting the right perch or prop to make sure it looks natural and attractive. 5Dmk3, 180mm, 1/160, f6.3, ISO 1000, -1/3 exposure compensation, tripod. Lincolnshire.

Before you run your trap make sure you have a good number of props to photograph the moths on. The moths you catch can be roughly divided into two groups - those that will cling to a twig (such as peach blossom, the spectacle or burnished brass) and those that rest with their wings flat open (such as the carpets or the blood vein). Make sure you have a collection of appropriately sized (in diameter) local twigs with attractive lichens or patterns. Elderberry bushes are often covered in delightful lichens. Also mentally make a note of any local bushes such as apple and hawthorn from which you can cut fresh twigs if you want some green leaves in the image.

For species that rest with their wings flat open have a stack of prepared bark such as birch and pine. You can collect these from dead trees. Simply soak them and unfold them so they are flat then weigh them down with bricks and let them dry. Flat stones with lichens or sandstone with swirls in the rock are also attractive. For more urban images have a selection of rusty garden implements and sheets of rusty metal. It is a good idea to spend a bit of time getting the props as photogenic as possible and try not to overly use one. Create variation where possible.

When you empty the trap have a good look around it. There are usually some moths roosting on nearby walls or plants. You may find props around the trap have some moths roosting naturally on them. It doesn't always happen but does occasionally.

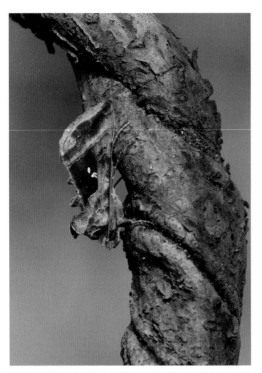

Plain golden Y. I always try to make the prop as attractive as possible. Here I have used some twisted stems from a creeper in my garden. Whenever I find any attractive props I save them at home. 5Dmk3, 180mm, 1/160, f13, ISO 800, tripod. Sheffield.

To photograph the moth set the twig in your clamp and get the camera with macro lens ready on your tripod. Always try to photograph the moths in overcast light or in the shade. They definitely don't like bright sunshine! Working at f16 is a good starting point and use your ISO to get a good speed. Live view can be advantageous for moth photography with a cable release or the 2 second timer. This means the camera has the mirror already up which allows you to use slower speeds without any camera shake as long as it's secure on the tripod.

The next bit is to coax the moth onto the twig. Use another thin twig to try to persuade it. It helps if you keep the small tub in the shade before you start so the moth hopefully has settled a bit. Some species go on very easily, others may simply fly away. It's a bit of luck of the draw. The more care you take the more you maximise your luck. Never cool them in the fridge, it does not work and probably harms the moths anyway. Once the moth is on the twig it often will stay put. The kittens (such as alder) and many of the prominents (such as iron) will stay all day. Others may be a bit more twitchy. As with all your photography the background

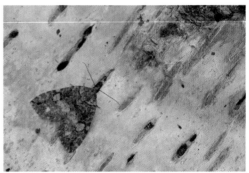

July highflier on birch bark. 5Dmk3, 180mm, 1/100, f11, ISO 800, live view, tripod. Sheffield.

is vital so make sure you have a good spot prepared before you start or use a board or sheet as a backdrop. Macro lenses have very shallow depths of field so you will need to experiment with high f numbers because even though the moth may be small it's got quite a big depth from the wing tip to the eye even when looking at it from above with its wings flat. Try to focus manually in live view and choose a spot half way between the wing tip and eye and experiment, reviewing images as you take them.

Moths that rest with their wings open tend to be more flighty. Set everything up with the sheet of bark or rock slab on the ground. Then invert the plastic tub the moth is in and try to get it to move onto the bark. Often it gets lively so do this carefully and eventually it will rest on the bark. Then leave the tub over it with a stone on for ten minutes so the moth settles. Work in a similar way as with moths on twigs but more quickly as many don't hang around for long - though some like, peppered moths, will stay put all day.

As with butterfly photography the key to getting sharp images from wing tip to wing tip is to get the plane of focus of the moth's wings exactly the same as the back of your camera. Try to work at high f numbers to maximise the dof. You will be amazed at just how shallow f4 is and that the moth may look flat but is actually not. Once you have finished photography let the moth go somewhere in the shade where the birds hopefully won't find it.

Swallow-tailed moths are often very flighty when I try to take them out of the moth trap so I have to move slowly and try not to knock any parts of the trap when emptying it. I chose to photograph this one backlit on some leaves from my garden. 5Dmk3, 180mm, 1/200, f8, ISO 800, +1 exposure compensation. Sheffield.

Vapourer moth male with stunning antennae. 5Dmk3, 180mm with extension tube, 1/160, f6.3, ISO 800, +2/3 exposure compensation, live view, tripod. Sheffield.

A few species like the thorns rest very similarly to butterflies so try to get these hanging from a twig. It is tricky but can be done, though many will fly off before you get your shot. You just need to remember that you will probably catch another one on another night.

Many moths have stunning eyes and lovely furry heads. Once one is resting comfortably on a twig it's simple to turn the twig 90° in the clamp and with extension tubes on a macro lens get frame-filling head and eye shots. As before choose a high f number and have the camera on live view with a cable release. Another option to get a large depth of field, yet keep a clear background, is to use image stacking

Image Stacking

The basic idea is to take a set of images, say 10, with the focus at very slightly different positions. The camera and lens must be on a tripod and fixed securely. It must not move at all. Focus on the front of the moth's head, the nearest part, and take one image. Move the focus forward 1 mm and take another shot. Repeat until you have a sequence of images that cover the whole subject at 1mm intervals. Use a low-ish f number like 4 to keep the background clean. A computer programme then combines all the images into one that has a massive dof of the subject with clean out-of-focus backgrounds. There are quite a few programmes that do this as either stand-alone or Photoshop plug-in. CS4 and above has image stacking built in though you will need to get a book or use a tutorial on the web to learn how to find it! The final image can be very dramatic though it loses a tadge of sharpness. It does not work for every situation but is something that you may consider in your macro invertebrate work and it's always worth a day playing with the idea.

Sugaring

Moth traps are the easiest and best way to attract moths but in the past sugaring was widely used. The idea is to cover a fence post or tree trunk with a heady, aromatic coating of sugary liquid that attracts moths to it. As with moth traps some nights are better than others. Warm, muggy evenings are good. Each expert has their own concoction and usually swears theirs is the best. Most brews contain the following - treacle or molasses for a sticky thick base, a few crushed pear

The image above of a elephant hawk moth larvae is one of six I took at f8. I couldn't extend the dof by increasing the f number without the back-ground becoming distracting. I therefore took a series of images and image stacked to produce the image on the top right. All with 5Dmk2, 180mm, 1/250, ISO 500, tripod. Sheffield.

drops and a splash of beer or rum. You then literally paint the brew onto a fence post or tree trunk and wait with a torch as it goes dark. When the moths arrive you select which species you want to catch and use a small tub to coax them in. You then put the boxes somewhere cool until the following morning for id and photography.

Dragonflies and damselflies

These are often referred to as odonata or odonts for short. They have become very popular as photographic subjects in the last 20 years. Odonts, like butterflies, are creatures of the summer and each species has its own season. The larval stage lives underwater in ponds, canals or sluggish rivers. When the larvae are due to change they crawl up a nearby stem which is often at the pond's edge, though some species can move a surprising distance away from the pond. They then transform in a similar way to butterflies. The best starting point is to get a good book about British odonts (see appendix) and learn about the various species and their behaviours.

Emerging odonts

The emergence and transformation from the brown larvae to the ultimate insect aerial hunter is spectacular and witnessed by very few. It is however, with a little preparation, not hard to photograph. Each species has its own month or two when it is most abundant so you first need to decide which species you want to work with.

A good starter species for photographing emergence would be the common darter. This species is very abundant and emerges in late July to late August. Most tend to emerge before dawn but often there are one or two which emerge just after dawn letting you work in daylight. Many dragonflies emerge around dawn so an early start is needed. A bit of research should allow you to find which local ponds or lakes near you have a good population of common darters.

Try to get there just before dawn and search all the larger plants that grow around

One afternoon I noticed that lots of common blue damsels were resting on rush stalks in a pond. I decided to add my own stalk in a photogenic place and 'cleaned' the water surface of any dead leaves and feathers. The damsels took to my perch in seconds and I had only to wait until they landed in an attractive arrangement. 5Dmk3, 180mm, 1/1200, f6.3, ISO 800, tripod. Lincolnshire.

the edges. You are looking for a small brown insect-like creature clinging onto the side of a sedge or reed. It will be about 50cm or so high up the plant so it can avoid moorhens and ducks. If the light is good enough have a close look. If it is translucent and there are small white threads and a split in the back it has already emerged. It might even be just above the shed case (called an exuviae). If it looks solid the chances are it has not started yet.

You now need to decide if you can photograph it where it is. The chances are it will be shielded by other sedges so either bend these out of the way or consider moving it. If you choose the latter have a clamp and stand with you and neatly cut the sedge 10 to 20 cm below the insect. Do this carefully and don't waggle the sedge about. Now clamp the sedge and get your camera ready. Use the same system and method

as with a butterfly emerging but obviously you will be out in the field. Choose a good background, use natural light and sit back and wait. Generally it will start to emerge in minutes, though you might have to wait an hour or two!

The back will split and the head will start to emerge and lean back. It's quite quick so keep taking images. The fastest part is when it pulls itself out of the case. It flips up really quickly and then proceeds to pull itself free. Have your motor drive set just to try to catch this part. Try to watch and wait with the cable release in your hand permanently. Now it's free it may crawl up the stem a bit and the wings (which look milky) will slowly expand. They stay closed until they are fully inflated then open into the characteristic dragonfly pose.

Once you have finished taking images place the adult dragonfly back into the vegetation at the side of the pool. Keep it slightly hidden and about half way up the plant. The juvenile adult has shimmery wings and is called a teneral at this stage. It takes a week or so before the wings fully harden and lose their silvery look. Many dragonflies leave the pond now and spend their early weeks in grassy fields or local woodlands before returning to the pond where they mate and breed. If you find one that has already started emerging leave it. The chances are you won't get it into a photographic position quickly enough before it has actually left the case and if you rush it you could end up damaging it.

Once you have completed a common darter emergence project the method is just the same for all other dragonflies. You need to pick ponds you know they breed in, be ready at dawn and get your dates correct. Most species are not as abundant around a single pond as common darters though scarce chaser and black darter often occur in large numbers in some situations. Most will only have a few emerging on any one day so it's a matter of putting the hours in. Most species tend to emerge at dawn though southern hawkers emerge in the afternoon. If you find emerged exuviae note the date in your wildlife diary because it helps you to know where and when to look in the future.

Emergence dates (table opposite) - these are general dates and will vary depending on the weather that year and if you're southern or northern based in Britain. Precise dates are difficult to state and vary annually but records from your local wildlife group or Country Park may help you.

Working with damselflies is very similar but they often emerge at far more respectable hours during the morning and afternoon. They are obviously smaller. Look for the larvae crawling up stem. Some will not be at the edge of the pond but towards the middle where there is any vegetation. As with dragons be aware that some species and individuals may crawl out of the pond so also search grasses and other plants up to 10m from the pond's edge. Most species emerge during the day.

Photographing the larval stage

Eggs are laid during the main flight period. Some hatch within a few weeks, others may wait till the following spring. Most larvae stay in the pond at least a year, some even two or three before they have grown enough to emerge.

Two stages of the emergence of a common darter dragonfly. This emerged 30 minutes after dawn. 1Dmk3, 1/60, f8, ISO 800, tripod. Derbyshire

Species	Date range and emergence time of day
Hairy dragonfly	Early May- early June, eam
Azure hawker	End June to mid July
Common hawker	August, night - eam
Migrant hawker	Late August - September, night - eam
Southern hawker	Late June – August, eam and during the day
Brown hawker	Late June - August, night
Emperor	Late June - July, mainly night, few eam
Club-tailed	Mid – late May, eam to mid pm
Golden-ringed	Late May - July, night
Downy emerald	Early May if it's warm, am to early pm
Brilliant emerald	Mid – late June, am
Northern emerald	June, (peak early July), am
Four-spot chaser	Late May – June, eam
Scarce chaser	Peak second half of May, sunny mornings, eam
Broad-bodied chaser	Mid May-early June, eam
Black-tailed skimmer	Late May - mid July, eam
Keeled skimmer	June - July, eam
Common darter	Late June-early September, eam
Ruddy darter	Late June-early September, eam
Black darter	Mid August, eam
Beautiful demoiselle	June to July
Banded demoiselle	Mid May - July
Emerald damselfly	Early August
White-legged damselfly	Late June – mid July
Large red damselfly	Late May – early June
Small red damselfly	Late July
Azure damselfly	Mid May – mid June
Variable damselfly	Mid June to mid July
Common blue damselfly	Mid May – early August
Blue-tailed damselfly	Mid June – early August
Red-eyed damselfly	June – early August

eam = emerges in the early morning

Larvae can be collected by sweeping a pond net through the submerged vegetation in early summer. Some species live in the mud so you may have to sweep through this as well. Try to keep the disturbance to a minimum. You will catch quite a wide range of water beetles, water boatmen and hopefully a few dragon and damsel larvae. Photography can be carried out in small tanks in the same way as described on p140.

You may decide to keep them for a while in a large tank but be aware that they are carnivores - eating other insects, frog tadpoles and even small fish so you will have to provide these! I once kept a southern hawker larva for a few months until it emerged. I kept a bunch of yellow flag iris

A larvae of the emerald damselfly photographed in a small tank in natural light. 1/200, f4.5, ISO 800, 5Dmk2, 180 macro tripod. Sheffield.

in the tank and got up at dawn every day to try to catch it emerging. You can imagine my frustration when one morning there was no sign of it yet when I got back home in the afternoon it had crawled out and emerged with the teneral hanging on the iris!

Working with adult odonts

Like butterflies these are sun worshippers and dull days rarely produce good sightings. However, when it's dull, cool and rainy they will be around roosting in a place in which they feel safe away from predators. Some roost around the pond but others roost a long way off, often in scrub or even high in trees. Conversely most adult damsels tend to roost in pondside vegetation so are much easier to find.

Finding roosting damsels is fairly straight forward. Go early in the morning or on a cold, dull day and carefully search amongst the sedges and grasses around the pond. It shouldn't take too long before you find some. They will be perched on the side of a piece of vegetation with their wings folded closed. However, whilst they may be too cool to fly they will probably be aware of your presence and may move further down the stem or around it using the stem to try to hide themselves.

With patience you should be able to find a few in photogenic spots with nice backgrounds. If it has rained recently or there has been a heavy dew they may be decked out in sparkling drops of water. Don't forget

to experiment with your composition and try more unusual images such as looking straight down onto their heads with a shallow depth of field such as f2.8.

Traditional odont photographers usually want to see the wings sharp right across both sets. When damsels roost this means getting your camera back parallel with the wings. Whilst this does produce great record shots

A traditional image of a male broad-bodied chaser showing the wings open. 1Dmk4, 180 macro + 1.4 converter, 1/500, f6.3, ISO 500, stalked. Derbyshire.

A male common darter resting on a dead reed. 1Dmk3, 1/800, f5.6, ISO 400, stalked. Derbyshire.

if you follow this dictate all the time you end up with a whole series of very similar images, so think outside the box where you can. Why not try to work in the evening and go for moody silhouettes against cloudy skies by under-exposing a stop or two? Both dragons and damsels have such a recognisable shape that silhouettes like this can work really well.

Roosting dragons can be treated in the same way as damsels for the most part but they roost with their wings open and are usually harder to find. Some species like the

A pair of mating azure damselflies. The male 'guards' the female (as she lays eggs) by holding her head with his claspers to stop other males mating with her. I took this image by lying down on the pond side and waiting until a pair came close enough to photograph. 1Dmk3, 180 macro, 1/2500, f5.6, ISO 400, beanbag. Derbyshire.

darters rest around the pond but many roost in vegetation, often high up and a long way from the pond. Cold searching usually can be a frustrating business. One method which works well is to watch the dragons on warm days when they are active. Try to choose a pond where they are around most of the day and, using binoculars, watch them in the late afternoon.

The aim is to try to watch them go to roost. It is not easy but you will get enough success to keep giving it another go. If you are lucky you can watch the dragon fly into grass or a bush/tree and roost. Don't go charging in but mark the spot as closely as you can and return the following morning. With luck it will still be there and nice and cool. If it's high up a tree it's virtually impossible to work with but if you persevere you will find the odd one low enough down and in a good photogenic position.

Once you have found a roosting dragon you need to decide on two issues. Are you able to bend any obstructing vegetation out of the way? Can you move the dragon or do you simply give up? Bending vegetation is done with a stick and hook and tent pegs to keep them bent over. However, the dragon may be in a situation that is not ideal so in some cases you may be able to move it. Many photographers tend not to move cool insects. It is really an issue for you to decide if you are comfortable with it or not. However, if it's done carefully no harm will come to the dragon. Gently persuade it to grip a twig and then place it onto a photogenic prop which you have found earlier. The dragon will grip onto this and allow you to take a range of images. If it's covered with dew do not move it because the dew gets knocked off. Once you have your shots either stay put and wait until the sun warms it up and it flies away or return it to exactly where you found it roosting.

Some photographers and wildlife recorders routinely catch dragons with butterfly nets. If it's a simple case of recording for conservation reasons the benefit is obvious. Dragons have hard wings and if one is netted correctly it won't come to any harm.

Dragonflies like this black darter go to roost in the late afternoon on cool days. If you can find one it will generally stay put and allow you to try a little more creative work such as under-exposing to produce silhouettes. 5Dmk3, 180 macro, 1/1000, f4.5, ISO 400, -21/3 under exposure, handheld. Derbyshire.

However, in the past, and still today to a lesser extent, some photographers cool them down. This is not appropriate and it is something you should not do. There are enough options for photography without resorting to catching them and cooling them artificially.

Warm and flying odonts

At first glance it can seem almost impossible to get really good images of fast moving odonts. With a few species this is certainly true. Emperors and brown hawkers never seem to settle for a rest. They are the most amazing Billy Whizzes, constantly on the move. However, a few species do like to perch up and you can use this to your advantage.

Males of a few species like broad-bodied chasers patrol their breeding pond incessantly during sunny weather. Every few minutes they will stop and rest. Often

these perches are not in good spots but the dragons are very adaptable. The trick is to set up a good photogenic stick, about 60 – 90cm long, on the pond's edge leaning slightly over the water. If you do this try to pick a spot where there are no competing perches or if there are snip these off so the dragon will naturally gravitate to yours.

Set up your camera and lens and focus on the top of the perch. Before you place the stick make sure the background is suitable with no messy vegetation in the way and the sunlight is providing the type of lighting you want. Try to use a longer lens than your usual macro one. A 300mm or even a 500mm with a converter and extension tube is ideal because you are now a little further away. Then simply sit and wait.

Usually within ten minutes the male is using the new perch and because you are already in position there is far less chance of scaring him away. Even now though still be careful. Dragons have amazing eyesight and if you move too quickly it will be away. So move slowly and carefully as you swing the camera round. The best ploy is to have the camera already trained on the perch so all you have to do is move your hands to it. Better still, have your hands already on the camera.

During the day vary the perch to create a series of images. Bullrushes can be very effective as well as lichen-crusted twigs. This method works well with four-spot chasers, scarce chasers, black and common darters and the occasional male of the more flighty species.

A few dragons, like black-tailed skimmers, like to sunbathe on the ground. A few minutes watching will usually show you their favourite spots. It's then a matter of lying down with the camera on a beanbag and waiting for them to return.

The only time I have photographed a female emperor laying eggs she had settled a few times on the same floating stick. When she left I waded out and simply crouched near to the stick hand-holding my camera. I got soaked but she came back in ten minutes and didn't bat an eyelid at me or my camera. 1Dmk3, 300mm, 1/400, f11, ISO 400. Derbyshire.

Some species, like the hawkers and emperor females, take a few minutes to lay their eggs and they like to settle on a floating object such as a stick. They then bend their abdomen into the water and lay their eggs onto water weeds. With a little work you can prepare your garden pond specifically to create this shot. Set up a stick floating amongst a bed of weeds near the side of the pond and lie down on sunny days when dragons are flying around it. A longer lens will allow you to get images if the stick is a little further away.

A number of species, such as broad-bodied chaser females, lay their eggs whilst they are in flight. This poses all sorts of challenges but is not impossible to photograph. The

females, when egg laying, cruise low over the water then dip their abdomen into the water for a spilt second, repeating the process a number of times. To capture this image choose a fast focusing lens (300mm 2.8) and a fast focusing camera. Lie on the bank of the pond and prefocus over the area where the females concentrate their egg laying. It is very hit and miss but if your camera has servo mode switched on it will lock on enough times to get some images. Choose a low f number (4) and use your ISO to get a fast speed, at least a 1/1600+. The hit rate is low but it does work enough times to keep you entertained. Great fun.

Possibly the most dramatic images are of odonts in flight. For many species this is difficult but challenges are what drive us on to better things. Many species are quite predictable in their flight paths. An hour or two spent around the pond will usually show you that some dragons regularly fly down the same routes. You then sit facing the route, choose servo mode and select the focus limiter.

A female broad-bodied chaser laying eggs in a dew pond in Derbyshire. 1Dmk4, 300mm, 1/1600, f5, ISO 500, handheld, lying on the pond's bank.

This means you tell the lens to focus only between two set points. On a 300 2.8 you can set it to only focus between 2.5 and 6.4m which means it won't go hunting off to infinity every time you press the shutter button. As long as the dragon is within that range there is a fair chance it will lock on. If you are very lucky it will actually hover for a few seconds allowing the lens to lock on. As long as the speed is high enough (1/2000+) there is a good chance some images will

A migrant hawker patrolling the edge of a pond in autumn. 1Dmk3, 300mm, 1/1600, f5.6, ISO 800. Yorkshire.

be sharp. Unfortunately, many lenses don't have focus limiters but you can improve your chances by pre-focusing on the area you think the dragon will fly into. This allows the camera to lock on a bit better because the insect is close to being in focus. If you can expand the central focus zone/sensor this may also improve your odds.

A few species will actually hover and investigate the photographer. The southern hawker will do this and can provide (as long as you are ready for it) some fantastic images. A number of the male hawkers patrol pond edges in the afternoons. They slowly fly around the pond and investigate any small bays and as they do so they often hover. Once you have found a suitable pond it's just a matter of having the camera set up on a tripod and pre-focused. Keep the camera low and sit on the ground. You should have your hands already on the camera so if the dragon appears you don't have to move, otherwise it will see you and fly rapidly away.

Some dragons mate by pairing up for a few minutes or even longer. Others (such as broad-bodied chasers) seem to get the whole thing done in literally a few seconds

in flight. By being in the right place alongside the edge of a pond you may be able to spot paired dragons. Black darters will stay paired for a while so a very careful stalk in a similar way to stalking butterflies should get you into a photographic position.

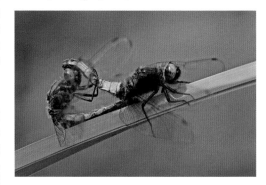

A pair of scarce chasers mating. They stayed on this reed stem for a minute or so and allowed me to stalk them. 1Dmk3, 180 macro +1.4, 1/1600, f5.6, ISO 800. Cambridgeshire.

One last tactic is worth a go if everything else fails. Make a dummy dragonfly male of the correct size and use a good identification guide to paint it accurately. It will keep you amused on long winter nights! Choose the larger species like emperors, chasers and hawkers. On your chosen day pop the dummy on a prominent perch and wait. With luck the resident male will fly over to investigate and hopefully give you a chance at a few shots.

Some photographers have the dummy on a line and waggle it about on a long stick. It is unclear how effective the method is but it is worth a go.

Spiders

Spiders are certainly an under-photographed group of invertebrates. They occur widely in all habitats and some can be quite large and very photogenic. Spider numbers, as a crude rule, increase until the autumn and the first frosts. A walk around natural grasslands, woods, heaths and gardens after a light misty rain in August or September should highlight large numbers of sparkly webs slung across the vegetation. However, not all spiders are web spinners.

An orb spider in autumn amongst bracken. The multiple eyes add so much to our fascination with them. 5Dmk2, 180macro, 1/500, f5, -2/3 exposure, ISO 800, tripod. Sheffield.

We have over 500 species of spider. Some are active hunters and stalk their prey like mini lions in the Serengeti. Others spin webs to trap their prey. Finding spiders should not be too much of a problem. Your garden should be full of them and some will be living with you in your house.

Most webs you come across are spun by a group of spiders known as orb spiders. These tend to have fat bodies, often with delightful markings, and medium length legs. The most frequently seen is the common garden spider which has a cross-shaped mark on the main body (abdomen). In late summer the larger females should be easy to find suspended in the middle of their webs.

I found this orb spider repairing its web in one of my local woodlands. I deliberatly chose to use the web at an angle to increase the 3D effect of the image. 5Dmk2, 180 macro, 1/100, f3.5, ISO 400, -1/3 exposure, tripod. Sheffield.

Photographing them is fairly straight forward. The main issues are distracting twigs or grass in the background and getting your camera level with the web to keep it sharp right across the image. If you look hard enough you should find an ideal web in the right situation. With care it is possible to bend the branch, twig or grass into a better position without breaking the web. The spider will retreat into cover on the edge of the web. Once it is still again and you have set up she should move back out into the middle.

Another approach that can work is to get the female to spin her web where you want it. Set up a twig/thin branch that has a side branch (v shaped) that extends so the gap runs to 30cm or so. You then wire this onto the bush she is living in. If you get the position correct she will eventually use this twig to spin her web. You can now unwire it and move it into a perfect position. Once you have completed your photography rewire it back. Try not to break the web but if you do it's not a disaster as many spin new webs on a daily basis anyway.

You can find orb spiders in the most amazing places. This one has built a nest in the head of a dead weed in the middle of a large field. 5Dmk3, 180 macro, 1/250, f16, ISO 1600, -1/3 exposure, tripod. Yorkshire.

Orb spiders are a huge group and make brilliant subjects. Many very photogenic ones live in a wide variety of habitats. If you search carefully through natural grasslands you should find some hiding in grass seed heads, bullrushes or weed heads. They make great camouflaged subjects. Some of them, such as the 4-spot orb weaver, can be quite large and are very photogenic. Another method to find them, along with a wide selection of other inverts, is beating. You place a large white sheet or tray beneath a bush and give it a few sharp raps on the branches with a stick. Many insects should fall out onto the sheet and you can pop any interesting ones into small tubs for photography later. Remember you don't want to damage the bush so shaking is fine but please don't try to thrash it to death!

Another group of spiders that are certainly fascinating are the crab spiders. Most are fairly dull coloured but with great body shapes. We do have one species though, Misumena vatia (the white crab spider), that is truly spectacular. Females are about the size of a pea with fat white or yellow bodies. They move like mini crabs (hence the name) and live in flowers. They are unfortunately fairly restricted in range in the UK occurring mainly in S England and Wales.

These spiders are active hunters and disguise themselves by being the same colour as the flower in which they lie in wait to capture any unsuspecting bee or fly. Once you find a bush with flowers and a few spiders set up with a macro lens and wait all day. Keep your eye on each female in her own flower until one has caught a fly or bee then lean in slowly taking images as you get closer.

Another group of crab spiders are common in grassland. To find these try sweeping a butterfly net through the grasses in August or September. You will catch a whole range of mini beasties and usually a few small crab spiders. Clamp a photogenic flower or weed head and let the spider roam around it. With the camera and macro lens on your tripod take images as it moves around or rests. Once you have finished put it back where you found it.

A male flower crab spider (Misumena vatia). 5Dmk2, 180 macro, 1/80, f5.6, ISO 500, +1 exposure, tripod. Worcstershire.

In September many houses are home to a number of male giant house spiders. These are probably the main species that elicits

A male house spider in my living room in the evening. 5Dmk3, 16-35mm, 1/30, f5.6, ISO 3200, -1/3 exposure, handheld. Sheffield.

the greatest fear among arachnophobes. They are all males that have matured over the summer and are now on the hunt for females. Most tend to come out in the evenings, especially when you're watching TV!

A good approach with these is to try to create an image that says something about the spider's world, such as your living room and TV. When you spot one on the prowl pop a small marg or yoghurt tub over it. Then set up using a wide angle lens such as a 17-40mm. You will need to set a high ISO and take a few images to get your speed and white balance sorted. Once you are sure you have all the settings correct lie on the floor and focus on the tub, then lift it up. Usually the spider will stay put for 10 seconds or so allowing you to focus on it and get a set of images. If you don't get what you want pop the tub over it again and have another go. You should really let them go in your house

but if they are a bit of a nightmare release them in the garden. Certainly never kill them. Just remember all the good work they have been doing all summer for you.

One spider that is possibly the most challenging is the zebra spider. These grow to 8mm so are very small and are common in many gardens. They look like peppery coloured, small animals zipping over walls in sunny weather. They are in fact hunting spiders with huge eyes. The main problem is that they are very mobile but they are faithful to their favourite spots. A search of warm, sunny walls in your garden in the summer should eventually allow you to spot one.

One challenge is their diminutive size. A 180mm or 100mm macro lens and extension tubes are needed to get the spider big enough in the frame. There are a few approaches you can adopt. One is to simply focus on the wall and wait until the spider walks into the area you are looking at. A bit hit and miss, but you will get results eventually. You can encourage them to wander where you want

A zebra spider on a wall in my garden. I deliberately photographed at a low angle to create the blur in the image. I must admit I love these tiny spiders. For something about half a centimetre in size they exude enormous character. 5Dmk3, 180 macro +1.4 converter and extension tube, 1/1600, f5, ISO 1000, tripod. Sheffield.

them to be with a fine bit of grass. Another approach is to find a freshly dead fly or very small moth and attach this to a very fine bit of grass. You then wriggle it around a bit on the wall where you want to photograph the spider. Believe it or not on the odd occasion it will approach and attack your prey!

Another method is to try to put a small tub over it but on the whole this is not very successful because they tend to simply walk under the edge or when you lift it up just scamper off. They are definitely worth persevering with though because those massive eyes are just stunning and make for a brilliant image.

Bees and wasps

In the UK we have 22 species of bumblebee, a number of different masonry bees, mining bees, various wasps and the hornet. All make great projects but a little knowledge about their lifestyles is needed to get to grips with them.

Queen bumble bees emerge in the spring to seek nectar and pollen before they start their small colonies. Bumble bees occur in a wide range of habitats as long as they contain flowers with pollen and nectar. They are fairing really badly in our modern, sterile, chemical-rich farmland. Gardens and wild

urban areas are their salvation until we can start a process of farming that sees wildlife as beneficial. The best place to photograph bumble bees (and many other bee species) is when they come to flowers to seek food.

There are two approaches you can adopt. The first is to use flowers like teasels and cow parsley that have open tops. Here the bee can approach from any direction so you concentrate on photographing the bee as it wanders around the flower.

They generally are very tolerant of the photographer as long as you move in slowly and keep fairly still. As with many wild insects the bigger the macro lens the better because your working distance is greater and disturbance less.

A common carder bee feeding on a teasel. 1Dmk4, 180 macro, 1/3500, f3.5, ISO 800, hand held. Lincolnshire.

The second approach is with flowers that restrict the bee's flight path so you can predict more reliably what direction they will approach from. Two excellent plants are foxgloves and Himalayan balsam. Both these flowers have deep tubes so when the bees approach they fly into the tube in a fairly predictable flight path.

To start set up with your macro lens or 300mm with extension tubes on a tripod with a cable release and the camera at 90° to the flight path of the bee. Choose a high speed, say 1/2000 (which shouldn't be a problem as you will be doing this in sunny weather anyway) and a low f number such

A white-tailed bumblebee arriving at a flower of Himalayan balsam. I used the middle of the lower part of the flower to pre-focus and just hit the cable release every time a bee flew in. When it works it produces amazing images. 1Dmk4, 300mm + extension tube, tripod, 1/1600, f3.2, ISO 800. Sheffield.

as 2.8 to 5.6. Pre-focus manually (switch auto-focus off) on what you think will be the bee's flight line. The front edge of the flower is a good guide to start. Choose the camera's fastest frame rate and every time a bee flies in fire a burst of shots. You then need to review them to see which parts of the bee are sharp and if you need to tweak the focus a bit. It is a bit of a lottery but if you give it a few hours you will get some delightful sharp images of bees in flight as they go into the flower.

Another approach with flowers that are visited frequently is to pre-focus on the flower, keep the auto-focus on with servo/AFC and the same settings as just discussed and try to get the lens to lock onto the bee. It can be fiddly but if you have lots of visits it will lock on every now and then.

A number of bees love feeding on the grape hyacinths in my garden. I simply sat down next to the flowers in the spring and pre-focused on one flower. Every time a bee flew in I hoped the auto-focus would lock onto it when I hit the shutter button. 1Dmk4, 180macro, 1/2500, f3.5, ISO 400, handheld. Sheffield.

There are a number of mining bees that inhabit the UK. Some are seldom seen but the tawny mining bee is a common species that is often found in gardens. The males emerge just before the females and then mate with them as they emerge. From now on the female is the sole worker.

Tawny mining bees are an early species appearing around early May. Look for small, mini pyramids of soil in areas of bare, undisturbed ground. During the night the female is below ground and the pyramid is closed. As the morning warms up she becomes active and will emerge from the top of the pyramid. You may find that if you move she is very aware you are there and will retreat back underground for a while.

One approach is to lie down with the camera on a flat-out tripod or beanbag. Focus on the top of the pyramid and wait till she emerges. As long as you keep your movements to a minimum she will emerge and fly off. If you have the frame rate high you should be able to catch her as she leaves or returns.

A female tawny mining bee taking off from her 'pyramid' in one of my flower beds. 1Dmk4, 180macro, tripod, 1/1600, f5, ISO 2000. Sheffield.

Masonry bees live either solitary lives or in loose colonies which can range from old snail shells and wooden structures to old walls. We have a large colony in an old wall in our garden. They are often incredibly docile and I find lots just sitting around during cold mornings on our paths and steps. I have to be very careful not to stand on them. However they can be easily moved. (Which I do anyway to pop them into a safer place). I like my images to have either an arty-moody feel or one that tells a story. The choice of where you place the bee and lens allows you a lot of creativity from straight macro shots to wide angle ones.

Wasps

Wasps are definitely not everyone's favourite insect, though they are amazingly beneficial to our gardens. They are strikingly attractive with their very distinctive yellow and black livery. In spring queens leave hibernation and start a small colony. This early nest is often found hanging from a rafter in an old shed and is very architectural. If you stand next to it and keep your movements slow and measured it's quite easy to get shots of the queen moving around the cells. As long as you don't startle her you shouldn't get stung. Later in the year the nests tend to be huge and hidden and the constant activity of hundreds of workers coming and going is a fairly strong deterrent to getting close.

A wasp visiting a blackberry in my garden in late summer. 5Dmk2, 180macro, tripod, 1/250, f8, ISO 800, -1 exposure compensation. Sheffield.

The best wasp photography is done later in the year in late August and September. Many of the colonies have now come to an end. New queens have left and are preparing to hibernate. The many workers are counting time before the first frosts send them to wasp heaven. These workers are partial to fallen fruits, sugary liquids and ivy flowers. You can set up a number of props in your garden such as small pots of jam, blackberries, ivy flowers etc. If you want the wasp to hang around a little longer make a solution of honey in hot water. When it's cool paint it onto a prop such as a blackberry. The wasps love this high energy tipple and as long as you move with care they won't sting you.

These wasps were visiting a number of small jam pots at an outdoor cafe. I don't think I was very popular as I spread a bit more jam around to increase the number of wasps visiting my table. I chose to create a wide angle image to try to show the whole situation. 5Dmk2, 16-35mm, 1/800, f11, ISO 400, handheld. Nottinghamshire.

Hornets

Hornets are far more scarce in the UK. I don't have any colonies near to where I live. All my work with them has been carried out further south. Like wasps they form large colonies and on cool days there are always one or two hornets hanging around the entrance. If you approach carefully it is not too difficult to work with these semi-torpid insects. I would be very cautious about approaching a large colony in mid summer on a hot day though!

If you don't know where the colony is but you keep coming across hornets (or wasps) then use a map and plot a line each time you see one fly off in a purposeful way. Hopefully it is going to the nest. If you do this from a number of places you can work out where the nest is. Another, more invasive, approach that was carried out in the past is to catch one and tie a thin piece of cotton to one of its legs. This hornet is now far easier to watch back to the nest. I have never done this but I do know insect researchers who have and tell me it's quite reliable.

Stag beetle

These are almost certainly the pièce de résistance of the beetle kingdom in Europe. The males and females fly in the evening and at night and are attracted to light. They are fairly restricted to areas of old woodland in the south of the UK. I have worked with them in the New Forest and in Bulgaria where they are quite common. If you are in the right habitat and the right time of year (mid May to late July) you may come across the odd one on warm evenings flying around or crash landing onto a lawn or pavement.

Stag beetles are protected in the UK because we have a significant population which is declining. You can handle them but not offer them for sale. Since they are vulnerable it is best that you confine your photography to a few minutes and allow the beetle to go about its short life as soon as possible. If you know you are in the right area have a few props handy such as nice

I found these two stag beetles in Bulgaria early in the morning before the sun had come up. I chose to under expose the image to create a feeling of twilight. 5Dmk3, 180macro, tripod, 1/2000, f8, ISO 400, -11/3 under exposure.

lichen encrusted branches. Then If you do find one you can quickly pop it onto this and photograph it before you let it go. If you come across one that has crash landed at night you could use artificial light from a torch.

Ladybirds

A 7 spot ladybird walking on a fly agaric toadstool. 1Dmk4, 180macro, 1/200, f5, ISO 1250. I often choose to use dull light in preference to bright sunshine to reduce shadows and stop the white parts of the image being 'blown out'. Sheffield.

We have a number of different species of ladybird in the UK. The most common and recognisable is the red 7 spot. In some years they can swarm and it would be a pity to miss out on such photographic potential. In years like this collect a number of props and place them around the garden.

A 7 spot launching from a small toadstool on my lawn. During the last invasion I used the opportunity to work quite intensively with the ladybirds in my garden. 1Dmk4, 180 macro, 1/500, f5, ISO 500, tripod. Sheffield.

You have two options really. Sit and wait until a ladybird walks onto your prop and photograph it there or catch a few and place them on the prop. During invasion years you will be able to sweep up lots that are stranded on local pavements. In a sense you are rescuing them. You can then release them around and on your props. Then wait with your macro lens for them to work their way onto them. Try to have the camera set with a high speed (such as 1/2000), a low f number (such as f4) and a fast frame rate.

If a ladybird gets to the top of a toadstool there is a fair chance it will open its wings and fly away. If it looks like it might do fire shots with the frame rate at it's highest until it is gone. With luck you will sometimes catch one just at the point of take off. It does take quite a few goes before you get lucky but during invasion years there can be literally hundreds around so your chances increase.

I chose to photograph this black phase of a harlequin ladybird against the reds of a rowan tree. 5Dmk2, 180macro, 1/640, f6.3, ISO 800. Sheffield.

Harlequin ladybirds are an invasive species that are spreading fast across the UK. As a conservation minded photographer you should join the Ladybird survey and send any records in. The harlequin is a new invader and its impact on other species of ladybirds is not fully understood so all records are vital to help form opinion and action (if any) in the future.

Snails and slugs

Snails have always been popular with the wildlife photographer, slugs far less so. Snails occur in a wide range of habitats and you should have quite a few by the end of summer in your garden. The best time to look for them is with a torch on wet nights during the summer and autumn. Snails as subjects purely on their own don't tend to get photographed too often. The more usual picture is when the snail forms part of a more complex image, for example on a shed window or crawling up an old garden boot.

Adult snails have thick shells. Some, like banded snails, have delightful patterns. Others, like the normal grey garden snail, are a little less attractive.

Young snails though have one lovely feature. Their small, thin shells are slightly transparent and allow some light to pass through. The use of a torch backlighting them as they crawl over small toadstools

A small snail backlit with a torch crawling on a toadstool. 5Dmk2, 180macro, 1/400, f8, ISO 1000, -2/3 under exposure, tripod. Sheffield.

As my photography has developed over the last decade I have started to explore new ideas and I am particularly drawn to the use of out of focus water droplets and the effects I can create with them. In this image the ants and droplets are backlit by the evening sun. By placing the lens very close (within the minimum focusing distance) the ants are silhouetted in the droplets. 5Dmk2, 180macro, 1/1000, f3.5, ISO 640, -11/3 exposure compensation, tripod. Derbyshire.

(particularly if you can get the background dark) is very dramatic and appealing. I find lots of baby snails in damp leaf litter in late summer.

Ants

Ant colonies occur in a wide range of habitats though most of the more familiar ones are found in woodland. They can make great photographic subjects though serious caution is needed to reduce the odd nip from the workers!

A large nest of the wood ant is very easy to find. During the colder autumn and spring months the ants are still active but very torpid. If you look closely at the surface of the nest you should see quite a few ants slowly moving around. The main problem is to get close enough to work with them and not get bitten. Long trousers tucked into socks is a good start. Make sure you are ever vigilant - they will scamper up tripod legs if given the chance.

One method that works well is to introduce a few twigs on their runs. If you watch the nest you will see that they have paths to it where a lot of ants are commuting to and fro. A small twig placed in the path will quickly have ants running up it. This should allow you to isolate an individual ant or two to work with.

Wood ants dragging a dead fly across the surface of their nest. 5Dmk2, 180macro, 1.125, f8, ISO 1250, tripod. Derbyshire.

Some ants tend aphids as if they are cows supplying milk. They swap protection for a sugary liquid that the aphids exude. If you find a number of ants patrolling tree trunks and branches its always worth looking out for this behaviour.

Another method is to find a few dead insects and place them on branches of the tree the ants are patrolling. If you have your camera and macro lens set up then hopefully you may get images of an ant as it stops to investigate the dead insect. If this is fresh it may carry it off to its nest giving you a good chance at an unusual and fascinating shot.

Glow worms

These have fascinated us for thousands of years. The idea that an insect can produce its own light (an eerie green one) is just mind boggling. Photographing them is not an easy affair. If you can find one in summer (they are about in July) and you decide to pick it up you will find that the glow slowly fades. This means you have to work with them where you find them.

Glow worms are not worms at all but beetle larvae that feed on snails. Most colonies are southern based in the UK and well documented so it should be possible to find one if there are any near to where you live. When you go to look for them be very aware of where you tread. You don't want to squash the very object you have come to photograph.

When you do find one you will need to use a tripod and slowly move it into position. Try not to shine the torch directly onto the glow worm. Once you are set up take one image (30 secs at ISO 100 or a variation of that ie. 15 secs at ISO 200 etc) to check for the green glow in your image. You won't see the beetle at all. Once you have the glow exposed correctly take another shot but 'tickle' the glow worm with mild torch light. It helps if you check how long to play this over an object first to calculate the desired exposure.

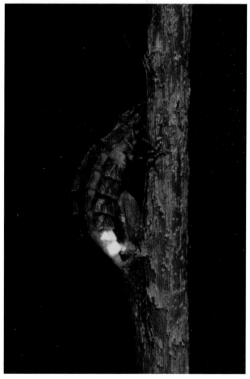

Glow worm. The top image is taken in normal daylight. The bottom is a combination of 30 secs at ISO 100 with the use of a torch to illuminate the body. You won't get many chances because it will probably stop glowing if you shine the torch onto it too much. EOS 5, 100macro, tripod, f8, 100 slide film. Derbyshire.

Lesser celandine, 1Dmk4, 180 macro, 1/2000, ISO 500, f5, -1/3 exposure compensation. Sheffield.

Plants and fungi

The use of field skills to photograph plants and fungi may seem a little over the top but good plant photography does require a number of skills. Britain has thousands of wildflower, fungus and lichen species. Choosing where to start is not easy. However, many wildlife photographers tend to specialise in one or two groups, such as orchids or fungi. As they become familiar with these well known groups they may later branch out to seek new subjects that offer something a little different.

Finding flowering plants, lichens and fungi is not difficult, they literally occur everywhere. The trick is to know where and when to look, as each species generally has its own season. Some, like trees, offer changing aspects all year round, others may only appear for a week or two. There are two approaches you can adopt. One is to simply take your gear for a walk without any precise species in mind and work on anything that interests you.

A different approach is to select a group or even a specific species and hunt for it. This will require a bit of research to find precise dates and potential sites. Luckily today there are a number of very specific site guides that will give you a good starting point. Some groups, such as the orchids, have a number of excellent field guides which will give you this precise data. Other groups like fungi, which can be hard to identify, have many good books which may help with the id process but won't give you the exact sites.

Many local Wildlife Trusts, RSPB and nature groups have websites that may help your research and possibly, even better, will often offer guided walks. Some of these will be themed, such as fungi forays. These are a brilliant way to find good sites and get great help with identifying tricky species. They will also allow you to meet local experts who may be able to help as you develop your interests further.

Photography

Traditionally the basic approach was to find the plant or fungus, set the tripod and camera up and select a big depth of field. Next the image would be checked through the view finder and if necessary any gardening would be carried out. Hopefully the wind would not be causing an issue and then the image would be taken. Today there are a number of variations on this as more photographers are looking for more artistic images.

A single flower of a fly orchid photographed with a 180 macro lens. 1Dmk4, 1/250, f8, ISO 500, tripod flat on the ground. Derbyshire.

Once you have found your desired plant or fungus you will have a number of decisions to make.

Lens choice

This will determine how the image will look and also how far away from the plant you will be working. There is no ideal lens. Many photographers like wide angle images

I photographed these large fungi with a 16-35mm wide angle lens. I was particularly drawn to the dappled light in the wood so chose the wide angle approach. I set the f number to f20 to create a sharp background (large dof), 5Dmk3, 1/60, ISO 1250, -1 exposure compensation, tripod. Derbyshire.

at high depths of field that show the habitat alongside the subject. In this case a 16-35mm on a full frame camera is ideal. If you have a cropped sensor (1.3 or 1.6) the wide angle effect is reduced. You may have to use an ultra wide angle like an 8-15 or an equivalent sized lens.

Probably the most commonly used lens is a macro because it offers the opportunity to get an image of the whole subject with the added bonus of going in very close to isolate a specific feature. Another option that is popular is to use a bigger lens with an extension tube (see p15). The tube allows the lens to be closer to the subject than normal. The bigger lenses (eg a 300 or even a 500) will produce lovely blurred backgrounds, though the dof at any setting is much shallower than with a smaller lens.

Position of view (pov)

The angle at which you approach the plant with your lens will alter dramatically the way it looks in the final image. This is also determined by the f number you choose and what size lens you are using. If you want to create blurred backgrounds you really need to be placing the camera and lens at the same height as the plant, not above it looking down. This means that the background will generally be further away and less in focus. With most plants you should have the option of approaching from a variety of directions so, taking the light into consideration, you should be able to select the best background.

I chose to use my 500 lens with an extension tube to photograph this thrift flower because I wanted to isolate the flower against the mass of pink in the background. 1Dmk4, 500mm, 1/2500, f4, ISO 500. Shetland.

If you are working in a situation where there are many examples of your plant (such as an early purple orchid colony) spend some time slowly walking round to choose the best subjects and the ones with the best background.

If you have decided on a low pov you will often find that looking through the view finder is difficult without lying on the ground and getting a cricked neck. A handy little bit of kit can work wonders here, the angle finder. Try to buy one that does not magnify the image so what you see through it is what the camera takes. The angle finder attaches onto the viewfinder and allows you to look down so you can kneel behind the camera. Be careful with the horizon. It's easy to get this sloping because the angle finder swivels.

An angle finder is a great gadget when your camera is very low to the ground.

Depth of field (dof)

This is determined by the f number you select. If you want a shallow dof choose a low f number, like f4 or f5.6. Generally this will give you the maximum blur in the background and help to set the plant off against it. The drawback is that most plants are not flat so low f numbers will mean parts of the plant will not be sharp.

Selecting a large f number, like f16 or f22, will increase the dof and the amount of sharpness across the plant. The big downside is that the background may now be very distracting. In some cases, especially if you're using a tripod and there is no wind, you could try image stacking (see p170). As with many aspects of wildlife photography

These two images of a lady orchid were photographed on a grassy roadside verge in France. The background was very messy, which at f10 (1/60) (top image) is very distracting. The lower image was taken at f3.5 (1/500) with the same 180 macro lens. The background is still not perfect but it is a vast improvement on f10. 1Dmk2, ISO 500, tripod.

there is a trade off between dof and the quality of your background.

195   Having a low pov increases the chances of better backgrounds and may allow you to try higher f numbers.

Stability

Hand holding your camera can be effective but to allow you to fine tune dof and sharpness a tripod is really necessary. Make sure you have one that is very stable and has no centre column so you can get the camera right down to ground level. If you are using slow speeds use live view or mirror lock up to reduce camera shake. If you do this use a cable release so you don't have to touch the camera.

My friend Mike is using a carbon fibre tripod that has no centre column to photograph this small plant in Scotland. The tripod is not fully open and will go lower.

Focussing

Unlike many other types of wildlife photography you will probably have ample time to experiment because the plant is not going anywhere. Many photographers in the past would have used the auto-focus option but today with live view another approach is now available. Live view will allow you to zoom right into the image and by using manual focus fine tune to get the exact bit you want sharp.

If you choose a low f number make sure you focus exactly on the part you want sharp. However, if you have chosen to select f16 or above you can focus a little into the plant by a few mm back from the front edge. Remember that when you focus the camera's dof is 1/3 in front of the point of focus and 2/3 beyond it.

Gardening

This is the term used by photographers to 'alter' the vegetation around the subject. It simply means removing distracting grasses that would show up next to the plant or in the background. Great care has to be shown here. The golden rule is that you want to try to leave the site as you found it. In reality this is very difficult, even if you simply kneel down you will flatten some vegetation. However, it is fine to remove a few intrusive grass stems. If you are cutting huge clumps out you are almost certainly going too far. Your choice of dof in part determines how much gardening you will have to do. Low dofs generally blur the background enough to reduce the amount of gardening.

This pasque flower was growing very close to the ground and had a number of white grass stalks in the background which I removed. By shooting from a low position and keeping the f number small I managed to keep the background clear. You can still see some of the actual leaves of the pasque flower itself but it would have been irresponsible to have removed these. 1Dmk2, 180 macro, 1/800, f3.5, ISO 400. Cambridgeshire.

Another point to remember is that many plants rely on the other plants, including grasses, growing around them. They may offer physical support so once removed your subject is more likely to be damaged by wind. The surrounding plants also raise the humidity within the local micro-climate that your subject lives in and they may help to disguise or hide the plant from animals and humans.

If you choose to garden try to bend distracting plants out of the way and use string and tent pegs to hold them down. Once you have finished 'fluff' up the grass again. The most likely thing you will garden out are dead white grasses which show up as white streaks in the image.

A few years ago I went to photograph some butterfly orchids that were growing in a field in the Peak District. I was told where I could expect to find them and that a camera club had been there a few days before. I thought I might have to search a bit for them because the field had a lot of long grass. However, I found them within a few minutes. All I had to do was spot the 3 metre 'crop circle' around each individual flower!

The problem of wind

One of the biggest headaches for the plant photographer is wind. Even on still days tall plants never seem to be actually still. You can end up sitting for ages with the cable release in hand just waiting for the plant to stop swaying! A couple of options exist to help. If you set a higher ISO you will get a faster speed. Double the ISO, you double the speed. If you can get a reasonable speed, say 1/250+, and take a few images on the fast frame rate you will probably have a couple of sharp ones.

An old trick is to carry a couple of thin (to reduce root damage) metal tent pegs and some flexible wire ties. If the plant is swaying too much push a tent peg into the soil next to it and loosely tie it to the peg with the wire tie. Make sure you don't pull it tight or you may damage the plant.

Even though this mountain pansy is a small plant it grows in upland areas where the grass is generally short which means that still days are very rare. I had to wait for quite a while before the wind dropped and I had to use my camera bag as a wind break as well. I have gardened out a few intrusive grass stalks but left a few to give a sense of place. I shot from a low pov and used my depth of field preview button to decide on the amount of dof I wanted. I found that f10 gave me enough depth for the flower but still left the background blurred. 1Dmk4, 180 macro, 1/350, f10, ISO 400, tripod. Derbyshire.

Another option is to use a wind break. Simply placing your camera bag next to the plant can work wonders. You can take this idea further and make a wind break with cloth and small poles. You can then set up the poles around the plant (but not in its background), run the cloth around them and attach it with small clamps. It can be a bit fiddly but the plant is not going to fly away!

A third idea is to make a wind tent. This is a collapsible box of fine cloth and supports which you erect around the plant. Personally I prefer the more simple method of sticks and cloth. It's far more versatile.

Lighting the plant

The photographer's perennial problem. What is the best light for plant photography? Oddly, bright sunshine, unless it's very early or late in the day, can be a nightmare, creating horrendous shadows and burning out subtle whites and yellows.

Strong sunlight also restricts the direction from which you photograph the plant. Bright, overcast days are probably as near to the ideal as you can get.

Lady's slipper orchid. I photographed this plant at a nature reserve where any gardening would have been out of the question. By choosing a low pov I have kept the background quite clean even though you can see out of focus flowers. I personally like these as they add a sense of the number of flowers. I chose a dull day because the yellows tend to burn out very easily in any bright light. I was lucky that it had been raining for part of the morning which left a couple of rain drops on the bottom of the flower. 5Dmk3, 180 macro, 1/1000, f3.5, ISO 800, -1 2/3 exposure compensation, tripod. Lancashire.

You can add additional light in a few ways. Flash can be effective. If set to a low power (under expose on the flash) it can put a bit of light into shadows and brighten colours.

A simple reflector is a really good gadget to have in your camera bag. You can make your own by scrunching up aluminium foil then flattening it and gluing it to a bit of card. Not only is it effective, you won't mind losing it either. However, for a few pounds you can buy a reflector that is silver on one side and gold on the other. The silver side reflects white light, the gold side warms up the image very nicely. These reflectors, such as those made by Lastolite, fold up (so don't

take much room) and are very light. They cost between £10 and £20.

Here I am photographing a common spotted orchid using a home made reflector. Derbyshire.

A third option is to use a torch. This has the advantage of being able to direct the light exactly where you want - reflectors are a bit limited here. Try to use an old fashioned torch that has the old filament bulbs which tend to produce a warmer light. Many of the neon types produce a bluer light. Simply by moving the torch closer or further away you can increase or reduce the amount of light. They are also excellent to add backlighting. The one thing to avoid is adding too much light and having an effect that looks like the subject has been blasted by a spotlight.

Hairy curtain crust is a common fungus growing on dead branches in the woods near to where I live. These woods tend to be quite dark so I chose to backlight the fungus with a torch to add some light and mood into the image. My camera was on a tripod so I could hold the torch and see the effect in live view as I moved it around. I chose a big dof because the fungus was small which meant I had a very slow speed. I used a cable release to fire the shutter. 5Dmk3, 180 macro, 0.3sec, f25, ISO 800. Sheffield.

When you use a torch or reflector you should find that the use of a tripod helps greatly because it frees your hands.

Fungi

Most of the preceding sections about plants apply equally to fungi. There is one difference though that is worth noting. With any plant photography you should never pick the plant. Often it will be protected under the Wildlife and Countryside Act. Even really common ones such as bluebells are protected by law. Weeds are not, but then a weed is only a plant in a place you don't want it. Weeds in an agricultural field are wild flowers somewhere else!

I backlit this small grass stem fungus with a torch to show up the gills. 5Dmk3, 180 macro, 1/10, f25, ISO 800, -12/3 exposure compensation (which you often need when backlighting), mirror lock up, cable release, tripod. Sheffield.

Fungi are picked quite extensively by many people to eat. Many are in part identified by their gills which are on the underside of the cap. Some traditional fungi photographers, especially if they want to use the images for identification purposes, pick one toadstool and place it next to another to show both sides of the cap. You need to be careful if you decide to do this - a few rare fungi are protected by law. I am also not sure it is the right way to go for the modern wildlife photographer. I get really frustrated when

I work in some of my local woods that are fungi rich and find many have been picked or left turned upside down by other photographers. My own personal view is that we shouldn't be doing this.

Colour

In most cases digital images are fairly faithful to the colours of the plants they depict. In the past when slide film was popular bluebells were a nightmare to get blue, they invariably looked pink. This is less of a problem now but a couple of orchids, such as early purples and marsh, can look too pinkish in some images. It probably depends on the light at the time but it always pays to keep an eye out and try to alter the white balance if you come across this effect.

I spent a lot of time working in this dune slack where huge numbers of southern marsh orchids grew a few years ago. The colours never looked correct on my monitor but they were close enough. However, when I projected them with my digital projector they took on a bluish cast. 1Dmk4, 180macro +1.4, 1/1250, f5, ISO 500, tripod. Lincolnshire.

Creative approaches

A few photographers work with white acrylic sheets to produce plant (and even insect) images that resemble Victorian botanical illustrations. There are a number of ways to go about this. Possibly the most complex is to use a white sheet, a wind tent and a number of flash guns to create the light. This is the most controllable method but it does involve a lot of equipment which will need lugging into the field. The more gear you use means more disruption to the

area you work in and increases the chances of damaging other plants.

Hedge bindweed photographed using a white acrylic sheet. 1Dmk3, 180 macro, F9, 1/320, ISO 500, +2 2/3 exposure compensation, tripod. Sheffield.

This image shows the approach I use to produce white images. The plant is on the other side of the sheet, through which sunlight is shining. Here the sheet is held in an old school science lab clamp.. The tripod is open fully to get the lens close to the ground to get the low pov I wanted.

A simpler approach is to use natural sunlight. Sunny weather is needed - just after dawn and before dusk being the best times when the sun is low in the sky. The idea is

I found this wax cap growing on the edge of a woodland. I chose to experiment with double exposures and found that 2 exposures worked well, one with the fungi sharp, the other with it slightly out of focus. The combined image (created in camera) has a lovely soft feel around the fungi and leaves. It is also more saturated. These are very much Marmite images. I love them but whenever I show them there are always a few negative comments from the more traditional photographers. 5Dmk3, 180 macro, low pov, 1/640, f3.5, -1 exposure compensation, ISO 800, tripod, Sheffield. The image on the right is the same fungus taken at the same settings but with a single exposure.

that you let the sun shine through the white sheet, then the plant, then into your camera. In a way it's backlighting the plant. You will need to use one or two small tent pegs or a clamp to hold the sheet up, which you place just behind your subject. A bit of gardening will normally be needed (particularly behind the sheet) because grasses etc will show up as shadows. The best method is to take a test shot and adjust the exposure compensation. You may have to go to +2 or even +3 to get the light right.

The choice of flower or plant is also critical. Try to choose flowers that are translucent and allow some light to shine through them.

Dark, thick plants don't work so well. If the flower is too dark against the white acrylic sheet you can add a bit of light by shining a torch onto it. You will certainly have to experiment before you produce images you like. I tend to use sheets of white acrylic of either A4 or A3 size. You will need to use a tripod with a medium size lens, like a 180 macro. You will also need to lie down on the ground. This in itself can cause problems because you will flatten what you lie on. Clearly you must make sure you don't lie on any of the flowers you or someone else will work with, so great care is needed.

Multiple exposures

Until fairly recently most DSLRs didn't offer this feature. Luckily today a few camera manufacturers have now added it to a number of the newer bodies. If you think you want to try this method make sure the camera body you buy has it as a feature.

You can select any number of multiple exposures in the camera. You also have a number of other options which include taking each image separately and getting the camera to balance the exposure of all the images so the final image is exposed correctly.

A different approach with double exposures is to take 2 images but move the camera between them and focus on 2 points. Here I first took an image of the fungus, then moved the camera and took an image of the trees. I had a few trial attempts before I managed to place the fungus between the trunks. I desaturated it and had to increase the contrast when I processed the image to remove the misty effect that double exposures can produce. 5Dmk3, 180macro, 1/250 and 1/25, at f3.5 and f11, ISO 400, tripod. Sheffield.

This is an area where you will need to experiment, which is great fun. You are never sure what the images will be like but as you gain confidence you will start to be able to predict and control the final image better.

A simple approach is to set the camera to 2 exposures. Make sure it's on a firm tripod and compose the image you want. Take one image by focusing on the plant then de-focus for the second image. You can experiment by how much out of focus you use or set 3 or 4 exposures and de-focus 2 or 3 by different

amounts. The effect you are looking for is an ethereal sense of blur around sharp flowers or fungi. They are a bit like Marmite though. Some will love them, others definitely won't. Another effect you will notice is that the final images seem far more saturated.

Another idea is to take repeated images of the same subject and move the camera slightly between each exposure so you get a series of images of the same subject across one image. All of these have a slightly veiled or masked quality which you may like. You can adjust the contrast later when you process the images at home to reduce this slightly.

It is possible to really let your imagination fly. You could change lenses between exposures (don't switch the camera off though!) to create giant or minute subjects in surrealistic situations. You can also try changing the background completely.

Backgrounds

In most cases you will photograph the plant or fungi exactly where it is and the background is whatever is behind it. You could though try to add a sense of place by trying to shoot slightly upwards. Fungi that grow on woodland floors are ideal candidates to try this approach. You will need to get the camera really low. You might even have to dig a shallow hole to lower it enough. You will find that it is easier to handhold it as well.

I lay down to photograph this honey fungus with some trees in the background. By using a low f number holes in the trees' canopy appear as circles with the odd branch. 5Dmk3, 180mm, 1/500, f3.5, ISO 1250, handheld. Derbyshire.

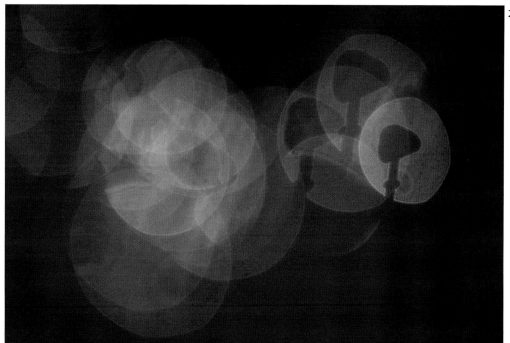

Experimentation can take you to so many places. I love playing around with the camera settings in different situations. Once when I was photographing some very small fungi against backlit raindrops I produced the image above. It did take a while before I perfected this style. The trick was to get the camera and lens within its minimum focussing distance when the sun was low in the sky, creating strong backlighting. When I show these images I get very mixed reactions. Some love them for the colours and interpretation of nature, others don't because they can't recognise the species. I guess I have moved away from this older view of wildlife photography and see it now much more as an art form where I try to evoke emotions more than simply recording the natural world. However, which approach you take is whatever satisfies you. You must like your own work. Don't let anyone dictate to you how it should be done and tell you that your approach is wrong. 1DX, 180 macro + 1.4 converter, 1/800, f5, ISO 800, -1 exposure compensation. Sheffield.

The idea is to shoot into the trees and create moody hot spots and shadows that convey a feeling of autumn woodland.

Another approach is to use prepared backgrounds on sheets of card. You can then select bizarre colours or nice warm tones when the natural background is too distracting.

Bokeh

Bokeh is about the quality of blur in out of focus parts of the image, usually the background. In many examples of this you can see hot spots like lights or raindrops rendered as circles in the image. It is easy to create by using backlit raindrops. If the sun is not strong enough a torch or flash can be used.

I photographed these small yellow fungi on a bright day after a period of rain. By using a small f number the raindrops are shown as out of focus circles. If you increase the f number they start to form small edges (like here) which is caused by the diaphragm that creates the aperture (hole size). 5Dmk3, 180 mm, 1/320, f7.1, ISO 250, tripod, +1 exposure compensation. Sheffield.

A black vulture attacking and greedily eating the black rubber window seal on a car in the Florida Everglades. It might not be the most attractive image but never overlook images that tell a story, particularly those that have a human interest angle. 1DX, 500mm, 1/800, f5.6, ISO 400, handheld.

Wildlife photography abroad

The wildlife opportunities on offer overseas today are incredible. In the past you would have had to plan every step of the way and have conducted a vast amount of research to find places where wildlife is both approachable and photographable.

Today a number of specialist companies take much of the load out of the equation and have a bewildering array of fantastic trips that now cover most of the planet. However, in virtually all cases you will still have to plan for your trip and get your photographic gear on a plane. Perhaps the most asked question concerning overseas trips is 'How do I get all my camera gear on the plane safely?'

A red fox walks across the snowy landscape in Yellowstone. For every trip that I run or go on I have to think carefully about how much gear I can take and which lenses will be essential. For Yellowstone there is no hide work and most of the time the animals can be distant so a 500mm lens was essential. However, many animals can approach you really closely as well so a 70-200 is ideal. This lens also allows you to frame animals in their environment and to take some landscape shots. 1DX, 500mm + 1.4 converter, 1/500, f5.6, ISO 2000, handheld.

With all plane journeys you can take two types of bag on the plane. One is called checked baggage and goes into the hold of the plane. The other is termed carry-on baggage which, as its name suggests, you physically keep with you all the time and carry it onto the plane.

Checked baggage can go missing. Anyone who has travelled a lot will have heard a number of tales about this and may have

experienced arriving at some destination only to find that their bag has gone astray. Generally the bag will turn up a day or two later and the airline will arrange to have it delivered to where you are staying. However, if you are moving around a lot this can be difficult.

One firm idea that many experienced photographers have is that whatever happens to their checked bag they can still photograph fully when they arrive at their chosen destination. This means that all the essential camera equipment is held in the carry-on bag. The problem here lies with the maximum size and weight allowed for this. You will have to plan carefully exactly which lenses and accessories you can take with you. Unfortunately the size of the carry-on bag and its weight allowance can vary from one airline to another.

Choice of camera bag

Most manufacturers state the exact outside dimensions of their bags and you need to look carefully at this when you decide which bag to buy. Some have wheels which can be great when you are walking miles down neverending corridors to the flight departure gate. However, these bags might not be so ideal if you intend to use them as your normal camera bag in the UK. The leading manufacturers of camera bags today are fully aware that many are used as carry-on bags and design them to fit the aircraft's overhead lockers.

I use a Think Tank Airport Addicted V2 and find it ideal. Other bag manufacturers such as Tamrac, Guru, Lowepro and Manfrotto all have their devotees and all make excellent bags. When choosing a bag try to go to a shop where you have a good choice and try out the various bags with your lenses in. You don't want to find out a few weeks later that you get a sore or stiff back every time you hoist it onto your shoulders. All these bags have internal dividers to keep your cameras and lenses safe plus a number of pockets for cards, cable releases and so on.

A Think Tank bag with two bodies, 500mm f4 and 300mm f2.8 lenses with battery charger.

To give an idea of bag and gear weights the following table is based on my own equipment (all Canon) and a Think Tank Airport Addicted V2 camera bag.

Bag + 7Dmk2 (body) + 1DX(body) + 500mm lens + 300mm 2.8 lens + 1.4 converter + battery charger + odds and ends (cable release, extension tube, cards, spare battery etc) = 12.8 kg

Bag + 7Dmk2 + 500mm lens + 1.4 converter + battery charger + odds and ends (cable release, extension tube, cards etc) = 8.2 kg

Bag + 1DX + 500mm lens + 300mm 2.8 lens + 70-200 2.8 lens + 1.4 converter + battery charger + odds and ends (cable release, extension tube, cards etc) = 13.4 kg

Some airlines allow 2 carry on bags but they may have a combined weight allowance - you need to check carefully before you book.

The biggest dilemma is when your gear and bag weighs more than the carry-on allowance. You have 2 choices really. One, choose an airline that has a larger allowance (though this may mean extra cost). Two, try to work around the problem. One solution is to put some of your equipment into your pockets which may sound a bit impractical. However, you could look at the use of specialist luggage jackets which you wear onto the plane, such as Bagket or Jaktogo. They retail around £70 and are a good way of solving the problem. You will need to check if the pockets are big enough to carry camera bodies and smaller lenses. In the past many photographers bought a photo vest for this exact purpose.

Airline baggage allowances

The following table shows some airlines and their carry-on and checked baggage allowance for economy flights (taken from each airline's website June 2015). Many airlines have more generous allowances for business and first class. This is a guide only. Things may and do change so please don't take this as gospel but check when you book your flight. Most airlines (including those in the table) allow a second carry-on bag for personal use, such as a handbag or laptop bag. The dimensions of this vary and its weight may be combined with the larger carry-on bag. Make sure you check when you book and also before departure because the airline may change the baggage weight allowance after you have booked. This has happened to me once and it took some convincing that I should be permitted the weight allowance at the time of booking. If you find that you have a problem check out the airline's website. You can often pay for an extra bag or extra weight allowance.

A hovering magnificent humming bird in Costa Rica. 5Dmk3, 70-200mm 2.8, 1/6400, f4, ISO 3200, handheld.

Airline	Carry-on bag dimensions cm	Carry-on bag weight	Checked bag weight
easyJet	56x45x25 + 45x36x20	As long as you can lift the bag into the overhead locker	20Kg
Ryanair	55x40x20 plus I small handbag 35x20x20	10kg	15 or 20Kg you select when you book
British Airways	56x45x25 + 45x36x20	23kg combined	23Kg
American Airlines	56x36x23 (extra personal bag under seat in front of you)	As long as you can lift the bag into the overhead locker	23Kg
Air France	55x35x25 plus I small handbag	12kg	23Kg
Air India	55x40x20 plus I small handbag	8kg	20Kg
Delta	114 (total of length + width + height) plus I small handbag	No max weight allowance apart from certain routes.	32Kg
Finnair	56x45x25 plus I small handbag	8kg	23Kg
Flybe	55x40x23	10kg	20Kg
Iceland air	55x40x20 plus I small handbag	10kg	23Kg
KLM	55x25x35 plus personal bag	12kg combined with second accessory bag	23Kg
Lufthansa	55x40x23 plus I small handbag	8kg	23Kg
Quantas	115 (L+W+H) plus I small handbag	7kg,	30Kg
United Airlines	56x35x22 + 22x25x43	no weight limit on website	32Kg
Wizz Air	large carry-on (pay a bit extra) 56x45x25	As long as you can lift the bag into the overhead locker	32Kg

A couple of further points will need checking out. In some cases when you book a trip that has a stopover you may find that the second leg or return journey is with a different airline. Make sure you check through your itinerary carefully and check their baggage allowance is sufficient.

A few airlines will point out that if the flight is full and there are a lot of carry-on bags some people will be asked to put theirs in the hold - a potential nightmare for a photographer! If the airline allows priority boarding (which only costs a few pounds more) you are usually exempt from this and you will be one of the first onto the plane so will find space for your camera bag. Check with the airline. This problem tends to apply more to the budget airlines.

Another issue when you change planes is that the second plane may actually have a much smaller space for the carry-on bags. This should not be a problem with international flights but it is one that catches many photographers out when they switch to a small plane for an internal flight. I remember once having quite a debate when I last flew to Shetland. I was eventually allowed to take my camera bag onto the plane but it had to go under the seat in front of me and it only just fitted.

You will find it difficult to get your tripod and head into your carry-on bag so most photographers consign it to the checked bag. A lightweight carbon fibre tripod is ideal for this. If you have a heavy head you either just have to put up with it or possibly have a second lighter head to use for travelling.

If you travel with a bean bag take it empty and buy a bag of rice when you reach your destination. Later, before you fly home, you can simply empty it.

Your choice of checked bag is a personal one but most people tend to either have a soft holdall/rucksack design or a hard plastic type. There are advantages for both. I use a soft style bag but when I had an extra lens in it once (which was carefully wrapped in its centre) I found later that the end glass had been pushed right into the lens. It must have taken an incredible knock or drop but probably if I'd had a hard style bag it might not have happened.

If you are going on a trip as part of a group try to find out if possible what gear the others are taking. You may be able to share lenses if they are likely to only be used infrequently and it's good to know that there are other battery chargers you could use if yours goes missing.

Never forget plug adaptors, take at least two. Some travellers have a short ganger with four plug sockets and need only one adaptor.

Backing up on a trip

A few years ago when laptops had smaller memories and cards were very expensive many photographers took a backup device

An Epson P7000. Unfortunatly now no longer available new. Small handheld backup storage devices are not as popular as they were a few years ago. However, if you don't want to take a laptop and want to copy your cards as a backup they are still very usefull. Newer models now provide up to 1 TB of hard drive space.

or two to store their images on the trip. Many brands were available at various prices from under a £100 to over £500 depending on the hard drive size and whether they had a viewable screen or not. Today it seems that far fewer photographers use them. I still use an Epson P7000 which has a 160 GB hard drive and love it. These are sadly no longer available but there are a number of alternative devices that take CF and SD cards and have capacities that go up to a 1TB. The alternative is to take your laptop on the trip, much bulkier and heavier but if you like processing your images and sharing them it is an ideal solution.

Many photographers today don't seem to back up their work when away but simply take enough cards to last the whole trip. It's not a bad idea. Cards, if tried before the trip, rarely fail and if they do backing them up wouldn't have helped anyway. The price of cards falls constantly and their capacities are always increasing. A word of caution though. It's tempting to get big capacity cards such as 128 GB ones. They will hold a lot of images, even if you shoot in RAW, but if they fail you will also lose a lot of images. Many people tend to compromise and use 16 or 32 GB cards. At least if one fails you won't lose all the trip's images. Failure is rare but it does happen.

Some trips can be a once in a life time adventure. It pays to spend a bit of time researching carefully exactly what the situation will be like. When I went to Rwanda a few years ago to photograph mountain gorillas I made sure I knew how much walking I would have to do, in what sort of terrain, which camera gear and lenses I would need and how to make sure I wouldn't suffer problems from high humidity and rain. When I got there I was fully prepared and consequently had a fantastic hour with an amazing group of gorillas. 1Dmk3, 70-200mm, 1/250, f4, ISO400, handheld.

Dust and humidity problems

Dust and humidity may be a problem on some trips so you will need to check out if they are potential issues and prepare for them. Dust can be a real issue when working from an open jeep such as in India or Africa. One way to reduce the problem is to take an old pillow case and keep the camera and lens wrapped in this when on the jeep, removing it only when photographing. It's also a good idea to try not to change lenses in these situations as well. A quick clean of your gear every evening will help to reduce the problem. You should consider every year or so getting your camera body professionally cleaned. It's not cheap if you go for a total body clean but it is worth it.

If you are travelling to a humid country then a plastic bag to cover the camera and lens will help. If you have the space take a bag of desiccant, like silica gel. Make sure you get the ones where you can see the colour change from pink to blue. You simply pop one into the plastic bag with your camera and lens overnight to absorb any moisture that may be causing a problem. You can dry the desiccant out in a warm oven, car engine or in the sun.

In an emergency if your camera gets wet and you are worried about it get a bag of dry rice and submerge it in the rice. Seal the bag and leave it. The rice will act as a desiccant.

Many photographers use UV filters on the front of their lenses to protect them from damage and dirt. This is very much a personal thing. Many don't see any benefit of adding another piece of glass in front of the lens. However, if the lens is dropped it may just save the front element.

A watchmaker's Phillips and normal screw driver can be a useful addition to your luggage to help with any of those small fiddly screws that may come loose. The other thing not to forget is your Allen key if your tripod head needs one. Don't pack it or the screw drivers in your carry-on bag though. They will almost certainly be confiscated when you go through security at the airport. Pack them in your hold luggage.

Which lenses to take

Which lenses to take can often be a bit of a headache. You will need to talk to your trip organiser closely. It's no good thinking that a 300mm is ideal and find out that everything is often miles away and a 500 with converter would be far better. You may not have a 500mm but there are now a few companies where you can hire one for a reasonable amount (approx £250+ for a Canon 500mm f4 for a week, much less for a Sigma 50-500 or Tamron 150-600mm). They may also deliver it to your door.

Using fixed position hides

The other issue to think about concerns fixed hides. The animal (usually a bird) is at a set distance from your lens. However, a recommended 500mm will give a very different image size if it's on a full frame or a 1.3 or a 1.6 cropped sensor. So when you book check carefully which lens is recommended with exactly which sensor size. A zoom lens such as a 100-400 or 200-400 can often be the answer and is far more flexible when you are not sure how close the animal is likely to be. However, if you have invested in a quality 500mm you will almost certainly want to take it and use it.

On many photo trips where you are working with birds at the nest or at a baiting site the folk on the ground will have the whole set running with perches in situ. This can be fine but you need to consider if you are happy with having all your images on the same perches as everyone else on that trip (and probably everyone on every other trip before and after yours). The reality is that most photographers don't seem that bothered but a few do like to try for more unique work so it's worth asking whether it's possible to change the perch for your photography. You may be able to find your own and get the guys on the ground to set them up for you. Once you have finished take your perch away and replace it with the original one.

Most perches tend to be of dead wood and often a bit white. Staining them can reduce any glare. A few tea bags can be a wonderful aid! Another tip is to take a small plastic bottle, some electrician's tape and cable ties. You can now set up perches with fresh leaves on them. Cable tie your new perch to whatever stake they have set in the ground, place the end of your perch into the small plastic bottle and either tape or cable tie it to the stake. Add water to the bottle and the leaves should stay fresh for a few hours. In hot weather they will often wilt in minutes and look terrible in your images without water. This tip is just as valid when working with living perches back home as well.

When you are using a hide it's essential that you have the right focal length lens. A zoom could be an ideal answer. In these two images from Hungary I took both my 500mm and 70-200mm 2.8, + a 1.4 converter. I used both with a 7Dmk3 (crop factor of 1.6) and a 1DX (full frame). Top, Red-footed falcon, 1DX, 500mm 1/1000, f4, ISO 800. Bee-eater, 7Dmk2 70-200, 1/1250, f4, ISO 640.

Workflow

When you start wildlife photography getting close to the animal and creating images you are pleased with unfortunately is not the whole story. Time has to be spent in front of a computer. For some this is great, for others it is a bit of a chore. Work flow describes the order in which you view, process and store your images. There are probably as many ways of doing this as there are wildlife photographers but most will work to a fairly standard system. Review - delete unwanted images – catalogue – process – store – backup.

The following system is how I do it. It is not necessarily the best system but it's the one that I find works well for me.

During a trip or a day's photographic work I review the images on my camera whenever I have any downtime and delete all those that are obviously duff. If I am not sure I leave them alone.

Once back in my office I load the card into a card reader and copy (not move) all the images into an empty folder on my C drive.

I use a programme called Breeze Browser to do an initial trawl. I like Breeze Browser because I can review four images at one time and magnify all four simultaneously. I use this to check for sharpness etc. I delete as I go along any soft images and any that are very similar. If in doubt I leave them.

Comparing 4 images of a hummingbird in Breeze Browser. I can zoom in on all 4 and compare for sharpness and choose which to keep.

I next batch rename them and often put the year into the title e.g. Blackcap 15. I keep the file name quite simple, possibly Blackcap, male singing, 15. I keep the name of the species first so it's easier to find later.

I then batch complete the IPTC data. This is the data hidden within the image that picture libraries and competitions may look at. Here I add my name as author. (Some people put their full address and phone number here as well). I then give it a file name and fill in the description with species name, Latin name, any behaviour and location e.g. Male blackcap in spring, Sylvia atricapilla, singing, S. Yorks, UK. Lastly I assign it copyright status and put my name in this box.

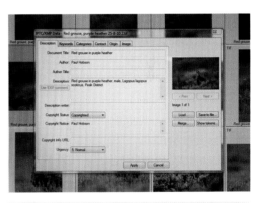

Filling in the IPTC data for a red grouse image. I can do this for individual images or select any number and batch complete to save time.

I have created my own filing system in a separate hard drive. It's fairly basic with folders named Birds, Mammals, Inverts, Reptiles etc. Each is then subdivided as I go along e.g. Birds – corvids – hooded crow – converted. For each species I have two folders, one into which I copy the RAW files and a second where I store all the converted TIFFS or JPEGS.

There are many alternatives to filing your images and many programmes can help set this up for you. I chose to do it my way so that I could create the style of filing system that I understood and I knew exactly where all the images were. Plus it does not depend on any programme as it stands alone outside them. I also found it was easier to back up this way. Saying this I can almost hear the chorus of comments giving alternative ideas and programmes. The thing is to explore a number of ideas before you settle on one that works for you.

Once I have moved (not copied) the images to the correct folder in my hard drive after the initial review and labelling I am ready to convert them. I don't delete the original images on the card until I have backed up the images in my computer (see later).

I use Lightroom for all my image processing as I find it quick and simple. I import all the RAW images I want to process and work through them. Once they have been processed I convert them to 8 bit TIFFS and export them to the converted folder for that species. I used to export them as 16 bit TIFFS in case I wanted to work on them later but found it didn't seem to make any difference and I had to convert them to 8 bit before I sent them to libraries anyway. I save them all as TIFFS but I think that there is no visible loss of quality in reality if I export them as high res JPEGS. All libraries seem to sell them as JPEGS anyway and all competitions seem happy with JPEGS.

Every time I have converted a new batch of images and stored them in the computer I back them up. I have two four TB external drives that at the moment can hold all my images. I simply copy the folder with the new images onto the external hard drive and let it replace the folder there. One of the hard drives is kept at home but is hidden. The other is kept at a separate address. This may seem a bit OTT but if the worse ever happens at least somewhere I will have all my images stored and up to date (relatively).

Every month I swap the two hard drives over and do a full backup of all my folders to the one I have brought home. I therefore have three copies of my images, one kept in the computer and two on external hard drives. Every few years I have to increase the hard drive capacity of my main computer and use larger external hard drives.

Processing Images

I use Adobe Lightroom V5 for this but there are lots of other programmes that will do a similar job. I prefer to stick to one programme and learn how it can work for me. I don't really want to have to learn how different programmes work and chop and change processing programmes. Lightroom allows me to alter quite a few parameters in each image before I store them. I rarely open them again in Photoshop for any further editing unless it's resizing them.

Part of the menu in Lightroom V5 when I have imported an image and am working on it in the Develop part of the programme.

A screen shot of Lightroom as I start to work on a Great Bustard image in Develop.

For each image I will review and potentially alter the following parameters.

I switch the main menu to Develop and work on one image at a time. I check the orientation and composition and use the crop tool to swivel it slightly if needed and crop for a better composition. I try not to crop too much, though this depends on the sensor size. I will crop a bit more if I need to if it's from a full sensor camera.

I then use the spot tool to remove any spots from the image. If I am processing lots of similar images I will use a right click of the mouse to go to settings and save the spot removal. I can then paste it for all the subsequent images which can save loads of time. You can do this for any of the settings if you are processing lots of images and even process them all at once if you want.

I then switch to the slider menu below. I may adjust the white balance a bit to warm up or cool down the image.

Exposure is obvious. I may use contrast if the image is flat (shot in dull light) but I tend to use the white and black sliders more to

get the effect I am looking for.

Highlights is good for any area that is overexposed and glary. You can choose to use the slider for the whole image or use the brush tool and brush over the area you want to dull down. The brush tool can be made to any size and you can choose (using the sliders once you have highlighted it) how far you want to go. You can also do this retrospectively to change the intensity of the effect before you close the brush tool.

Shadows will lighten up any dark areas. Again it's a choice between doing the whole image or using the brush. I may add a small bit of saturation.

The clarity tool is similar to contrast but works well in the mid tones. I will often give it a tweak instead of using contrast or the black and white slider.

If the image is a challenging one with lots of dark and light areas and needs a lot of work I will play around with the tone curve and sliders a bit. I must admit that unless it's a once in a lifetime image I hope to keep the processing to a minimum.

The next menu down is the HSL one and here I sometimes slide one of the colours a bit. Generally this is to intensify one colour to

If it's too good to be true it usually is. All these birds genuinely landed on this footpath sign on the same morning but not together. I had set up the sign next to one of my winter bird feeders. I was asked to create this image to illustrate a talk/debate about the authenticity of wildlife images and how easy it is to clone and 'cheat'. However, cheating is a harsh word and if you are always honest about what you do there is nothing wrong with playing around with the power of your image processing programmes.

add a bit more punch or I use the blue one to give the sky a bit more colour.

I always note what ISO I shot the image on. If it's high (1000+) I will expect a bit of noise so I will use the mask tool under sharpening. I hold the alt key down and slide the mask until the outline of the subject is sharp and the noise in the background (thousands of white dots) disappears. I may also slide the luminance a small amount (under noise reduction) first. I try not to slide it too much as it does soften the image a bit. Sharpening is pre-set to 25 and I always leave it as this. If I want to sharpen more I will open the converted image in Photoshop and work on it there.

That's pretty much all I do. The vast majority of my images will be close to what I want them to look like. That's the art of getting it right in the camera. All my processing is to improve it a bit, not to radically change

the image. Once I am satisfied I export the image. If I need to do any more work such as cloning any distracting elements out I open the image in Photoshop and work on it.

How much should you change in an image?

This is a hotly debated issue with no obvious answer. It all really depends on your own beliefs and what you intend the image to be used for. If you are in a camera club and showing creative images the world is your oyster, you can do anything. In natural history there are firm, though slightly changeable conventions, depending on where the image is to be used. Competitions will have rules you should study before you manipulate any images and enter them.

Most people feel that gentle alteration of white balance, contrast, sharpness and saturation are fine. The basic idea is that the processed image still looks like the original but has a bit of an improvement. If it has altered radically and bares little resemblance to the original you have gone too far. Cloning things in and out is a bit of a 'no no' for many though I will do it every now and then. I don't do it for competition images but I believe that cloning out a bit of grass or a twig in the background is not wrong. The inherent natural history of the image remains intact. It is still real (in my eyes). I will

I and the group I was co-leading to Yellowstone spent an incredible hour with this bobcat in the most gorgeous light. Bob (as our guides called him) had one of his ear tufts missing. It's how he is and is part of his character. However, I can understand that some people would be tempted to clone a tuft onto his left ear to match the one on his right. It may increase sales and it may help with a competition entry. Who would know? Well, I would and everyone else who photographed Bob that winter would. But does it change the natural history value of the image? I would argue not but I know that many people would disagree. 1DX, 500mm, 1/1600, f5.6, ISO 200, handheld.

clone dirt from perches and muck from birds' beaks. Im aware however that not everyone feels like this. I still see lots of images every year that never quite ring true. I would never accuse someone of manipulating or falsely changing their images but I suspect it does go on a lot of the time. Shadows that run in two directions, unbelievable depths of field, images with two or more animals together that you strongly suspect never occurred in reality and barn owls with legs where you know a falconer's jess has been cloned out are often seen. Again there is nothing wrong with any of the above if it is declared and the end use is a suitable one.

One argument that is often presented is that the image should look the same as the reality of the situation - if someone else was there with you they would recognise the image. This doctrine has a serious flaw though. Creative techniques done 'in camera' such as creating bokeh and combining multiple images never resemble the scene you see with your eyes. If five photographers stood next to each other each may shoot their images differently, in some cases very differently. This is part of what photography is all about, not faithfully copying what you see but manipulating it 'in camera' to create the style you want.

The bottom line is to be honest to yourself and the natural history of the image and if necessary declare what you have done. Remember, keeping the original RAW is your proof of the level of your manipulation. If you are entering competitions make sure you read and stick to the rules.

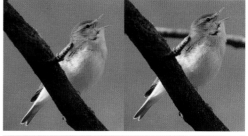

Wood warbler singing. The left image has had the twig behind the bird removed. The natural history has not been altered, or has it? And is this so bad?

Appendices

RPS Nature Photographer's code of conduct

Written by The Nature Group of The Royal Photographic Society. Revised in 1997 and 2007 in consultation with the RSPB and the three Statutory Nature Conservation Councils.

Introduction

There is one hard and fast rule, whose spirit must be observed at all times

"The welfare of the subject is more important than the photograph."

Photography should not be undertaken if it puts the subject at risk. Risk to the subject, in this context, means risk of disturbance, physical damage, causing anxiety, consequential predation, and lessened reproductive success.

Photography may be seen as a criminal offence with relation to some species, since disturbance will be occasioned.

Many species are afforded special legal protection. The Law as it affects nature photography must be observed. For Great Britain the main legislation is listed at the end of this leaflet. In other countries one should find out in advance any restrictions that apply.

Apparent lax or absence of local legislation should not lead any photographer to relax his/her own high standard.

The photographer should be familiar with the natural history of the subject; the more complex the life-form and the rarer the species, the greater his/her knowledge must be. He/she should also be sufficiently familiar with other natural history subjects to be able to avoid damaging their interests accidentally. Photography of uncommon creatures and plants by people who know nothing of the hazards to species and habitat is to be deplored.

With reference to Sites of Special Scientific Interest (SSSIs): anyone who intentionally or recklessly destroys or damages any of the flora, fauna, geological or physio-graphical features by reason of which a site is of special interest, or intentionally or recklessly disturbs any of those fauna, is guilty of an offence and is liable on summary conviction to a fine.

It is important for the good name of nature photography that its practitioners observe normal social courtesies. Permission should be obtained before working on private land and other naturalists should not be incommoded. Work at sites and colonies which are subjects of special study should be coordinated with the people concerned.

Photographs of dead, stuffed, homebred, captive, cultivated, or otherwise controlled specimens may be of genuine value but should never be passed off as wild and free. Users of such photographs (irrespective of the purpose for which it is thought they will be used) should always be informed, regardless of how little they may seem to care.

Birds at the nest

The terms of the Wildlife and Countryside Act 1981 must be complied with at all times. It is an offence to recklessly or intentionally disturb a Schedule 1 species while it is building a nest, or is in, on or near a nest containing eggs or young; or to disturb the dependant young of such a species. In Scotland it is an offence to recklessly or intentionally disturb or harrass any Schedule 1A bird (ie White-tailed Eagle) or any Schedule 1 bird which leks (ie Capercaillie).

A licence is necessary to photograph Schedule 1 birds in certain circumstances. Licences can be obtained from the appropriate Statutory Nature Conservation body - see addresses at the end.

Photography of birds at the nest should only be undertaken by those with a good knowledge of bird breeding behaviour. There are many competent photographers (and bird watchers) who lack this qualification.

Scarce species should only be photographed in an area where they may be relatively frequent; it is therefore preferable to photograph British rarities overseas where they may be commoner. Photographers working abroad should exercise the same care as they would at home.

A hide should always be used if there is a reasonable doubt that birds would continue normal breeding behaviour otherwise. No part of the occupant should be visible from the outside of the hide.

Hides should not be erected where the attention of the public or a predator is likely to be attracted. If there is any such risk, an assistant should be in the vicinity to keep potential intruders away. No hide should be left unattended in daylight in a place with common public access.

Visits to a site should be kept to a minimum to avoid damage to vegetation and the creation of new tracks or pathways. The site should be restored to naturalness between sessions.

Reported nest failures due to nest photography are few, but a high proportion of those that occur are due to undue haste. The maximum possible time should elapse between stages of hide movement or erection, introduction of lens or flash equipment, gardening and occupation. Many species need preparation at least a week in advance; this should be seen as the norm. Each stage should be fully accepted by the bird (or birds, where feeding or incubation is shared) before the next stage is initiated. If a stage is refused by the birds (which should be evident from their behaviour to a competent bird photographer) the procedure should be reversed at least one stage; if refusal is repeated photography should be abandoned.

The period of disturbance caused by each stage should be kept to a minimum. It is undesirable to initiate a stage in late evening, 216 when the birds' activities are becoming less frequent.

Remote-control work where acceptance cannot be checked is rarely satisfactory. Resetting of a shutter or manually advancing film is even less likely to be acceptable because of the frequency of disturbance.

While the best photographs are often obtained about the time of hatching this is not the time to start erecting a hide - nor when eggs are fresh. It is better to wait until the reactions of the parent birds to the situation are firmly established.

The birds' first visits to the nest after the hide is occupied are best used for checking routes and behaviour rather than for exposures. The quieter the shutter, the less the chance of birds objecting to it. The longer the focal length of the lens used, the more distant the hide can be and the less risk of the birds not accepting it.

Nesting birds photographed from a hide can be put under pressure if too many photographers are waiting for 'their turn' in the hide. Each change of photographer causes fresh disturbance and should be avoided. Ideally two photographers working together should be the norm - two to enter the hide and one to leave, although more may be required for some species. Disturbance should always be kept to an absolute minimum and should never be caused during bad weather (rain or exceptionally hot sun).

The trapping of breeding birds for studio-type photography is totally unacceptable in any circumstances and an offence under the WCA.

It is an offence to remove nestlings or eggs from the nest for photography even on a temporary basis; when photographed in situ care should be taken not to cause an 'explosion' of young from the nest. It is never permissible to artificially restrict the free movement of the young.

General

The use of playback tape or stuffed predators (to stimulate territorial or alarm reactions) should not be undertaken near the nest in the breeding season. Additionally the use of bait or song tapes to attract birds to the camera, even though this is away from the nest, should not be under-taken in an occupied breeding territory. Use of such methods may be considered illegal with respect to Schedule 1 species.

Predators should not be baited from a hide in an area where hides may later be used for photography of birds at the nest.

Wait and see photography should not be undertaken in an area where a hide may show irresponsible shooters and trappers that targets exist; this is particularly important overseas.

Mammals and Birds away from the nest

The capture of even non-breeding birds for photography under controlled conditions is not an acceptable or legal practice. Incidental photography of birds taken under licence for some valid scientific purpose is acceptable provided it causes minimal delay to the bird's release. If any extra delay is involved it would need to be covered by the terms of the licence.

Taking small mammals for photographic purposes is not recommended. In exceptional cases where captivity is necessary it should only be carried out provided they are not breeding (either sex) and are released with minimum delay in their original habitat. No attempt should be made to tame any animal so taken as it jeopardizes their survival.

Hibernating animals should never be awakened for photography.

Threatened species such as Otters, Red Squirrels and Dormice are given full protection under Schedule 5 of the Wildlife and Countryside Act. The restrictions on photographing these species at their places of shelter are exactly the same as those for nesting birds. Not all protected species have regular places of shelter; these include two reptiles, two amphibians and several very rare butterflies and moths. The best rule is, 'if in doubt, don't'. For example do not move objects in the habitat in search of smooth snakes to photograph.

Bats need special care. Disturbance at or near a breeding colony of any bat may cause desertion of an otherwise safe site; all bats are specially protected and none may be disturbed or photographed in a roost except with a licence from the appropriate Statutory Nature Conservation body. Bats are acutely sensitive to disturbance. There is evidence that important hibernation sites have been permanently deserted as a result of disturbance caused by photography. Licences to photograph are normally issued only to experienced bat workers.

No fully protected species may be taken from the wild without a licence, and taking means any form of capture including the use of butterfly nets.

Some further animals, included on Schedule 6 of the Act, are protected from trapping, and these include shrews, hedgehogs and pine martens. If you need to trap these species in order to photograph them you must apply for a licence.

Disturbance of any European protected species anywhere is an offence under the Habitat Regulations 1994.

For cold-blooded animals and invertebrates, temporary removal from the wild to a studio or vivarium (or aquarium) for photography is not recommended, where practicable field photographs are to be preferred. If a subject is removed from the wild for photography it should be released as soon as possible in its original habitat.

It is illegal to take from the wild, species listed on Schedule 5 of the Wildlife and Countryside Act, or take by means such as live-traps, species on Schedule 6. Insect photographers should be familiar with those species which may not be taken without a licence.

Chilling or anaesthesia for quietening invertebrates should not be undertaken.

When microhabitats (e.g. tree-bark, beach rocks, etc.) have been disturbed, they should be restored after the photography.

There should be no damage to habitat; any that does occur may be illegal on nature reserves, or SSSIs, even if the landowner has given permission.

Plants

Photographers should be clear about existing legislation. It is an offence to uproot any wild plant without the permission of the landowner or his tenant. For over a hundred very threatened plants, including the rarest orchids, the law extends to picking, so any damage to surrounding vegetation, which may include young plants, must be avoided. If photography comes to be seen as a threat, rather than an aid, to rare plant conservation, pressures may mount for more restrictive legislation such as giving protected plants at flowering time similar protection to that enjoyed by Schedule 1 birds at nesting time.

No rarity should ever be picked (still less dug up) for studio photography, or to facilitate the in situ photography of another specimen. Nor should any part of one be removed to facilitate the photography of another plant.

For some subjects (botanical/fungi/etc) some 'gardening' (i.e. tidying up of the surrounding vegetation) may be necessary. This should be kept to a minimum to avoid exposing the subject to predators, people, or weather. Plants or branches should be tied back rather than cut off and the site restored to as natural a condition as possible after any photo-graphic session. The aim should always be to leave no obvious signs of disturbance.

If an image of a rarity is to be published or exhibited, care should be taken that the site location is not accidentally given away.

Take care that your photograph does not contain any clues as to the whereabouts of the specimen; this is particularly important in wide-angle photographs. Sites of rarities should never deliberately be disclosed except for conservation purposes.

Fungi

Other than a few very common species, it is rarely possible to identify fungi either in situ or from a photograph; a photograph of an unidentified or incorrectly identified species is of very limited value. Therefore it is usually necessary to collect a specimen after photographing them. This should be done with a knife rather than the fingers, taking care to collect the entire specimen including any base which may be immersed in the substrate. Notes should be made of the substrate (in particular for mycorrhyzal genera) and any associated organisms, as this may aid identification.

One of the first principles of collecting is to leave the environment as close as possible to the state in which it was found. Any logs which are rolled over should be returned to their original position.

If working as a group, then only the most experienced mycologist should collect specimens as his analysis can later be communicated to the other photographers. He/she may need to collect five or six specimens of differing ages to enable a mycologist to make an accurate identification after microscopic analysis, and also have sufficient specimens left over to store in a herbarium for future reference. It may not be necessary to collect the entire specimen in the case of very large species, i.e. brackets, as a wedge taken from the side is often sufficient.

Be aware that some public open spaces are subject to local bye-laws that may prohibit collecting. Four species are legally protected from collection anywhere in England, Scotland and Wales, even for scientific purposes, by Schedule 8 of the Wildlife and Countryside Act 1981 (species covered are

219 Hericium erinaceum, Piptoporus quercinum, Boletus regius and Battarea phalloides).

The Truth of the final Image

A nature photograph should convey the essential truth of what the photographer saw at the time it was taken.

No radical changes should be made to the original photograph, nor additions made from any source, whether during processing in the darkroom, or through digital/electronic manipulation. The removal of minor blemishes or distractions is permissible.

The photographer should be aware of the appropriate sections of the following, and any subsequent 'amendments':

The Wildlife and Countryside Act 1981.

The Wildlife (Northern Ireland) Order 1985.

Protection of Badgers Act 1992.

The Butterfly Society Conservation Code.

Botanical Society of the British Isles (BSBI) list of rare plants and Code of Conduct.

The RSPB leaflet 'Bird Photography and the Law'.

The Conservation (Natural Habitats, etc.) Regulations 1994.

The Countryside & Rights of Way Act 2000

Natural Environment & Rural Communities Act 2006

For more information on the protection of species and habitats:

The Royal Society for the Protection of Birds, The Lodge, Sandy, Bedfordshire, SG19 2DL www.rspb.org.uk

Natural England,

1 East Parade, Sheffield, S1 2ET

www.naturalengland.org.uk

Scottish Natural Heritage,

Great Glen House, Leachkin Road, Inverness, IV3 8NW

www.snh.org.uk

Countryside Council for Wales,

Maes y Ffynnon, Penrhosgarnedd, Bangor, Gwynedd, LL57 2DW

www.ccw.gov.uk

Partnership for Action against Wildlife Crime (PAW)/DEFRA

www.defra.gov.uk/paw/

Bird photography and the law

Photography of wild birds in Britain is limited by law where it involves the disturbance of rare breeding species, as explained in paragraph 9 below. Other legal and moral restrictions, such as those affecting access to nesting colonies, or feeding and roosting sites, may also be relevant to photographers seeking close views.

The birds' welfare must always come first—photography should not disturb their normal activity. At times this will mean not taking photographs.

Some extra considerations apply to photography at the nest:

1   Ensure you have the landowner's permission.

2   Keep the nest site secret. Choose a site away from public view, and if a hide is used, camouflage it well. Leave no tracks or signs that may lead predators to the brood.

3   Keep visits to the nest as few and as short as possible. Changes of photographer should be kept to a minimum and should not take place in bad weather.

4   Leave the nest as you find it. Any

'gardening' of a nest should be kept to a minimum to avoid exposing the nest to predators or adverse weather. Tie back vegetation rather than cutting it so it can be restored to its original position.

5   When using a hide, erect it some way off, moving it closer over a period of days so the birds grow used to it. Ensure at each stage that the hide has been accepted. If there is any doubt, move it back. Many species will need at least a week's preparation.

6   The use of a friend is recommended as a 'walk-away', accompanying the photographer to and from the hide. Certain species may require two people for this purpose. This is often the only responsible method to minimise disturbance.

7   Fingers and lenses suddenly poked out of a hide, flapping cloth and loud noises scare birds. Get them used to small sounds, talk to them perhaps, before taking pictures.

8   Remember that public opinion generalises actions, and that the thoughtlessness of one bird photographer may damage the reputation of others.

9   To protect rare breeding birds, the law prohibits intentional disturbance of any species included in Schedule 1 of the Wildlife and Countryside Act 1981. This applies while such a bird is building a nest, or is in, on or near a nest containing eggs or young. It is also illegal to intentionally disturb dependent young of Schedule 1 birds. Photographers cannot visit such nests unless they obtain the appropriate licence from the relevant authority.

These are as follows: English Nature,

Northminster House, Peterborough PE1 1UA. Tel: 01733 340345

Countryside Council for Wales, Plas Penrhos, Fford Penrhos, Bangor, Gwynedd LL57 2LQ. Tel: 01248 370444

Scottish Natural Heritage, Research and Advisory Service, Bonnington Bond, 2/5 Anderson Place, Edinburgh EH6 5NP. Tel 0131 554 9797

Northern Ireland env agency, http://www. doeni.gov.uk/niea/other-index. Tel 028 9056 9515

SCHEDULE 1

Avocet, Bee-eater, Bittern, Bittern – little, Bluethroat, Brambling, Cirl Bunting, Lapland Bunting, Snow Bunting, Honey Buzzard, Capercaillie (Scotland), Chough, Corncrake, Crake – spotted, Crossbills (all species), Divers (all species), Dotterel, Duck - long-tailed, Eagle – golden, Eagle - white-tailed, Falcon – gyr, Fieldfare, Firecrest, Garganey, Godwit - black-tailed, Goldeneye, Goose - greylag (Outer Hebrides, Caithness, Sutherland & Wester Ross only), Goshawk, Grebe - black-necked, Grebe – Slavonian, Greenshank, Gull – little, Gull – Mediterranean, Harriers (all species), Heron – purple, Hobby, Hoopoe, Kingfisher, Kite – red, Merlin, Oriole – golden, Osprey, Owl – barn, Owl – snowy, Peregrine, Petrel - Leach's, Phalarope - red-necked, Pintail, Plover – Kentish, Plover - little ringed, Quail – common, Redstart – black, Redwing, Rosefinch – scarlet, Ruff, Sandpiper – green, Sandpiper – purple, Sandpiper – wood, Scaup, Scoter – common, Scoter – velvet, Serin, Shorelark, Shrike - red-backed, Spoonbill, Stilt - black-, winged, Stint - Temminck's, Stone-curlew, Swan - Bewick's, Swan – whooper, Tern – black, Tern – little, Tern – roseate, Tit – bearded, Tit – crested, Treecreeper - short-toed, Warbler - Cetti's, Warbler – Dartford, Warbler – marsh, Warbler - Savi's, Whimbrel, Woodlark, Wryneck.

Box hide plan

A simple box hide plan

All measurements in metres.

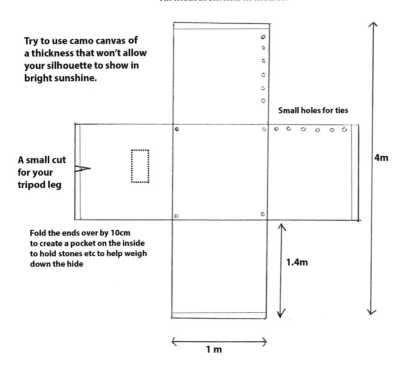

Try to use camo canvas of a thickness that won't allow your silhouette to show in bright sunshine.

Small holes for ties

A small cut for your tripod leg

4m

Fold the ends over by 10cm to create a pocket on the inside to hold stones etc to help weigh down the hide

1.4m

1 m

The poles can be bought from a camping store. Try to get ones that are adjustable in height. Fishermen's poles are an alternative.

To stabilise the hide when it is put up use tent pegs through the bottom of the canvas and use 4 guide ropes from the top of the poles secured to the ground with rocks or tent pegs.

The measurments are only suggestions, adapt to suit your body height and how much room you want in the hide.

An alternative front opening made of soft material, which is stitched to the front of the hide

The front opening can be a simple rectangle cut out with scrim held in place with safety pins.
Don't forget small openings in the sides so you can see in other directions.
Two openings in the front are ideal, one for your lens and one to watch from.

Bird box plan

Basic bird box design

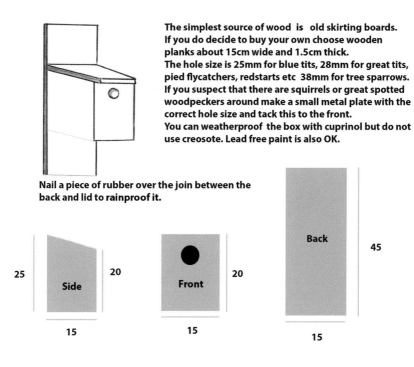

The simplest source of wood is old skirting boards. If you do decide to buy your own choose wooden planks about 15cm wide and 1.5cm thick.
The hole size is 25mm for blue tits, 28mm for great tits, pied flycatchers, redstarts etc 38mm for tree sparrows. If you suspect that there are squirrels or great spotted woodpeckers around make a small metal plate with the correct hole size and tack this to the front.
You can weatherproof the box with cuprinol but do not use creosote. Lead free paint is also OK.

Nail a piece of rubber over the join between the back and lid to rainproof it.

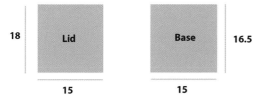

25 — **Side** — 20	**Front** — 20	**Back** — 45
15	15	15

18 — **Lid**	**Base** — 16.5
15	15

Situate the boxes at a convenient height for your hide. They don't need to be high - one to two metres is fine. Put them up where they won't have strong sunlight or driving rain on them.

All measurements are in cm

You can either nail the back to a tree or use wire. If you choose wire use a piece of rubber to stop it cutting into the tree.

You can hinge the lid and hold it down with a small hook. This will allow you to check it and clean it next winter.

Mammal tracks

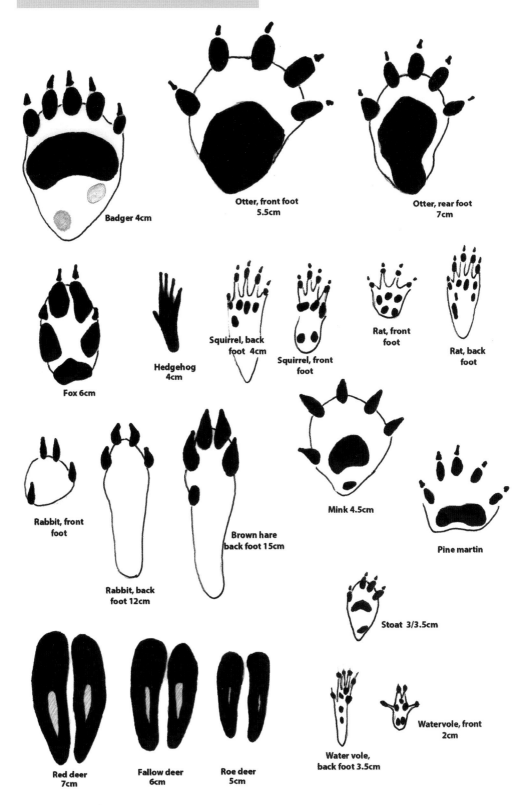

Badger 4cm

Otter, front foot
5.5cm

Otter, rear foot
7cm

Fox 6cm

Hedgehog
4cm

Squirrel, back
foot 4cm

Squirrel, front
foot

Rat, front
foot

Rat, back
foot

Rabbit, front
foot

Rabbit, back
foot 12cm

Brown hare
back foot 15cm

Mink 4.5cm

Pine martin

Stoat 3/3.5cm

Red deer
7cm

Fallow deer
6cm

Roe deer
5cm

Water vole,
back foot 3.5cm

Watervole, front
2cm

Useful resource sites and books

Websites

Anglian Lepidopterist supplies
www.angleps.com/mothtraps.php
Suppliers of a wide range of moth traps.

Insect lore www.insectlore.co.uk
Source of painted lady caterpillars.

Worldwide butterflies www.wwb.co.uk/
Supplier of live butterfly eggs, larvae and pupae. Many native species.

LBS www.lba.uk.com/aboutus.aspx
Suppliers of live butterfly eggs, larvae and pupae. Many native species.

Natural England www.naturalengland.org.uk/

Scottish Natural Heritage www.snh.gov.uk/

Natural Resource Wales
naturalresourceswales.gov.uk/

Northern Ireland Environment Agency
www.doeni.gov.uk/niea/

Ladybird survey http://www.ladybird-survey.org/

Wild boar http://www.britishwildboar.org
Great for info about wild boar.

CJ bird foods http://www.birdfood.co.uk/
An on-line bulk bird food retailer.

Haith's bird foods http://www.haiths.com
An on-line bulk bird food retailer.

Live foods direct http://www.livefoodsdirect.co.uk/Category/Mealworms
A great supplier of mealworms and other insect foods.

Natural History bookshop www.nhbs.com/
Online book store.

Ispot http://www.ispotnature.org/
Online wildlife identification site - just brilliant!

Guide site for moth identification, http://ukmoths.org.uk/

Books

A Field Guide to Bird's Nests Campbell + Ferguson-Lees, 1972, Constable. Essential guide for information about bird's nests, incubation times and nesting dates.

The Millennium Atlas of Butterflies in Britain and Ireland Asher, Warren etc, 2001 Oxford. A great ref for distribution and breeding biology of our native butterflies.

Butterflies and Dragonflies, A Site Guide Hill + Twist, 1998, Arlequin. Essential site guide.

Practical Entomology Ford, Warne, 1963. Out of print but available second hand, a brilliant little book full of great ideas.

Field Guide to the Dragonflies and Damselflies of Great Britain and Ireland Brooks and Lewington, BWP, 2014. Ideal guide with good behaviour tips and some sites.

Watching British Dragonflies Dudley, Dudley and Mackay, 2007, Subbuteo. Good information and excellent site guide.

A Field Guide to the Bumblebees of Great Britain and Ireland Edwards and Jenner, CELLI, 2005.

Wild flowers of Britain Marjorie Blamey, Richard SR Fitter, Alastair H Fitter, AC Black. The definitive plant id guide.

Collins Bird Guide, Lars Svensson, Killian Mullarney, Dan Zetterström, Peter J Grant, David A Christie. An excellent bird id guide.

Mammals of the British Isles handbook. 4th Ed, Stephen A Harris, Derek W Yalden, Guy Troughton, The mammal soc. The best resource for British mammals.

Collins Butterfly Guide, Tom Tolman, Richard Lewington. An excellent guide for the UK and Europe.

Britain's Dragonflies Dave Smallshire, Andy Swash. Wild guides. An up to date guide book.

British Moths Chris Manley, 2nd ed Bloomsbury. A Photographic Guide to the Moths of Britain and Ireland. Essential guide to help id moths, particularly good because it gives so many variations and actual images of moths as they rest naturally.

Collins Field Guide to the Spiders of Britain and Northern Europe Michael J Roberts.

Britain's Day Flying Moths David E Newland, Robert Still, Andy Swash, Wild guides.

Collins Fungi Guide Stefan Buczacki, Chris Shields, Denys W Ovenden.

Orchids, A Field and Site Guide Anne and Simon Harrap, 2005, AC Black.

Field Guide to the Micro Moths of Britain and Europe Phil Sterling, Mark Parsons, Richard Lewington, British Wildlife Publishing.

British Wildlife. A bi-monthly magazine. The only one dedicated to British wildlife. One, if not the best, source of news, articles about British Wildlife. Kemp House, Chawley Park, Cumnor Hill, Oxford, OX2 9PH, subs@britishwildlife.com

How to Find and Identify Mammals Gillie Muir, Pat A Morris, Guy Troughton, Rob Strachan, Sarah Wroot, Amy-Jane Beer, Jackie Savery, Mammal Soc.

Butterflies of Britain and Ireland, a Field and Site Guide Michael Easterbrook, A+C Black.

Britain's Reptiles and Amphibians Howard Inns, British Wildlife.

Guide to Bees of Britain Chris O'Toole, Chris Shields. Field studies council.

Ants Gary J Skinner, Geoffrey W Allen. Naturalists handbooks.

Grasshopper V Brown, Naturalists handbooks, Vol 2, Richmond publishing.

Ladybirds Helen E Roy, Peter MJ Brown, Richard F Comont, Remy L Poland, John J Sloggett, Sophie Allington, Chris Shields, 2013. Naturalists handbooks, Vol 2, Pelagic publishing.

Feathers. Identification for conservation. Marian Cieslak, Boleslaw Dul, 2006, Natura publishing house.

A guide to the caterpillars of Britain and Ireland John Bebbington and Richard Lewington. 2002, Field studies council.

Guide to Freshwater Invertebrates Michael Dobson, Simon Pawley, Melanie Fletcher, Anne Powell, Alan Crowden, 2012, Fresh Water Biological Association.

Track and Signs of the Animals and Birds of Britain and Europe Lars-Henrik Olsen, Marc J Epstein. 2013. Princetown University press. Essential guide for those difficult footprints and feathers.

A Guide to British Mammal's Tracks and Signs Simone Bullion, 2001, Field Studies Council. Well worth having.

A Guide to the Identification of Prey Remains in Otter Spraints JWH Conroy, J Watt, JB Webb and A Jones, 2005, Mammal Society.

Guide to the Reptiles and Amphibians of Britain and Ireland Froglife and Peter Roberts, 2003, Field Studies Council.

The Mammal Society Species Guides Great value (£4.99) if you intend to spend a bit of time on one species or want a bit more background information. Some of these are now out of print. A good source of second hand books is **abe books** (www.abebooks.co.uk/)

Squirrels John Gurnell, Peter WW Lurz, Luc Wauters.
The Hedgehog Pat Morris.
The Brown Hare Stephen Tapper and Derek Yalden.
The Badger Michael Woods.
Muntjac Stephen Harris and Norma Chapman.
Bats Dean Waters, Ruth Warren.
The Dormouse Paul Bright and Pat Morris.
Fallow deer Jochen Langbein and Norma Chapman.
The Pine Marten Jochen Langbein and Norma Chapman.
Sika Deer Rory Putman.
Chinese Water Deer Arnold Cooke and Lynne Farrell.
Roe Deer John K Fawcett.
Stoats and Weasels Robbie McDonald and Stephen Harris
The Edible Dormouse.
The Wildcat A Kitchener.
The Red Fox S Harris and P White.
Otters Paul Chanin.
Moles David Stone.
Mink Johnny Birks.
Shrews S Churchfield.
Foxes Stephen Harris.
Woodmice John Flowerdew.

The British Natural History Collection. A new set of books, with volumes constantly added. Each is an in-depth monograph.

Owls Volume: 1 Chris Mead, Mike Toms, Guy Troughton.
Otters Volume: 2 Paul RF Chanin, Guy Troughton
Moles Volume: 3 Rob Atkinson, Belinda Atkinson.
Hedgehogs Volume: 4 Pat A Morris, Guy Troughton.

Bird/wildlife photography books

 Some of these were written in pre-digital days but still have valuable ideas.

The Bird Photography Field Guide David Tipling, 2011, Ilex publishers.

Bird Photography choosing the best destinations, planning a trip, taking great photos, David Tipling, 2005, Guild of Master Craftsmen.

RSPB Guide to Digital Wildlife Photography D Tipling, 2011.

RSPB Guide to Bird and Nature Photography 1996 L Campbell.

Photographing Birds Mark Sisson, 2014, Crowood press.

The Illustrated Guide to Bird Photography Bob Gibbons, Peter Wilson, Blandford, 1990, pre-digital but full of good info.

The Art of Bird Photography Arthur Morris, 2003, Amphoto.

Wildlife Photographer, A Course in Creative Photography Chris Gomersall, 2012, Francis Lincoln.

Photographing Wild Birds Chris Gomersall, 2001, David and Charles.

Wildlife Photography, Stories from the Field George Lepp and Kathryn Vincent Lepp, 2011, USA based. Lark books.

British Wildlife Photography Awards AA publishing. Award winning photographs from the annual competition.

Simon King's Wild Guide 1994, BBC books, S King. Out of print but a great reference guide.

Chris Packham's Wildshots C Packham, 1993, Collins and Brown.

The Art of Wildlife Photography Fritz Polking, 1998, Fountain Press.

Beyond the basics, Vol 1 and 2 George Lepp, 1997.

The Art of Photographing Nature Martha Hill and Art Wolfe, 1993, Crown Trade.

Index

Acknowledgements

A great many people over the years have given me support, advice or allowed me access to one of their sets. The list is a long one and to all these people I am very thankful. The following is a list of friends and acquaintances that I have worked with extensively, have directly helped with the content of the book or have given fully of their knowledge which has built up my own personal set of fieldskills.

Paul Batty, Pete Cairns, Cal Cotteril, Roger France, Danny Green, Russell Hague, Mark Hamblin, Joy Hales, Ian Haskel, Jim Hodson, Dave Jones (biog image), Chris Knights, Mike Lane, John Lintin-Smith, Andy Parkinson, Mark Sisson, Ian Shaw, John Tinning, Geoff Trinder, Russell Wade and The Royal Photographic Society.

The person who has given freely of his time and advice and has been a friend for many years and to whom I have so much to be grateful for is Mike Muddiman.

And lastly I must thank my better half, Judy, who spent many long hours painstakingly correcting my vocabulary alongside making some very useful suggestions about layout and design.

Biography

Paul grew up with a love of wildlife. He can't remember a time when he wasn't fascinated by the wildlife around him. Probably the first time the environment he lived in seemed to make sense was when (at school) he read My Family and Other Animals by Gerald Durrell. His world expanded exponentially as he took his early interests further and searched the countryside around his childhood home for living animals. Like his childhood hero, Gerald, Paul not only spent countless hours watching the lives of the creatures around him, he also caught and kept as pets a great variety of animals including voles, mice, grass snakes, newts and many insects. He talks about this time as the beginning of his love of fieldskills with this hands-on approach which he took to a further level as he became a wildlife photographer 30 years ago.

Today he works as a professional wildlife photographer after a successful career as a lecturer in Environmental Sciences in Sheffield, where he now lives.

Paul works extensively in the UK as well as abroad and he has travelled widely pursuing his love of wild animals, places and images. He leads trips for Nature's Images, writes articles and is represented by a number of picture agencies including NPL and FLPA.

Paul has had some success in wildlife photography competitions with -
Highly Commended, Wildlife Photographer of the Year 2008.
Category Winner, European Wildlife Photog-

rapher of the Year 2010.
Highly Commended, European Wildlife Photographer of the Year (2 images) 2014.
Public's favourite image, Festival de L'oiseau 2014.
Finalist Commended, British Wildlife Photography Awards 2009,10,11,12,14 and 15.

His images regularly feature in many magazines, including BBC Wildlife, and he writes a monthly article for Derbyshire Life along with occasional articles in the photographic press.

Wildlife Photography Field Skills and Techniques is Paul's second book. His first, Wild Derbyshire, was published in 2012.

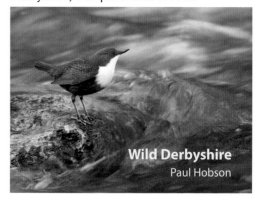

Wild Derbyshire
Paul Hobson